CAMBRIDGE
Brighter Thinking

Spain in the Age of Discovery, 1469–1598
A/AS Level History for AQA Student Book

Max von Habsburg
Series Editors: Michael Fordham and David Smith

CAMBRIDGE
UNIVERSITY PRESS

University Printing House, Cambridge CB2 8BS, United Kingdom

Cambridge University Press is part of the University of Cambridge.

It furthers the University's mission by disseminating knowledge in the pursuit of education, learning and research at the highest international levels of excellence.

www.cambridge.org
Information on this title: www.cambridge.org/ukschools/9781107587281 (Paperback)
www.cambridge.org/ukschools/9781107587328 (Cambridge Elevate-enhanced Edition)

© Cambridge University Press 2015

This publication is in copyright. Subject to statutory exception and to the provisions of relevant collective licensing agreements, no reproduction of any part may take place without the written permission of Cambridge University Press.

First published 2015

A catalogue record for this publication is available from the British Library

ISBN 978-1-107-587281 Paperback
ISBN 978-1-107-587328 Cambridge Elevate-enhanced Edition

Additional resources for this publication at www.cambridge.org/ukschools

Cambridge University Press has no responsibility for the persistence or accuracy of URLs for external or third-party internet websites referred to in this publication, and does not guarantee that any content on such websites is, or will remain, accurate or appropriate. Information regarding prices, travel timetables, and other factual information given in this work is correct at the time of first printing but Cambridge University Press does not guarantee the accuracy of such information thereafter.

NOTICE TO TEACHERS IN THE UK

It is illegal to reproduce any part of this work in material form (including photocopying and electronic storage) except under the following circumstances:
(i) where you are abiding by a licence granted to your school or institution by the Copyright Licensing Agency;
(ii) where no such licence exists, or where you wish to exceed the terms of a licence, and you have gained the written permission of Cambridge University Press;
(iii) where you are allowed to reproduce without permission under the provisions of Chapter 3 of the Copyright, Designs and Patents Act 1988, which covers, for example, the reproduction of short passages within certain types of educational anthology and reproduction for the purposes of setting examination questions.

Message from AQA

This textbook has been approved by AQA for use with our qualification. This means that we have checked that it broadly covers the specification and we are satisfied with the overall quality. Full details of our approval process can be found on our website.

We approve textbooks because we know how important it is for teachers and students to have the right resources to support their teaching and learning. However, the publisher is ultimately responsible for the editorial control and quality of this book.

Please note that when teaching the A/AS Level History (7041, 7042) course, you must refer to AQA's specification as your definitive source of information. While this book has been written to match the specification, it cannot provide complete coverage of every aspect of the course.

A wide range of other useful resources can be found on the relevant subject pages of our website: www.aqa.org.uk

Contents

About this series iv

Part 1: The establishment of a 'New Monarchy', 1469–1556   1

1 The forging of a new state, 1469–1516   1
- The condition of the Iberian Peninsula in 1469   2
- Royal authority   4
- Social issues and policies   9
- Dealing with the religious minorities   12
- Economy, trade and exploration   18
- Changes in Castile and Aragon by 1516   23

2 The drive to 'Great Power' status, 1516–56   27
- Charles V's inheritance   27
- The workings of empire: government and administration   33
- Foreign relations   39
- Religious policies and the Church in Spain   46
- The expansion of empire   48
- The political, economic, social and religious condition of Spain in 1556   51

Part 2: Philip II's Spain, 1556–98   54

3 The 'Golden Age', 1556–98   54
- Philip II as ruler   55
- Opposition: faction and internal rebellions   61
- Religion and society   68
- Economic developments   72
- Social and cultural developments in Spain's 'Golden Age'   75
- The condition of Spain by 1598: what were its political, economic and social strengths and weaknesses?   76

4 The 'Great Power', 1556–98   80
- Philip's inheritance and ambitions; ideas and pressures   81
- Relationships with European neighbours   83
- Mediterranean relationships   88
- Beyond the Mediterranean   94
- Spain in the New World: the impact of empire   100
- Spain's international position by 1598: illusion or reality?   101

Who's who?   105

Glossary   109

Bibliography   112

Acknowledgements   113

Index   114

About this Series

Cambridge A/AS Level History for AQA is an exciting new series designed to support students in their journey from GCSE to A Level and then on to possible further historical study. The books provide the knowledge, concepts and skills needed for the two-year AQA History A Level course, but it's our intention as series editors that students recognise that their A Level exams are just one step to a potential lifelong relationship with the discipline of history. This book has further readings, extracts from historians' works and links to wider questions and ideas that go beyond the scope of an A Level course. With this series, we have sought to ensure not only that the students are well prepared for their examinations, but also that they gain access to a wider debate that characterises historical study.

The series is designed to provide clear and effective support for students as they make the adjustment from GCSE to A Level, and also for teachers, especially those who are not familiar with teaching a two-year linear course. The student books cover the AQA specifications for both A/AS Level. They are intended to appeal to the broadest range of students, and they offer challenge to stretch the top end and additional support for those who need it. Every author in this series is an experienced historian or history teacher, and all have great skill in conveying narratives to readers and asking the kinds of questions that pull those narratives apart.

In addition to high-quality prose, this series also makes extensive use of textual primary sources, maps, diagrams and images, and offers a wide range of activities to encourage students to address historical questions of cause, consequence, change and continuity. Throughout the books there are opportunities to criticise the interpretations of other historians, and to use those interpretations in the construction of students' own accounts of the past. The series aims to ease the transition for those students who move on from A Level to undergraduate study, and the books are written in an engaging style that will encourage those who want to explore the subject further.

Icons used within the series include:

 Key terms

 Speak like a historian

 Voices from the past/Hidden voices

 Practice essay questions

 Chapter summary

About Cambridge Elevate

Cambridge Elevate is the platform which hosts a digital version of this Student Book. If you have access to this digital version you can annotate different parts of the book, send and receive messages to and from your teacher and insert weblinks, among other things.

We hope that you enjoy your AS or A Level History course as well as this book, and wish you well for the journey ahead.

Michael Fordham and David L Smith

Series editors

PART 1 THE ESTABLISHMENT OF A 'NEW MONARCHY', 1469–1556
1 The forging of a new state, 1469–1516

In this section, we will study how far Ferdinand and Isabella forged a new state and assess the nature and effectiveness of their domestic and foreign policies.

Specification points:

- the political, economic, social and religious condition of the Iberian peninsula in 1469
- the restoration of royal authority, royal government, unity and confederation, relations with other European powers
- social issues and policies: the nobility, the peasantry, urban communities and the Church
- Muslims/*Moriscos*, the *Reconquista*, Jews/*conversos* and anti-Semitism
- economic stagnation and change: trade and exploration in Europe and North Africa, discovery and first settlements in the New World
- the degree of political unity and social and economic change by 1516.

The condition of the Iberian peninsula in 1469

Politics

In the 15th century, European countries did not possess centralised political systems, concrete frontiers or the kind of concept of nationhood that developed in later centuries. Although France had only recently recovered territory lost in the Hundred Years' War, it was still politically decentralised and the monarchy remained peripatetic. In consolidating its lands, conflict with France's southern neighbours seemed likely as each power sought to control border territories, such as the kingdom of Navarre. Having suffered decades of civil wars (the Wars of the Roses), England was unlikely to engage in warfare abroad, though the new Tudor King Henry VII was eager to open diplomatic channels with foreign territories. At the same time, the marriage alliance between Maximilian of Habsburg (later Holy Roman Emperor) and Mary, duchess of Burgundy, heralded the rise of a major European power. The wealth and cultural pre-eminence of the Italian city-states encouraged the major European dynasties, notably the French Valois and Habsburgs, to take an active interest in the Italian peninsula. This brought them into contact with the Aragonese, who controlled Sardinia and Sicily. At this point, as separate kingdoms, Castile and Aragon pursued very different foreign policy objectives. The Mediterranean was of far greater strategic and economic importance to the latter. By 1453, Constantinople had fallen to the Ottoman Sultan, Mehmed II, leading to Muslim expansion in the northern Balkans and in the Mediterranean.

Figure 1.1: Europe, 1500.

The Iberian Peninsula lacked both political unity and uniformity, and there was not even a willingness, let alone any attempt, to centralise the governmental systems. In fact, 'Spain' was no more than a geographical expression and the term was not used at the time. Setting aside Portugal, which remained a separate kingdom, the provinces of Castile and Aragon were dominant in political and economic terms and were also

1 The forging of a new state, 1469–1516

recognised as independent kingdoms. They contained over 75 per cent of the Iberian Peninsula's population. The Castilian monarchy wielded greater political power than its counterpart in Aragon. Kings of Aragon were expected to respect the privileges and liberties of their nobles and towns, which were upheld by a more powerful *Cortes*. Yet in the second half of the 15th century, both provinces were debilitated by civil wars. Motivated by a disputed succession, powerful nobles challenged the authority of Henry IV of Castile and John II of Aragon respectively.

> **Key term**
>
> **Cortes:** The *Cortes* was a provincial representative assembly consisting of nobles, clergy and town officials. There were different Cortes in Castile, Aragon, Catalonia and Valencia, all of which were generally summoned to raise taxes and to approve legislation.

Figure 1.2: The political disunity of the Iberian Peninsula, *c.*1480, and the towns and cities that elected the *Cortes*.

The foundations for a symbolic, if not a proper, political union were laid by the timely marriage between John's son Ferdinand of Aragon and Henry's half-sister Isabella of Castile in 1469, though the marriage did not represent a union of equal partners. The stronger imperial tradition of monarchy in Castile obliged Ferdinand to confirm that he would not give away Castilian lands or offices without Isabella's consent. In Aragon, the king was contracted to provide effective government in return for loyal service and he was expected to appoint viceroys in his absence. The marriage did not usher in an immediate end to the civil wars and collusion between the nobles left the Iberian Peninsula profoundly unstable. During the wars, some influential nobles, such as the Cardinal-Archbishop of Seville and the Count of Benavente, changed sides twice and their loyalty was not guaranteed. The motives of the nobility in the civil wars were varied and significantly affected by local circumstances. Such was their power that they sought to fill the vacuum left by the political turmoil; for example, **Archbishop Carrillo of Toledo** had such influence over the Church that he not only sought a cardinal's hat but also to dictate affairs to the king. While the nobility remained divided, the towns were more united in their support of Ferdinand and Isabella.

Economic and social conditions

Economic and social trends were dominated by rural conditions: the peasantry represented at least 95 per cent of the population. There was a boom in sheep farming,

A/AS Level History for AQA: Spain in the Age of Discovery, 1469–1598

Key term

Mesta: The *Mesta* was the powerful organisation that controlled the movement of sheep across the Iberian Peninsula, defended and promoted the interests of the wool trade.

which was partly due to serious water shortages, primitive agricultural methods, and the preponderance of infertile terrain. The interests of sheep owners were represented and promoted by the powerful *Mesta* organisation, which granted numerous privileges in exchange for financial contributions. Merchants and professionals remained a minority and tended to reside in the coastal towns. Politically and economically, towns competed with local nobles, the Church and even the Crown.

Religion

The religious conditions of the peninsula were affected by the Church's possession of extensive property and land. Senior clerics formed an integral part of the Iberian Peninsula's social and political hierarchy. Owing allegiance to the Pope in Rome, the Spanish church was in need of reform, especially in its monastic communities. Prior to Ferdinand and Isabella's accession, the key provinces of Castile and Aragon already had a strong tradition of royal intervention in ecclesiastical affairs.

Royal authority

The restoration of royal authority

Royal authority could not be established before the conclusion of the civil wars. For all its apparently powerful symbolism, the marriage between Ferdinand and Isabella did not immediately bring peace to the peninsula. In fact, following Henry's death, Isabella's coronation in 1474 drew Castile into a civil war. The rival claimant, **Juana 'la Beltraneja'**, had substantial support, including King **Afonso V** of Portugal, Archbishop Carrillo, and the **Marquis of Villena**. In response, Ferdinand and Isabella mobilised

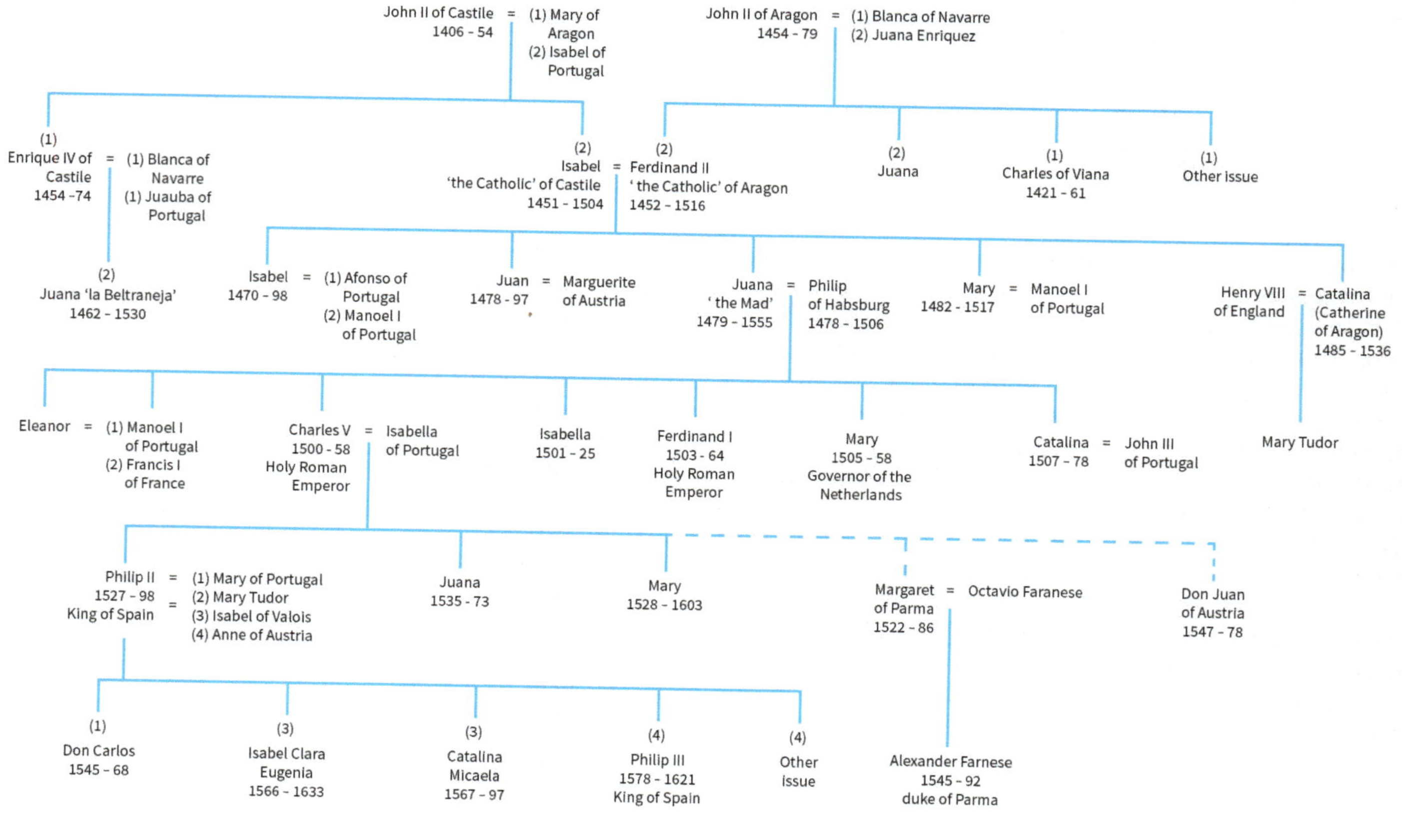

Figure 1.3: The kings of Castile, Aragon, Spain and Portugal.

their urban supporters by commanding royal representatives firstly to respect local privileges and then to coordinate resistance in all the major towns and fortresses. The civil war was eventually concluded by the Treaty of Alcáçovas in 1479, by which time royal influence and personnel had been effectively extended to the provinces. With the death of John II of Aragon in the same year, Ferdinand was unchallenged when he acceded to the Aragonese throne. With the termination of the civil wars, Ferdinand and Isabella were in a position to consolidate their authority and power.

Given the nature of their political inheritance, successful government would depend on effective collaboration between Ferdinand and Isabella. The absence of centralised political institutions reinforced the importance attached to the actual presence of each monarch. As Henry Kamen has argued, 'if the monarchy had a centre, it was located only in their persons and not in any fixed capital city'.[1] Throughout their reigns, Ferdinand and Isabella were noticeably diligent in visiting the various localities. Ferdinand and Isabella spent the majority of their time in Old Castile, often visited New Castile and Andalusia, but rarely went to Aragon.

ACTIVITY 1.1

Research and identify other contemporary rulers, such as the French Valois, English Tudor and Habsburg dynasties, and Ottoman sultans, and compare and contrast their political systems and territorial possessions.

Figure 1.4: Royal itinerancy: the extent of Ferdinand and Isabella's travels.

The theories of kingship devised by the *letrados* (lawyers) on the royal council further empowered Ferdinand and Isabella. Monarchy was defined not purely in political terms, but as an institution that maintained a unique relationship with God: 'God is called King over all the Kings because from him they derive their name and by him they reign and he governs and maintains them and they are his vicegerents, each one in his kingdom.'[2] In spite of this special relationship, there were limits to Ferdinand's and Isabella's power. It was perceived that kings could make laws on their own initiative (particularly in Castile), though they were certainly not absolute rulers in the modern sense, especially in Aragon where their power was restricted by the **fueros**.

Ferdinand and Isabella were seemingly driven by a unity of purpose, though they had rather different personalities. While the former was considered cunning and pragmatic (securing praise from **Machiavelli** himself), the latter was renowned for her piety

 Key term

Fueros: The *fueros* were the existing laws, traditions and liberties of a province. In contrast with the Castilian Crown, there was greater pressure on the kings of Aragon to observe the *fueros*.

and determination. Contemporary writers described Isabella as 'the most feared and respected' of leaders (Bernaldez) and as imposing her will with a mixture of 'love and fear' (**Castiglione**).[3] Ferdinand's infidelities were contrasted with Isabella's integrity, though Lucio Marineo labelled her as being 'vigilant in jealousy'.[4]

The consolidation of royal authority was neither immediate nor a foregone conclusion. While the nobility were primarily responsible for prolonging the civil wars, the signing of the Treaty of Alcáçovas did not secure their unconditional subservience to Ferdinand and Isabella. The Crown was hesitant and unable to challenge the powerful Castilian aristocracy directly, so Ferdinand and Isabella opened diplomatic channels. The monarchy restored its authority by making strategic alliances with leading noble families, such as the **Mendozas** and **Velascos**, and by granting various new titles and offices. Ferdinand and Isabella were by no means complacent and sought to strengthen their control of the coastal regions and improve their access to the Mediterranean and the Atlantic. For example, Castile's most important naval bases, Gibraltar and Cartagena, were seized from the Duke of **Medina Sidonia** and Don Pedro Fajardo in 1502 and 1503 respectively. Although both were compensated for their significant losses, the former conspired against Ferdinand and Isabella only five years later. Medina Sidonia's rebellion was unsuccessful, though his conspiracy was a timely reminder that monarchical authority remained insecure without the complete submission of powerful nobles.

Royal government

Counsel for the monarchs

As one would expect, royal government was characterised by Ferdinand's and Isabella's direct intervention in government. Although often perceived to be new, modern and bureaucratic, the royal government under Ferdinand and Isabella remained essentially medieval and personal. Their active involvement in government enhanced their own power, in particular, because Isabella controlled the appointment of treasury officials, the masterships of **military orders**, and the major ecclesiastical promotions in Castile. From 1475, Ferdinand was also empowered to appoint royal officials. Ferdinand and Isabella chose royal secretaries, who became increasingly important in the late medieval period. Secretaries, such as Hernando de Zafra and Luis de Santangel, could represent the crucial point of contact between the sovereigns and the Royal Council.

> **Key term**
>
> **Military orders:** The military orders were chivalric organisations, established in the late Middle Ages to facilitate the reconquest of southern Spain. By the 1480s, these orders had accumulated land, property, fortresses and even the control of some towns. The most influential military orders were Santiago, Calatrava and Alcántara.

Both Ferdinand and Isabella inherited court systems that served political and legal functions. The Castilian government was centred on the royal household and the court. It consisted of household officials, who performed political and administrative functions. The aristocracy dominated the court, though few nobles resided there on a permanent basis. As was the custom in the Middle Ages, the Castilian court remained itinerant. Rather than presenting a disadvantage for the Crown, the absence of a capital made it very difficult for nobles to collaborate and seek to impose their will on the monarchy. While the Crown paid for the movement of the court, the localities hosting the sovereigns would cover the remaining costs. Ferdinand and Isabella's itinerancy meant that the costs tended to be spread across the peninsula. With more distant territories, Ferdinand and Isabella introduced viceroys to act as royal representatives, though Catalonia, Aragon and Valencia also had viceroys by 1516.

The Royal Council (*Consejo Real*) was Ferdinand and Isabella's main advisory body. It was subdivided into five departments, dealing with foreign affairs, justice, finances, the *Santa Hermandad* (which survived until 1498), and Aragon. It was the single most important organ of government in Castile, and met on a daily basis. Bishops, leading nobles and heads of military orders were allowed to attend, though they were not allocated voting powers. The aristocracy was not only permitted but obviously encouraged to provide counsel. Initially, most of the leading councillors were lawyers,

Figure 1.5: Portrait of Isabella of Castile in her youth.

and by 1493 all of its members were expected to hold a university law degree. The key officials included the *contadores* (officers of the royal counting house), treasury officials, working chancellors and secretaries, and the judicial members of the Royal Council.

The employment of lawyers was not innovative, though their dominance was more pronounced under Ferdinand and Isabella, transforming them into the elites of the Castilian administration. Lawyers could not pose a direct threat to monarchical authority, owing to their lack of inherited political and financial power. On the contrary, they were and continued to be utterly reliant on royal patronage. In certain cases, there was a tendency towards corruption because the monarchs could not afford to pay them what they arguably deserved. Their interpretation of the law allowed them to promote the royal theory of kingship, enforce law and order within the realm and provide a legal framework for the increase in royal revenues. Ferdinand and Isabella were eager to impose their will directly by attending council meetings where possible. During the course of the reign, other councils emerged, responding to the particular needs of the kingdom, including the Councils of the Inquisition (1483) and of the Orders (1489). The authority of each council was derived and stemmed from a delegation of royal power, which was largely inspired by the Aragonese model. Aragon relied on conciliar government in order to administer its distant lands in the Mediterranean.

The *Cortes*

Royal authority was restored partly via the effective management of the *Cortes* (see Figure 1.2). Ferdinand and Isabella were intent on acknowledging the political influence of the *Cortes* and exploiting it as a channel to re-establish royal power, especially in the towns. The Crown retained full control of the *Cortes* in Castile, particularly with regard to its composition and even the right of representation. The *Cortes* in turn lacked substantial legislative power and retained only the right to petition. Its financial power was no greater, and unlike some early modern parliaments, it was unable to make the supply of money dependent on the redressing of grievances. A full meeting of the Castilian *Cortes* was summoned to Toledo in 1480, though it would not meet again until 1498, meeting another 12 times before 1516.

Despite their dominant position, Ferdinand and Isabella handled the *Cortes* very effectively and even sensitively. The Crown tended to make laws in the presence of the *Cortes* and usually with its consent. Ferdinand and Isabella 'legislated in, rather than outside, the *Cortes*', even though they wielded sufficient power to ignore it.[5] In 1505, for example, the *Cortes* issued 83 laws by its own authority and Ferdinand himself subsequently ratified them. The main function of the *Cortes* was to vote subsidies, from which the nobility and clergy were exempt, hence their frequent absences. The Crown took full advantage of its commanding position over the *Cortes*. At the 1480 *Cortes*, Isabella declared that all major Castilian towns should elect a **corregidor** for two years, a royal official appointed to impose law and order. While *corregidores* were not introduced to Aragon, there were 54 towns with *corregidores* by 1494, and a further 32 Castilian towns had been added by 1515. Although the *corregidores* did not secure complete royal control of the towns, they certainly contributed to the maintenance of peace and boosted the status and profile of the monarchy.

Ferdinand and Isabella reinforced royal authority by managing the province of Aragon. Unlike Castilian monarchs, the kings of Aragon were reliant on the *Cortes* to legislate and to introduce new taxes. The Aragonese *Cortes* retained greater privileges and power than its Castilian counterpart. Aragonese kings could not operate without its consent. Given that all the *Cortes* in the eastern kingdoms (Aragon, Catalonia and Valencia) could be used to resist royal authority, Ferdinand sensibly chose not to threaten their independence. Nor was there any pressure on Ferdinand and Isabella to secure political unity because the eastern kingdoms had relatively little to offer. The

> **Key term**
>
> ***Santa Hermandad:*** In the late medieval period, some Castilian towns established *hermandades* (brotherhoods) to keep the peace. In 1476, Ferdinand and Isabella placed these organisations under royal control. The *Santa Hermandad* was coordinated by a general council (the *Junta General*) and financed by local communities, including the clergy and the nobility.

Figure 1.6: Portrait of Ferdinand of Aragon.

resources available in Aragon and Catalonia were 'little more than useful additions to what the crown already possessed in Castile…if the crown of Spain had been deprived of essential power in its peripheral kingdoms then it would have been forced to take issue with them'.[6] Ferdinand's long absences from the eastern kingdoms are very revealing, given the importance attached to the royal presence in the Iberian Peninsula; in 37 years, Ferdinand spent four years in Aragon, three years in Catalonia and only six months in Valencia. In order to make up for his frequent absences, Ferdinand established the Council of Aragon in 1494, arguably his most important administrative innovation and an attempt to bypass the *Cortes*. The tradition of independence was far stronger in Aragon, which explains why the kings of Aragon were less powerful than the rulers in Castile. The King of Aragon ruled by consent, and the power of the nobles made any substantial political and legal reforms very difficult. Aristocratic support for the monarchy was largely dependent on the Crown preserving regional privileges. For those reasons, Ferdinand and Isabella were reluctant to insist on a comprehensive political union of the Castilian and Aragonese crowns. As a result, serious conflict was avoided and Castile and Aragon maintained harmonious relations.

Justice

Ferdinand and Isabella restored royal authority by setting a framework for justice. From 1489, the **Audiencia** sat in Valladolid to deal with civil and criminal cases and was composed of a President and eight judges, appointed on an annual basis. A second appeal court was established in Ciudad Real (1494), which was moved to Granada in 1505, with lesser courts created in Santiago and Seville. In some towns, the Crown had the right to appoint *regidores* (town councillors) and *alcaldes* (town magistrates), though this did not inevitably strengthen the Crown. In the province of Aragon, the **Justiciar** was considered to be guardian of their *fueros* and liberties. These judicial developments encouraged a steady increase in the number and influence of lawyers throughout the peninsula.

Key term

Audiencia The *Audiencia* was the highest court in Castile.

The establishment of the *Santa Hermandad* in 1476 was of even greater significance to the extension of royal power. As a centrally organised constabulary and judicial tribunal, it was intended to provide security and justice for local communities. The *Santa Hermandad* facilitated the increase of royal control over urban and rural affairs and quickly became one of the most significant institutions in the localities. Every city, town and village with over 50 inhabitants was expected to form a local brotherhood. The *Hermandad* helped to link together the different localities in the peninsula, for each brotherhood was expected to send representatives to a central assembly (*Junta General*) that directed policy. The *Hermandad* was very powerful (including the authority to execute those who committed crimes) and was used both to raise finances and to establish militias. As time progressed, it formed an integral part of the royal army, becoming a permanent citizen militia, if not a regular army.

Unity and confederation

The marriage of Ferdinand and Isabella brought a semblance of unity to the provinces of Aragon and Castile, though neither monarch sought to impose a rigid process of political centralisation. Isabella was queen in Castile, though Ferdinand was permitted to give orders there. Major political decisions required both their signatures. It was never their objective to secure a new united Spain. Ferdinand and Isabella respected the political and legal variances of their respective territories. In particular, Ferdinand respected the *fueros* of his Aragonese subjects. His lack of absolute power is manifest in the Aragonese oath of loyalty, which highlighted the restrictions on his power. While the Castilian *Cortes* did not represent a check on royal power, the parliamentary tradition in the eastern kingdoms was stronger. The *fueros* were a constant barrier to centralising policies, especially since they were given institutional backing in the *Cortes*. They were also upheld by the *Justiciar*, who would actively question and resist royal legislation. It is not surprising that the different realms developed successfully but separately under Ferdinand. Although he was based in Castile, Aragon was not completely neglected and its *Cortes* was summoned in later years (1510, 1512 and 1515). As Lynch has noted, 'the emergence of Castile as the dominant partner in the union was not due to a narrow nationalism, but had the fullest support of Ferdinand – a measure of the King's realism, not of the Queen's prejudice'.[7] While Aragon and Castile remained separate states, Catholicism provided an important unifying link across the two provinces.

The political stability provided by Ferdinand and Isabella was gravely threatened by the succession crisis that followed the latter's death in 1504. Her death had the potential to break up the union of the Castilian and Aragonese Crowns. With Ferdinand forced to renounce the Castilian Crown, Juana the Mad and Archduke Philip of Habsburg were proclaimed rulers. The future looked bleak as Juana was incapacitated by illness and Philip was a foreigner with little understanding of Castile. The breakdown of relations with Philip was sufficiently serious for Ferdinand to encourage Louis XII of France to attack the Habsburg-controlled Low Countries, or Netherlands. A crisis was averted because Philip died the year he arrived in Castile and Ferdinand was appointed governor of Castile on the understanding that Juana was unfit to rule. Ferdinand successfully deflected any criticisms by accommodating and appeasing the diverse interests of his Castilian and Aragonese inhabitants. He was sufficiently wise not to exploit his considerable power in Castile in order to fulfil Aragonese goals. While he was clearly devoted to the strengthening of Aragonese power in the Italian city-states, he was equally dedicated to Castilian expansion in the New World. His annexation of southern Navarre to the Castilian Crown, rather than the Aragonese Crown, is indicative of his sensitivity to the divergent priorities of each province.

Relations with other European powers

Ferdinand and Isabella certainly exploited the diplomatic advantages that arose from their symbolic union. The securing of northern borders reinforced their royal authority. They had used the treaty of Medina del Campo (1489) with Henry VII to target Cerdagne and Roussillon. Charles VIII of France, who was seeking to secure a presence in the Italian city-states, agreed to hand over the provinces in the Treaty of Barcelona (1493). Less than a decade later, in 1512, Ferdinand led an invasion on his northern border and agreed to partition Navarre with the French. Ferdinand had by then remarried, to **Germaine de Foix**, giving him a claim to Navarre. The French were again too preoccupied with Italian affairs to resist the Spanish takeover of Navarre and Ferdinand was shrewd enough to promote and protect Navarrese laws and customs.

Social issues and policies

The nobility

Noble dominance in the civil wars reminded Ferdinand and Isabella that aristocratic power needed to be both contained and harnessed. The wealth and influence of the 300 or so grandees meant that they could not be ignored, especially given that nobles remained a military class. By the 1470s, 15 families dominated the Castilian aristocracy, owning more than 50 per cent of the land in Castile. This included the dukes of Infantado (Mendozas) – who controlled as many as 90 000 vassals – and Medina Sidonia. Out of necessity, Ferdinand and Isabella secured alliances with key nobles, but in the process they ensured that the aristocracy did not accumulate too much political power. Ferdinand encouraged the intermarriage of Catalan and Castilian noble families to engineer greater political and social unity across the peninsula. Hesitant to introduce any innovations, he and Isabella strengthened their hold on nobles by using pre-existing institutions such as the *hermandades*. In some instances, Ferdinand and Isabella adopted more direct methods to curtail the powers of the aristocracy. Some fortified castles were destroyed, frontier governors

ACTIVITY 1.2

Write a short biography of Archduke Philip of Habsburg.

> **ACTIVITY 1.3**
>
> What were the origins of the military orders? How did they become so powerful? How effectively did Ferdinand and Isabella deal with them? Use examples from this book and combine them with your own research.

> **Key term**
>
> *Reconquista:* After Muslim Arabs conquered the Iberian Peninsula in the eighth century, Christians from the north began a long process of reconquest that often took the form of a crusade. The military subjugation of the Moorish kingdom of Granada by Castile in 1492 marked its end.

> **ACTIVITY 1.4**
>
> What were the principal grievances of the peasantry? Research and identify the 'six evil customs'. How far did the Sentence of Guadalupe improve the livelihood of peasants?

(*adelantados*) were targeted and removed, and private wars were declared illegal. The political influence of magnates at court was greatly restricted and few leading nobles were allowed to contribute to the formulation of policy. Ferdinand and Isabella encouraged nobles to seek royal patronage. They promoted **mayorazgo** (prohibiting the division of inheritances), which was a much sought after form of patronage.

The monarchs called on the aristocracy to celebrate their dominant social and economic position in society, instead of aspiring to a major political role. Chivalric activities were given prominence at court, and this led to the revival of the knightly culture of John II of Castile, the promotion of bullfighting, and the popularity of Arthurian legends (famously inspired by the books of Amadís de Gaula). Despite Ferdinand and Isabella's attempts to curb aristocratic power, the greater nobles with their enormous estates remained a potential and very real threat. For example, following Isabella of Castile's death, the Duke of Medina Sidonia offered 2000 cavalry and 50 000 **ducats** to Ferdinand's rival, Philip of Habsburg. While the nobility was perceived to be a threat in the heartlands of the kingdom, Ferdinand and Isabella aimed to work in partnership with the aristocracy in the southern part of the peninsula. Following the completion of the *Reconquista*, the nobility received over 50 per cent of conquered Moorish lands in Granada. The monarchy was shrewdly dispensing land to the aristocracy without diminishing the royal patrimony.

Ferdinand wanted to capitalise on the power and wealth of the different military orders (Santiago, Calatrava and Alcántara in Castile, Montesa and St John in Aragon). The military orders had substantial property in towns and in the countryside, including fortresses, and their combined wealth equated to that of the kingdom of Naples. With their ability to raise troops, the military orders had wreaked havoc in the civil wars. By 1500, Ferdinand had taken over the mastership of the orders of Santiago, Calatrava and Alcántara, opening up an important and substantial new field of **patronage**.

The peasantry

In contrast with the aristocracy and the Church, few peasants owned land. Most peasants were relatively free, though the traditions of serfdom were stronger in Galicia. There were no substantial efforts to redress peasant grievances, with one notable exception in Catalonia. After peasant unrest in the years 1484–85, Ferdinand produced the 'Sentence of Guadalupe' (1486), which identified and removed the 'six evil customs', securing greater rights and liberties for the peasantry. While the six evil customs had kept the peasantry in relative serfdom, the Sentence outlined contractual obligations between tenants and landlords. As a consequence of their rebellion, they were expected to pay a large sum for the privilege. Overall, the regime never resolved the considerable economic inequalities, which were scarcely unrepresentative by European standards.

The urban communities

The major towns and cities were a genuine force in the localities because they tended to govern outlying territories under royal jurisdiction. In the 1480s, three of the four largest cities were in Castile – Seville and Granada with a population of 50 000 each and Toledo with 30 000. Yet with the exception of the 17 royal corporate towns, there were no other towns with concentrations of more than 8000–10 000. In Aragon, the situation was similar, with the dominant towns being Valencia with 30 000, Barcelona with 25 000 and Zaragoza with 15 000 in 1500. The towns were often dominated by that small fraction (4 per cent) of the population who were neither peasants nor nobles, namely merchants, professional men and clerics. The *Santa Hermandad* mobilised the collective resources of the towns into a potent political force. It was an influential body because it incorporated many towns that were outside the sphere of the Castilian *Cortes*.

From the outset, Ferdinand and Isabella made every effort to control the towns and cities. The willingness and regularity with which the monarchs visited and resided in the towns illustrates their importance, at least in the minds and actions of Ferdinand and Isabella. They sought to consolidate their power by intervening as mediators between factions and by making concessions to the urban elites. The resulting changes confirmed the local gentry in power and secured peace. Towns were otherwise contacted via the *Santa Hermandad*. Royal influence was also extended through the existence and intervention of *corregidores*. Acting as judicial officers or military officials in the most strategic towns, the *corregidores* were nominated by the King and appointed for two years. This allowed Ferdinand and Isabella to gain a far greater insight into the inner workings of urban society. Although resentment existed because the towns had little apparent control over an appointee whose salary they paid, in reality the *corregidores* were overwhelmingly local officials, who were sensitive to the traditions and customs of the urban commune. Ferdinand and Isabella did not introduce the *corregidores* into the eastern kingdoms, where the monarchy needed to tread more carefully out of respect for Aragonese privileges and liberties.

ACTIVITY 1.5

Assess the political significance of the towns during Ferdinand and Isabella's reign. In what ways and with what success did Ferdinand and Isabella control Castilian and Aragonese towns?

The Church

The Church was a key institution in the newly united provinces of Castile and Aragon. In December 1496, Ferdinand and Isabella were given the title of Catholic Monarchs (*Los Reyes Católicos*), which they merited on account of their personal initiatives. They insisted on daily worship at court. Isabella's own piety was exemplary and she took care in adding the key devotional works of the age to her library, including Castilian editions of Ludolph of Saxony's *Vita Christi* and Thomas à Kempis's *Imitatio Christi*. Ferdinand and Isabella were determined to increase royal control over church structures and personnel. This was marked by the timing and measures taken by the Ecclesiastical Council in Seville, summoned in 1478. The Council confirmed the royal appointment of bishops and archbishops, including the key archdioceses in Castile (Toledo, Santiago and Seville) and Aragon (Zaragoza, Tarragona and Valencia). The subsequent royal appointments were almost uniformly successful. The competence and capabilities of these ecclesiastical leaders, such as **Hernando de Talavera, Jiménez de Cisneros** and **Diego de Deza**, helped to reduce the levels of anticlericalism.

In addition to gaining control of church structures and personnel, Ferdinand and Isabella sought to improve the quality of pastoral supervision. The condition of the secular clergy (priests) was arguably worse than that of the regular clergy (clerics in religious orders). Anticipating the later disciplinary decrees of the **Council of Trent**, significant emphasis was placed on the reform of the episcopacy. In particular, it was insisted that bishops reside in their diocese so that they could personally supervise clerical reform. Avoiding foreign appointees meant that bishops such as Talavera in Ávila (later moving to Granada) became strong and effective advocates of reform. As ever, there were exceptions to the rule, notably Ferdinand's illegitimate nine-year-old son, Alonso de Aragon, who secured the see of Zaragoza (Alonso's own illegitimate son went on to succeed him). Not all bishops undertook exclusively spiritual functions. Some were actively involved in royal administration, for church and state were inseparably bound. Juan de Fonseca directed the expansion in the New World, whereas Juan de Ortega, bishop of Almeria, supervised the *Hermandad*.

As well as embarking on a reform programme, Ferdinand and Isabella were adamant that the Spanish Church should not pose a threat to royal authority. The Church's judicial, financial and military power meant that it had the potential to undermine the Crown. Ferdinand and Isabella intended to secure greater jurisdiction over the clergy by challenging the independence of the ecclesiastical courts. The monarchs achieved some success by 1502, by which time all church courts were expected to employ lay judges or to refrain from imposing merely spiritual penalties for temporal offences.

A/AS Level History for AQA: **Spain in the Age of Discovery, 1469–1598**

> **ACTIVITY 1.6**
>
> Why was the Church so powerful and influential? How successfully did Ferdinand and Isabella harness its power?

> **ACTIVITY 1.7**
>
> Research the following religious orders: Benedictines, Augustinians, Franciscans, Dominicans and Jeronimites. For each, identify the founder, the date of their foundation, their expansion in Spain and their main characteristics.

> **ACTIVITY 1.8**
>
> How did Ferdinand and Isabella maintain control of the different social groups in Spain? Focus on the nobles, urban dwellers, peasants and the clergy.

> **Key term**
>
> **Luther(an):** The German reformer and monk, Martin Luther (1483–1546), challenged the financial corruption of the Roman Catholic Church in October 1517 and his revolt developed into an outright rejection of the Church's authority. Lutheranism thrived within the Holy Roman Empire, though it was less successful in the Italian city-states and on the Iberian Peninsula.

Ferdinand and Isabella were also able to gain control of church taxes, notably tithe payments. Even after the fall of Granada, citizens continued to pay the *cruzada* tax. With the memories of civil war relatively fresh, Ferdinand and Isabella also targeted the military power of the Church. The archbishops of Toledo and Santiago had previously had the power to mobilise small armies. Following the war of succession, Isabella ordered Alfonso Carrillo, the Archbishop of Toledo at that time, to hand over all of the Church's fortresses to the Crown.

Much of the evidence points to the Spanish Church's increasing independence from Rome, though the papacy was not excluded from the Spanish reform programme. At various times during the reign of Ferdinand and Isabella, the popes actively supported their religious work through the promulgation of **papal bulls**. In 1486, Pope Innocent VIII granted Ferdinand and Isabella complete control over the Church in Granada. Seven years later, the Crown was granted a monopoly for missionary activity in the New World (the bull *Inter Caetera*) and Christopher Columbus, accordingly, took friars on his second journey. In 1501, a papal bull gave the Crown the right to collect tithes. Energised by papal support, Ferdinand and Isabella were keen to promote a properly functioning church in the New World. Nicolas Ovando (governor of Hispaniola, 1502–09) was given detailed instructions about church administration and Seville was made the centre for the Archbishopric for the New World churches. The monarchs saw themselves as champions of Christendom.

Cardinal Cisneros launched a major initiative to reform the monasteries. Having secured a papal bull in 1493, Cisneros started with his own order (the Franciscans) then continued with the Dominicans and the Augustinians. It was not, however, a straightforward process as many monks had to be forcefully expelled from their communities and the Dominicans at Salamanca even defended themselves with weapons. By 1517, the year that **Luther** posted his 95 theses in Wittenberg, nearly all Franciscan conventual houses had become **Observant**, a process that had royal backing in Spain. Although Ferdinand and Isabella were clearly supportive of these changes, the impetus for these reforms did not lie with them. The inspirations for the Observant reform movement came from the reforming trends of 15th-century spirituality. Within Spain, this was characterised by the success of the Jeronimite order, with its foundation in 1373 at Guadalupe, as well as its remarkable proliferation, amounting to 49 religious houses by 1516. The Benedictine foundation of San Benito de Valladolid was a major centre for monastic reform, from its foundation in 1390. The Observant reform movement was also inspired by external influences, particularly the *devotio moderna*. The leading Spanish promoter of monastic reform was García Jiménez de Cisneros, cousin to the cardinal, and abbot of the Benedictine community at Montserrat. Advocating reform to the Benedictine and Cistercian orders, Montserrat became a beacon for reform, as well as the key location for the channelling of the *devotio moderna*'s writings in Spain. The two cousins inspired the translation and publication of numerous devotional works, dominated by the *Vita Christi* and the *Imitatio Christi*. In addition to commissioning the **Polyglot Bible**, Cardinal Cisneros had forbidden the preaching of indulgences in Spain before Martin Luther's protest in 1517. Cisneros, unlike Luther, was not driven by theological motives. He argued instead that there were more important priorities in Spain than the rebuilding of St Peter's in Rome.

Dealing with the religious minorities

Muslims/*Moriscos* and the *Reconquista*

The Iberian Peninsula contained a large number of Muslims, particularly in Granada and Valencia. The majority of Muslims lived in the countryside and worked as agricultural labourers. Although Christians and Muslims coexisted with a degree of harmony, the **Moors** were perceived to be a threat because of their potential links

1 The forging of a new state, 1469–1516

with the **Ottomans** and corsairs who dominated the Mediterranean. Inevitably, royal officials who lived in areas where Muslims prevailed remained constantly on their guard. The greatest potential challenge to royal authority came from the Moorish kingdom of Granada. In the words of Fernando of Zafra, Ferdinand's secretary who was largely responsible for much of Granada's administration after the conquest, 'I could wish all of them would leave...I like them better there than here.'[8] Ferdinand and Isabella shared Zafra's concerns and had decided on war from an early stage. In 1481, Ferdinand remarked to a Galician official that 'we now intend to put ourselves in readiness to toil with all our strength for the time when we shall conquer that kingdom of Granada and expel from all Spain the enemies of the Catholic faith'.[9]

There were numerous motives and reasons for embarking on the Granada campaign. Given the relatively recent fall of Constantinople in 1453 and the increasing Ottoman stranglehold on the Mediterranean, Ferdinand and Isabella were eager to prevent the emergence of a strong alliance between the Ottoman and corsair Muslims and Granada's Moors. After all, Ferdinand was already King of Sicily and about to target Naples. Traditionally, popes conferred the status of crusades on wars against the Moors. As well as justifying the use of the *cruzada* tax, it had the advantage of securing spiritual benefits for those who participated. While nobles in particular might be motivated by a crusade against the Moors, there were obvious financial opportunities from conquering Granada. The southern kingdom managed part of the Saharan trade in gold, which was controlled by North African Muslims. The wealth emanating from the silk trade was even greater. For Ferdinand and Isabella, there were tremendous opportunities for generating patronage. The monarchs were beholden to the law that while a ruler's Crown lands could not be distributed, any territories gained by conquest could be freely bestowed on any subjects. By the end of the reconquest, over 50 per cent of lands in Granada had been redistributed to the nobility.

It is unlikely that complete conquest was either the initial or, considered to be, a realistic objective, despite Granada's marked vulnerability. Yet war began rather unexpectedly as a response to the fall of the frontier castle of Zahara in 1481. Ferdinand and Isabella's reaction indicates that this was an opportunity that could not be missed: 'we are taking counsel to determine how war shall be waged against the Moors on every side [so that] very soon not only shall the town be regained [but] others will be won'.[10] The political benefits of reintegrating Granada were obvious. Without Granada, reconquest was incomplete and Spain itself would remain forever disunited. The campaign would also distract attention away from the internal disputes of Andalusian nobles, thereby reinforcing peace within the peninsula.

Already weakened by a lack of artillery, the Moors' prospects were not helped by the intra-family rivalries of their ruling dynasty. The ruling emir, Mulay Hassan, was dethroned in a palace revolution and was driven away to Malaga. His son Boabdil took his place, even though Mulay Hassan had abdicated in favour of Boabdil's half-brother. When Boabdil was temporarily held captive, he swore an oath of vassalage to Ferdinand in the Treaty of Córdoba (1483). Despite the disunity of the Moors, Boabdil finally surrendered only after an extraordinary 10 years of fighting.

The longevity of the conflict can be explained partly by the sheer numbers of Moors (approximately 500 000) in Granada. The political skills of the Moors, combined with the economic and technical limitations of the Castilian war machine, meant that the Castilian economy was at breaking point by 1487. Even territorial advances and military successes brought their own obvious problems for Ferdinand and Isabella, such as how to deal with the conquered lands and peoples. It would take time for Castile to establish a clearly delineated structure of government and a legal and fiscal administration within Granada.

Yet Castilian forces successfully overcame their Moorish rivals. Ferdinand and Isabella remained personally involved throughout the campaign and responded decisively

Key terms

Moors: The major Muslim power at this time was the Ottoman Empire. Its power was in the eastern Mediterranean, but Muslim influence extended all-round the southern shores and into Spain, which had been in Islamic hands since the 8th century. The Muslims living on the Iberian Peninsula were referred to as the **Moors**. Muslim pirates, known as **corsairs**, were much feared by Christian European seaborne traders and travellers.

ACTIVITY 1.9

Identify the strengths and weaknesses (political, military and financial) of Castilian forces and Moorish rebels and explain their relative importance in determining the outcome of the Granada War.

from the outset. There was far greater political substance to their leadership than the respective contributions portrayed by the contemporary poet, Juan del Encina: 'she with her prayers, he with many armed men'.[11] The military campaign was not merely supported by leading nobles (such as the Count of Cabra, the Duke of Medina Sidonia, the Marquis of Cadiz, the Duke of Infantado), but the Andalusian aristocracy in fact took the lead. Even well-established noble rivals, such as the Marquess of Cadiz and the Duke of Medina Sidonia, cooperated and fought together. Perhaps their willingness to set aside personal animosities can be attributed to what they hoped to gain from the campaign.

The Granada war led to the emergence of a national army, which was mobilised with the help of great magnates, gentry and their dependants, the militia of the *hermandad* towns and soldiers, including Swiss mercenaries, raised by the Crown. The biggest single source of troops was the municipalities. At the height of the conflict, Ferdinand and Isabella had 50 000 foot soldiers and 10 000 cavalry under their command. By 1487, Spanish use of heavy artillery in sieges was the norm. Castile contributed the most to the campaign, though the resources and supplies that came from Aragon, Catalonia and Valencia were not insignificant. Ferdinand and Isabella's campaign benefited greatly from the capture of Malaga in 1487, which was of considerable strategic importance. Castilian men and supplies could now be directed by sea. This allowed the Castilians to disrupt the Moors' communications with their fellow Muslims in the Mediterranean.

Financially, the Castilian war effort was supported by church taxes, and especially the *cruzada* introduced by **Sixtus IV**. Although the total income from papal grants was substantial, amounting to 800 million *maravedís* between the years 1484 and 1492, they did not cover the costs of war, particularly a conflict that lasted a decade. The campaign was also financed by heavy taxes imposed on members of the Jewish communities, who provided 58 million *maravedís* between 1482 and 1491. The sale of slaves from Malaga produced 56 million *maravedís*, while there were sizeable contributions from prominent nobles (17 million from the Duke of Medina Sidonia alone) and 27 million from the *Mesta*. By the early 1490s, the *Santa Hermandad* was giving 32 million *maravedís* per annum, and donated 300 million during the period 1482–90. Booty was an alternative and important source of finance, especially prisoners who could be held to ransom for cash. Despite these impressive amounts and varied sources of revenue, the quantities were not enough to effect a speedy conclusion to the war.

 Voices from the past

The Surrender Treaty of the Kingdom of Granada

Read the following extract on the Surrender Treaty of the Kingdom of Granada, 1491, and answer the questions that follow:

Their Highnesses and their successors forever shall let [the Moors] live under their own law, and [keep] their mosques, nor shall they interfere with their ways and customs … No Moor shall be forced to become Christian against his will.[12]

Discussion points:
1. What do the nature of these terms suggest about the *Reconquista*?
2. Why were the terms so favourable to the Moors?
3. What is your assessment of the value of the words 'and their successors forever'?

1 The forging of a new state, 1469–1516

Ferdinand and Isabella consolidated their victorious *Reconquista* by granting generous terms to Boabdil and his supporters. Initially, they were permitted to live under Muslim law in the Alpujarra Mountains, and to continue practising the Islamic faith. Moorish leaders were given their own lands in the southwest of Granada. These conciliatory policies were necessary in the short term but secondary to the ultimate objective of persuading the Moors to emigrate. Talavera was responsible for reintroducing Catholicism in Granada, and employed a conversion strategy that was respectful and tolerant of Muslims. By 1499, Talavera had lost the initiative to Cisneros, who adopted a more uncompromising stance towards the Moors. Cisneros played a prominent role following the Moorish uprisings in 1499, which had broken out in response to the increasing taxation demands on Muslims. Again Catholics in Granada feared potential links between the Granada Moors and their co-religionists in the Mediterranean. Cisneros himself acknowledged and articulated this fear by highlighting their proximity to the Spanish coastline, as well as the sheer numbers that could come to the assistance of the Moors. In order to strengthen the position of Christianity, 40 000 Christian settlers moved to Granada between 1485 and 1498, the majority of whom were Andalusians.

The departure of Boabdil for Africa in 1493 did much to encourage the movement of Moors abroad, but eventually Ferdinand and Isabella replaced the policy of emigration with one of expulsion. This was largely the result of the rebellions between 1499 and 1501, which convinced Ferdinand and Isabella to take a harsher line. By 1501, it was officially assumed that Granada's Moors were being Christianised. The following year, all of Castile's Muslims were forced to convert or to leave, with many of the Muslim elites moving to North Africa. During the course of the war, 100 000 Moors had been killed and 200 000 had fled Granada. This left the remaining 200 000 converted Moors (*Moriscos*) in Granada still subject to discrimination; there were now 500 000 *Moriscos* on the Iberian peninsula out of a population of 7 million.

The flight of so many *Moriscos* facilitated the political developments that followed. Iñigo Lopez de Mendoza was put in charge of the Granada government, while Hernando de Talavera was appointed Archbishop of Granada. *Corregidores* were appointed to the chief cities and an *audiencia* was fixed in Granada in 1505. It has previously been asserted that much of the kingdom of Granada was given over to the leading magnates, yet in fact only a few areas were handed over to the **señorios** and they tended to be territories with a large *Morisco* population. The conquest and Christianisation of Granada strengthened royal authority by linking the Church and the nobility to the royal cause. The *Reconquista* certainly enhanced the status of the Crown, which gained an additional population of 300 000 inhabitants, as well as the wealth of Granada and the security of its southern coastline. There were obvious military benefits, as Castile's troops became battle-hardened and gained invaluable experience.

The Jews/*conversos* and anti-Semitism

The other significant religious minority with which Ferdinand and Isabella's regime had to deal were the Jews. Spanish Jews had enjoyed considerable success in the Middle Ages, but their peaceful coexistence with Christians was greatly undermined by the economic depression that occurred in the middle of the 14th century. Anti-Semitic prejudice clearly predated the accession of Ferdinand and Isabella. Most striking were the anti-Jewish riots of 1391, which culminated in numerous forced conversions.

With over 100 000 converted Jews (*conversos*), many of them living in urban communities within close proximity to unconverted Jews, it was feared that the *conversos* were practising Judaism in secret. The persecution of former Jews did not cease with their conversion and there were frequent clashes in the 15th century, notably Toledo in 1467 and Córdoba in 1473. In late 15th-century Spain, no serious heresy existed so the Inquisition was founded in order to address the problem of the

ACTIVITY 1.10

How well did Ferdinand and Isabella's regime deal with the Moorish kingdom of Granada? Create a 2 × 2 table, heading the sections Strengths, Weaknesses, Opportunities and Threats to make a SWOT analysis. Were they successful?

Key terms

Moriscos: The *Moriscos* were people of Moorish descent who had converted to Christianity. Labelled as New Christians, they were granted legal equality to Old Christians, though they were not allowed to possess weapons. The sincerity of their conversion was frequently questioned.

A/AS Level History for AQA: Spain in the Age of Discovery, 1469–1598

Key terms

Conversos: The *conversos* were formerly Jews, who converted to Christianity. Like the *Moriscos*, they were labelled as New Christians, and the sincerity of their conversion was also questioned.

Spanish Inquisition: The Spanish Inquisition was established to eradicate heresy from the different provinces in Spain. In the early part of Ferdinand and Isabella's reign, the Inquisition predominantly targeted the *conversos*. The Inquisition had the right only to investigate Christians, and therefore not Jews and Muslims.

conversos. The **Spanish Inquisition** differed from the papal inquisition both in its origin and organisation.

The foundation of the Spanish Inquisition was directly encouraged by Ferdinand and Isabella, who were determined to promote and enforce a degree of religious unity on the Iberian Peninsula. Ferdinand and Isabella had petitioned the Pope to give them full authority over the Inquisition. Although Pope Sixtus IV was reluctant to empower the Spanish Crown in that way, the Spanish Inquisition was finally established with papal approval in 1478. Masterminded by Alonso de Hojeda, the prior of the Dominican community in Seville, the Council of Inquisition (known as the *Suprema*) was the Inquisition's key institution. All members of the Council owed their position and allegiance to Ferdinand and Isabella and were considered to be royal officials. To that effect, the Inquisition represented another strand of conciliar government. By 1492, there were over 10 tribunals situated in the main towns, staffed by clergy, but controlled by the Crown. There were no inquisitors appointed until 1480, owing to opposition within Spain. Once established, the first **auto da fé** was held in Seville and six *conversos* were burnt. In addition to the two Dominican friars who became inquisitors in 1480, a papal bull of 1482 promoted a further seven inquisitors, including the Inquisitor General, Tomás de Torquemada.

By 1483, the Inquisition had spread to Aragon, so Torquemada had gained authority in Castile and Aragon, a jurisdiction that no other official on the Iberian Peninsula controlled. Torquemada's appointment defied the Aragonese *fueros* because non-native officials were forbidden to function. Inevitably, there was considerable opposition from Zaragoza's influential community of *conversos*. The Inquisition in Aragon was seen as an alien institution, an agent of Castilian intervention and also a possible threat to Aragonese economic interests. As early as 1484, the Valencian *Cortes* denounced the new tribunal as a violation of its *fueros*.

Timeline: Spanish Inquisition

Year	Events
1478	Spanish Inquisition founded by Papal Bull
1482	Inquisitors appointed, including Tomás de Torquemada
1483	Inquisition established in Aragon
1484	Valencian *Cortes* rejected the new tribunal in defence of its *fueros*
1485	Inquisitor Pedro de Arbues assassinated in Aragon
1488	1000 killed in Valencia alone

Torquemada was obviously not the architect of the Inquisition, but once appointed Inquisitor General, he took responsibility for giving the Inquisition its definitive organisation. He was empowered to appoint and dismiss individual inquisitors and, in turn, his authority was subordinate to that of the Crown. It was intended that papal intervention should be avoided where possible. Interestingly, the inquisitors were mostly secular clergy and university graduates, and not completely dominated by the Dominicans. Although there were strict rules for the gathering of evidence (two witnesses and hearsay were insufficient), testimony from the prosecution was allowed to be anonymous (which was different from **Roman** and **Canon law**). While the early activities of the Inquisition were concerned more with enquiry than punishment and focused exclusively on the threats of heresy and apostasy, it later became dominated by personal animosities, and social and economic rivalries.

1 The forging of a new state, 1469–1516

In their desperate defence, *conversos* appealed to Rome, regional immunities, local magistrates and to the monarchs themselves. In certain cases, they resorted to violent counter-measures, including the assassination of the Inquisitor of Aragon, Pedro de Arbues, in the cathedral of Zaragoza in 1485. Despite this resistance, between 1481 and 1488, 700 Judaizing *conversos* (those found to be covertly practising Judaism) were convicted and burnt. By 1480, 4000 *converso* families had fled from Andalusia. Such was the violence of the early tribunals that Sixtus IV regretted the extensive powers that he had granted to the Spanish Crown. Yet Henry Kamen has suggested that the proportion of *conversos* actually executed was relatively small; 2000 were executed between 1480 and 1530 compared with a population of 70 000 Jews in Castile and 10 000 in Aragon. It is worth noting that the numbers executed were far smaller than those arrested. Between 1480 and 1500, 40 per cent of those arrested in Valencia and Ávila were executed. The Inquisition in Valencia claimed almost 1000 victims in 1488 alone. In Córdoba, 107 were burnt in a single *auto da fé* in 1504. It is beyond doubt that the *conversos* became the main target of the Inquisition during Ferdinand and Isabella's reign. Out of the 1200 tried in Barcelona in the years 1488–1505, all but eight were *conversos*.

The jurisdiction of the Inquisition was restricted to Christians and it was certainly not a means of converting unbelievers by force. It punished heresy and apostasy, but not the profession of a different faith. Baptism remained a precondition of heresy so Jews, Muslims and American Indians were excluded from its authority. The pressure on *conversos* and the forcible conversion of Moors did, however, generate social pressure for purity of blood (*limpieza de sangre*). Although it never attained official status in public law, it was supported by Salamanca University in 1482, the Jeronimites from 1486 and Seville Cathedral from 1515. The promotion of purity statutes may well have been a response to *converso* attempts to seek political advancement.

With significant pressure exerted on the *conversos*, the Jewish communities did not escape attention. They were often used as scapegoats and accused of cannibalism and infanticide, and contemporary sermons often alluded to the Jews being collectively guilty for the death of Christ. Relative to other European states, there was greater tolerance towards Jews in Spain, largely due to their economic importance. They were protected throughout the *Reconquista* because they provided significant financial support when circumstances demanded it. They were frequently employed as rent and debt collectors, tax farmers and moneylenders. The sheer numbers and influence of *conversos* conveyed the impression that society was being overcome by Judaizing influences. Town authorities imposed ever harsher sanctions on Jewish communities, who were expected to wear distinctive clothing and to be confined to their Jewish quarters. Contemporary writers such as Bernáldez lamented local populations being 'infected' with Jewish customs, the 'result of the constant contact they had with the Jews'. That said, some municipalities (including those of Seville, Toledo, Barcelona, Valencia and Zaragoza) complained about the excesses of the Inquisition, mainly because the expulsion of Jews and *conversos* had a detrimental impact on the local economy. Given the negative economic consequences, the expulsion of Jews from Spain was undoubtedly motivated by well-established religious motives.

At the end of 1482, the Inquisition ordered a partial expulsion of Jews from Andalusia, in 1484 they were driven out of Seville, and by the mid-1480s all Jews were under attack. During 1484–91, the church authorities expelled Jews from Andalusia in order to raise funds for the Granada campaign. The Jews were obliged to sell their property cheaply. Inevitably, the persecution of *conversos* was counter-productive and undermined royal finances. There was a reluctance to allow Jews to stay, even if they promised to pay a ransom; a collection of rabbis had offered the substantial sum of 300 000 ducats. By 1492, royal legislation decreed that Jews should be expelled from the peninsula on the grounds that their presence was preventing *conversos* from practising Christianity properly. Out of 200 000 Jews, about 75 per cent left the kingdom and they were forbidden from taking gold, silver, money, weapons and

Speak like a historian

Ferdinand, Isabella and General Franco

Extract from the introduction to John Edwards's biography of Ferdinand and Isabella:

Generally respected in Spain, both in their own time and subsequently, Isabella and Ferdinand became political and cultural role models during the dictatorship of General Francisco Franco, between his victory in the Spanish Civil War, in 1939, and his death in 1975. For Franco and his ideologues, the 'Catholic monarchs', as they were entitled by Pope Alexander VI in 1496, represented all that was virtuous. They were, indeed, devout Catholic Christians, whose religion was claimed to give the lie to the secularist creeds of socialism, communism and anarchism, against which Franco's war was supposedly fought. They 'unified' Spain – Castile, Aragon, Navarre – under one government, thus like Franco, attempting to suppress the culture and national identity of minority peoples, notably the Basques and Catalans, and securing the political, linguistic and cultural dominance of Castile. By means of war in Granada, they ended Muslim rule in Spain and they also affirmed the country's Catholic Christian identity by expelling from their domain those Jews who would not become Christians and enforced religious orthodoxy by means of a new Inquisition.[13]

Discussion points
1. Why were Ferdinand and Isabella well regarded during the Franco era?
2. How important is it to review and revise interpretations of historical figures and periods?
3. Should historians entirely dismiss historical accounts that are ideologically driven?

horses. Ferdinand and Isabella also successfully exerted diplomatic pressure on King Manuel of Portugal to expel the Jews from his kingdom in 1497, since many Spanish Jews had fled there in the first instance.

Economy, trade and exploration

Economic stagnation and change

Castile was much larger and more powerful than Aragon, and had greater natural resources and wealth. Yet the lack of political unity brought with it economic disunity, and a strong sense of particularism profoundly affected the economy. The *Mesta*, for example, refused to collaborate with the Catalans because the Genoese, their chief rivals for the Mediterranean trade, had more to offer. The Catalans were not treated as equal partners nor were they invited to the commercial fairs at Medina del Campo. On a similar theme, the kingdom of Castile dominated the trade with the New World; Spain's American empire remained primarily a Castilian empire.

The consequences of the *Reconquista*

The Crown sought to counterbalance the detrimental impact caused by the departure of the *conversos* by publishing edicts inviting foreign workers to Spain in 1484. They were initially granted exemption from all taxes for 10 years. In order to promote trade, Ferdinand and Isabella granted licences for commercial voyages to those who had financial independence and therefore the capital, especially foreign merchants. Genoese merchants were considered to be even more important than Jews, and Castilian overseas expansion would have been impossible without their assistance. Genoese merchants supplied much of the funding for the conquest of the Canary Islands and the voyages of Columbus. These increases in revenue occurred in spite of the economic crisis in Granada, which resulted from 10 years of warfare, the economic impact of Muslim emigration, and the collapse of traditional trade with North Africa.

The crisis in agriculture

Much of Castile's strengths stemmed from her powerful trading structures, notably the *Mesta*, as well as her control of the towns. The *Mesta* controlled Castilian sheep-farming and wool marketing, so in 1500 Ferdinand and Isabella promoted presidents of the *Mesta* to a senior position on the Royal Council. The Crown did not merely sanction the status quo; 'it short-sightedly worsened it', blindly defending the *Mesta* against all opposition.[15] Owners of livestock, and especially migrant merino sheep, dominated much of southern and central Spain. The wool trade was also coordinated by the *Hermandad de las Marismas* (seafaring towns) and an intricate network of agents was established, connecting Spanish towns with key European cities, including Bruges, La Rochelle, London and Florence. In 1488, the government's chief tax farmer, the Jewish financier Abraham Senero, was made treasurer-general of the *Hermandad*, whose officials were used to collect the *cruzada* and the tax on sheep. The *Mesta*'s dominance led to a law of land lease in 1501, granting the *Mesta* the right to use, in perpetuity and at fixed rents, any land it had once used as pasture.

The predominance of pastoral farming caused the neglect of the arable sector; inevitably, Spain developed such serious grain shortages that by 1506 the population was dependent on large-scale imports of wheat. Pressurised by the demands of military campaigns abroad and the *Reconquista* at home, the Crown was reluctant to promote agriculture and effect substantial reforms. In that enterprise, Ferdinand and Isabella had the support of the landed aristocracy, who turned the majority of their lands to pasture, which required little investment of money and manpower.

Revenues and taxes

Castilian financial affairs were controlled by the Council of Finance, which was directed by Alonso de Quintanilla. Although there were few innovations in the way that royal income was generated, more effective leadership led to a remarkable increase in revenue, from 800 000 *maravedís* in 1470 to 22 million in 1504. These achievements

> **ACTIVITY 1.11**
>
> Why was there a crisis in agriculture and how serious was it?

Voices from the past

Andrés Bernáldez

Read the extract about the Jews from the chronicler, Andrés Bernáldez, and consider the following questions:

The Jews were 'merchants, salesmen, tax-gatherers ... tailors, shoemakers, tanners, weavers, grocers, pedlars, silk-mercers, smiths, jewellers, and other like trades; none tilled the earth or became a farmer, carpenter or builder: all sought after comfortable posts and ways of making profits without much labour'.[14]

Discussion points:
1. What does this extract tell us about the Jews?
2. Bernáldez was a parish priest near Seville. How does this affect our reading of the source?
3. Should we completely disregard the source as a result? If not, why?

occurred in spite of the economic challenges encountered during this period. Ordinary revenues were traditionally based on Crown lands, which expanded during the course of the reign. They were partly raised via customs duties, which were also extracted from within the kingdom on the movement of sheep. A substantial amount of revenues (estimates range between 80 and 90 per cent) came from the *alcabala*, a tax on sales and purchases, from which the Church and the nobility were exempt. Over two-thirds of the revenues came from Old and New Castile, which included the important trading centres, such as Burgos, Valladolid, Medina del Campo, Segovia, Toledo, Córdoba and Seville.

Far from being a modern state, a large part of the royal financial administration was farmed out, rather than being centralised and under immediate royal control. There is no doubt that existing taxes were collected more efficiently. With a central record of taxes, the accounts of tax farmers (*arrendadores*) were audited every two years. Yet the fiscal system remained basic, and tax farmers were certainly prone to corruption. The Castilian *Cortes* also played an important part in raising extraordinary taxes. This was more difficult in Aragon, where the King could not raise revenue or troops without summoning each individual *Cortes*.

In the latter part of Isabella's reign, 70 per cent of Castilian royal revenues were drawn from extraordinary sources, having previously stood at 30 per cent. Like their European counterparts, Ferdinand and Isabella were also dependent on extra-parliamentary means, especially the fund-raising of the *Santa Hermandad* and the exploitation of the military orders of Santiago, Calatrava and Alcántara. Ferdinand and Isabella greatly benefited from the wealth of the Church, as well as its taxes; the revenues from the *cruzada* had doubled to 112 million *maravedís* by 1504.

Royal expenditure

Royal expenditure was considerable during the reign of Ferdinand and Isabella. Sustaining the war effort in the Granada and Italian campaigns, including the mobilisation of armies and the deployment of artillery, was prohibitively expensive. Military expenses within the kingdom amounted to 500 million *maravedís* during 1495–1504; two expeditions to Naples cost 454 million, while the Crown had spent 80 million on the royal militia by 1504. Consolidating territorial gains was also costly, particularly the building and maintenance of fortresses. The numbers of fortresses increased from 70 in 1474 to 160 by 1492. Ferdinand and Isabella also showed interest in shipbuilding, arms manufacture and horse-breeding. These different demands led Ferdinand and Isabella to borrow. By issuing *juros* (government bonds) to royal creditors, the Crown agreed to pay 10 per cent interest, which was costing 131 million *maravedís* by 1516. By 1504, the Crown had spent 35 million on their royal residences, ambassadors and court ceremonial, and Catherine of Aragon's journey to England cost a staggering 60 million.

Foreign policies of the two realms

Despite the dominance of Castilian resources, Ferdinand and Isabella's foreign policy was, from the 1480s onwards, dominated by Aragonese and Catalan priorities. This reflected an anti-French stance, which ran counter to the traditional Castilian policy towards France. In pursuing defensive objectives, Ferdinand sought alliances with any potential enemies to France, such as England, imperial Burgundy and Brittany. In particular, he was eager to secure the northern frontiers, especially Navarre, Roussillon and Cerdagne. Ferdinand and Isabella also sought to dominate the western Mediterranean, to prevent the French from attacking the Italian city-states and to drive back the Ottomans. In order to secure stronger and more effective diplomatic relations, Ferdinand and Isabella employed resident ambassadors abroad, a practice only previously seen in the Italian city-states. For that reason, Henry Kamen has described Ferdinand as one of the 'pioneers of the European diplomatic system'.[16]

As a result, Ferdinand and Isabella had permanent diplomatic agents at the papal, Venetian, Imperial and English courts. The differences between Castile and Aragon were clearly evident in the realm of foreign policy.

Historically, the English presence in Gascony had united France and Castile against England in the Hundred Years' War, while Aragon's lengthy frontier with France made them enemies. Aragonese affairs in the Italian city-states were of no interest to the Castilians, who were more preoccupied with expansion in the Iberian Peninsula and in Africa. Castile and Aragon inevitably had different trading partners, with the latter almost exclusively focused on the Mediterranean.

Matrimonial alliances

Diplomacy formed an integral part of Ferdinand and Isabella's foreign policy and they made the very most of matrimonial alliances. Their eldest daughter Isabella was married in 1490 to Afonso, son of King John II of Portugal. When Afonso died a year later, Isabella married his successor Manoel, though she herself then died in 1498. That same year, Manoel married their fourth daughter Maria, illustrating the importance that was attached to that alliance. In 1496, Ferdinand and Isabella sought to strengthen their relations with the Habsburgs via two strategic marriages. Their only son, John, married **Margaret of Austria**, daughter of **Maximilian I**, in 1496 (though he died in 1500). Also in 1496, Archduke Philip (Emperor Maximilian I's son) married their second daughter, Juana, which was to prove the most decisive of the matches they arranged. Their youngest daughter, Catherine, was betrothed to Henry VII's eldest son, Arthur, and married him by proxy in 1499. The fact that the marriage alliance was renewed with Henry's younger son Henry following Arthur's death in 1502 showed how significant it was to both countries.

France, Navarre and North Africa

There were undoubtedly significant achievements in Ferdinand and Isabella's foreign policy. Roussillon and Cerdagne (under French occupation since 1462) were secured via the Treaty of Barcelona in 1493. Ferdinand managed to take full advantage of Charles VIII's priorities; the French king was willing to compromise owing to the preparations for his Italian campaign. Navarre was Ferdinand's last major territorial acquisition, during which he exploited the disputed succession between his second wife Germaine de Foix and the French Albret family. He reinforced his claims with the help of an army commanded by Fadrique Alverez de Toledo y Enríquez, the second Duke of Alba that quickly occupied the kingdom. Briefly integrated into the territories of Aragon (1512–15), Navarre subsequently belonged to Castile. Shrewdly, Ferdinand did not seek to undermine Navarrese privileges, he did not disregard the Council of Navarre and their *Cortes* continued to function.

Following the fall of Granada, Ferdinand was eager to attack the North African coast in order to give further protection to the newly conquered kingdom of Granada. In this objective, he collaborated with Cardinal Cisneros and achieved some important territorial gains, including the ports of Mers-el-Kebir (1505), Oran (1509), Bougie, Tripoli and Algiers (1510–11) and the fortress of Peñon de Vélez (1508). Wisely, Ferdinand refused to support Cisneros's ambitions to extend their African conquests inland. Possession of these strongholds also greatly strengthened Spanish control of Mediterranean trade. Further west, Castilians provided 70 ships to an alliance that successfully expelled Ottomans from Otranto in 1481. In that enterprise, Ferdinand was largely motivated by Sicily's security. In 1501, Castile helped the Venetians to expel the Ottomans from the fortress of St George in Cephalonia.

Timeline: Ferdinand and Isabella's Foreign Policy

Year	Events
1479	Treaty of Alcáçovas
1481	Ottomans expelled from Otranto
1492	Christopher Columbus's first expedition to the New World
1495	Charles VIII annexed Naples
1498	Charles VIII died, and succeeded by Louis XII
1500	Treaty of Granada
1503	Spanish victories at Cerignola and Garigliano; *Casa de Contratación* established
1505	Treaty of Blois
1512	French driven out of Navarre

Naples

Ferdinand's greatest achievement in the Mediterranean was the acquisition of Naples. In the first instance, Ferdinand organised a Holy League against France on the pretext of supporting his brother-in-law King **Ferrantel** of Naples and the papacy (Naples was traditionally a **papal fief**). In reality, Ferdinand did not divulge to his allies that he sought to annex Naples for himself. He was given his opportunity when Naples was invaded by Charles VIII in 1495. In response, Ferdinand secured a strategic matrimonial alliance between Philip and Juana with Emperor Maximilian I, who had recently claimed Milan. In the first phase of the war (1495–98), Ferdinand intervened to support his cousin Ferrante II, who became entirely dependent on Spanish military assistance for his political survival. Ferdinand then benefited from the death of Charles VIII in 1498 because his successor Louis XII was more interested in the duchy of Milan. Despite a Franco-Spanish agreement to divide up Naples (as signed in the Treaty of Granada in 1500), when fighting was renewed the French were driven out following the Spanish victories at Cerignola and Garigliano in April and December 1503 respectively.

Thanks to Gonzalo de Córdoba's brilliant campaigns, Ferdinand was secure as King of Naples by the time Isabella died. At the Treaty of Blois in 1505, Louis XII gave his rights to Naples to his niece Germaine de Foix, who married Ferdinand that year. The acquisition of Naples was invaluable not only for strategic reasons but also for the resulting increase in revenues and agricultural resources. Yet in the longer term, possession of Naples not only involved Spain in Italian affairs (and an ongoing conflict with France) but also brought her even closer to the Ottoman Empire. The continuing tensions with France are evidenced by the creation of another Holy League in 1511. The following year, the French were driven out of Navarre while in 1513, a combined force of German and Spanish troops drove Louis XII out of Italy.

The New World and Christopher Columbus

Arguably, Ferdinand and Isabella's greatest legacy came with their territorial gains in the New World. Partly motivated by their rivalry with the Portuguese, they targeted the New World for commercial and economic reasons. It would provide space to cultivate land (and to grow sugar and corn). With the Ottomans gaining an increasing stranglehold in the Mediterranean, and the establishment of settled colonies in North Africa becoming increasingly difficult, the suggestion of an alternative was welcomed. The opportunity was provided by the Treaty of Alcáçovas (1479), whereby Portugal

1 The forging of a new state, 1469–1516

renounced its claim to the Canary Islands. This encouraged Ferdinand and Isabella to send expeditions to seize Grand Canary, La Palma and Tenerife. Although the islands were not completely pacified until 1496, they became vital stepping stones for future exploration and conquest. Ferdinand and Isabella benefited from the improvement of relations between Castile, Aragon and Portugal, which were cemented by yet more marriage alliances.

Christopher Columbus was eager to access the wealth of the Indies by sailing west around the globe. Since the Portuguese monarchy was reluctant to support anything other than southern and eastern expeditions, Ferdinand and Isabella agreed to commission Columbus to undertake his journey. Partly driven by religious motives, Ferdinand and Isabella managed to secure a papal bull in 1493, granting them control of any newly discovered lands. In his four expeditions (1492, 1493, 1497 and 1502), Columbus sought to establish trading posts in the lands he called the 'Indies' (he did not realise he had discovered a New World) and selected men with technical skills to accompany him, including soldiers, sailors, craftsmen, miners and farmers. It was intended that the natives would provide hard labour. While Columbus wanted to establish only a small permanent population of Spaniards, Ferdinand and Isabella were eager to colonise the new territories at all social levels. '[W]e have commanded Don Cristobal Colon to return to the island of Hispaniola and the other islands and mainland which are in the said Indies and supervise the preserving and peopling of them', they wrote in a letter to the Castilian municipalities in anticipation of Columbus's third voyage, and they made their intentions quite clear: 'thereby our Lord God is served, His Holy Faith extended and our own realms increased'.[17]

Figure 1.7: Portrait of Christopher Columbus, painted by Domenico di Tommaso Bigodi, better known as Ghirlandaio (1449–94).

Columbus was a less than reliable agent of the Crown. He was not a statesman and his political delegation to his brothers Bartolomé and Diego led to the mistreatment of natives, which was undoubtedly counter-productive to the Spanish cause. When Columbus was named viceroy, he was given economic concessions and administrative rights, though the colonies were so underdeveloped that he had few opportunities to exploit his jurisdictional powers. Earlier expeditions were reliant on public finance, but as time progressed, private sources of finance started to dominate as *conquistadores* were promised a share in the spoils. For that reason, economic factors came into conflict with more noble missionary motives. Successive governors of Hispaniola, Francisco Bobadilla and Nicolás de Ovando, were more effective in consolidating Spanish gains. After testing the abilities of the Indians, Ovando became convinced that they were incapable of self-government. Equally significant was the regulation of trade from the New World, and it was Juan Rodriguez de Fonseca's idea to centralise the Indies trade in Seville. The *Casa de Contratación* (House of Trade) was established in Seville in 1503 under Fonseca and Francisco Pinelo. By 1516, Spanish possessions in the New World included Hispaniola (1500), Puerto Rico (1508), small settlements in Central America (1509) and Cuba (1511).

Changes in Castile and Aragon by 1516

Political, social and economic change

Ferdinand and Isabella neither unified Spain nor created any significant political institutions by 1516. Their symbolic marriage did not lead to the emergence of a powerful political body that united the provinces of Castile and Aragon. John Lynch noted that: 'Ferdinand and Isabella gave Spain a common government but not a common administration.' The union of Crowns, he explains, 'was personal, not institutional: each kingdom preserved its identity and its laws … the union of crowns was only the beginning of the unification of Spain'.[18] Yet that union was unfavourable to Aragon. Ferdinand was normally absent and the key imperial institutions were controlled by Castile. Isabella did not make any notable interventions in Aragon's affairs, though Ferdinand may have contributed to the impression of joint rule.

 Key term

Conquistadores: The *conquistadores* were ambitious adventurers, who sought to discover and explore new lands primarily for the sake of their self-advancement. The most important territorial conquests were against the Aztec and Incan empires in Mexico and Peru respectively.

Ferdinand never acted individually as King of Castile without Isabella's consent. The continuing separation of the kingdoms was evident in the territorial expansion that occurred during the reign of Ferdinand and Isabella: the New World, Granada and Navarre were annexed by Castile; Aragon controlled Cerdagne, Roussillon and Naples.

In truth, there were no institutions common to both Castile and Aragon, with the exception of the Inquisition. One of their major achievements was to bring peace and order to Spain, which Henry Kamen accredited to Ferdinand and Isabella – the 'basic ingredient was the firm use of direct personal authority'.[19] This is impressive given the lack of a standing army and reliable income. They created stability out of disorder mainly because of their control over the nobility. The pre-eminence of the nobility in society was confirmed by the size of their estates and private armies, though Ferdinand and Isabella shrewdly restricted their political responsibilities. In their place, they were increasingly reliant on lawyers, who became an essential element in the transition from medieval government to the later bureaucratic state of the Habsburgs. For all Ferdinand and Isabella's strengths, it should not be forgotten that, following Isabella's death in 1504, the cause of unity was only saved by a combination of largely fortuitous events, including the death of Philip of Habsburg (who reigned as Philip I in Castile) in 1506, the madness of Juana and the infertility of Ferdinand's second marriage. As a result, Ferdinand was left in charge of Aragon, Castile and Italian claims. By 1516, Castile and Aragon were perceived to be a significant power in Europe.

The supremacy of Castile was reflected also in the expansion of her language. The literature of Spain's golden age was written in Castilian and its foundations are rooted in Ferdinand and Isabella's reign. Based in that centre of excellence, the University of Alcalá, the humanist and philologist Antonio de Nebrija published a Castilian grammar book in 1492. In the prologue to that book, dedicated to Queen Isabella, Nebrija expressed his conviction that 'language was always the instrument of Empire'. Nebrija believed that Castilian should be learnt by 'the Basques, the Navarrese, the French, the Italians, and all others who have any traffic and communication with Spain'.[20] It was at Alcalá that the project to complete the Polyglot Bible was begun, though it was completed only in 1522. By 1516, numerous towns and cities had acquired printing presses. The first book printed in Spain appeared in Segovia in 1472, and there were 800 titles published in Spain by 1501.

Financially, Ferdinand and Isabella left a somewhat unstable legacy. A third of ordinary income was used to service royal debt. Economic disunity reigned, with three different coinage systems and internal customs barriers in force. While parts of the Castilian economy prospered (especially wool production), the Aragonese economy largely went into decline. The regime had seemingly tolerated the diversion of taxes into private hands, especially with the *alcabala*.

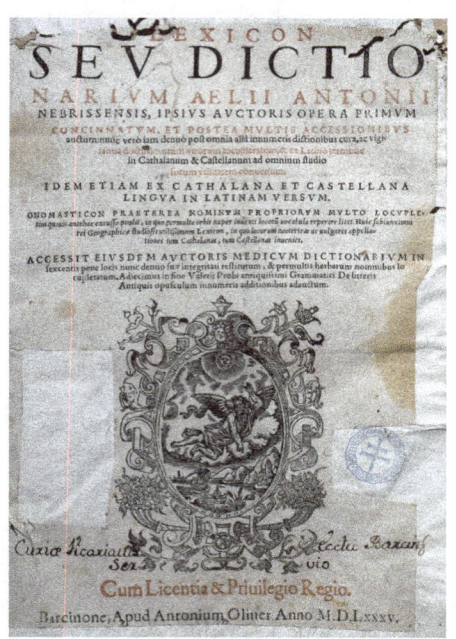

Figure 1.8: Nebrija's grammar book, printed in 1486.

Practice essay questions

1. 'Ferdinand and Isabella forged a "new monarchy".' Explain why you agree or disagree with this view.
2. 'Ferdinand and Isabella's reputation for greatness has been exaggerated.' Assess the validity of this view.
3. 'Ferdinand and Isabella's domestic and foreign policies were driven by religious motives.' Explain why you agree or disagree with this view.
4. With reference to these extracts and your understanding of the historical context, which of these two extracts provides the more convincing interpretation of the impact of Columbus's voyages of discovery?

1 The forging of a new state, 1469–1516

Extract A

By 1510 Spanish settlement in the Americas was becoming established and royal authority was being strengthened. Thus Diego Columbus was never permitted to inherit his father Christopher's powers as 'Admiral of the Ocean Sea' and in 1511 a further crucial step was taken, in the establishment of a Royal High Court (audiencia) for the 'Indies' at Santo Domingo, on the island of Hispaniola. Already, in 1503, a central 'trading office' (casa de contratación) had been established in Seville, to secure royal control over all trade between Europe and the newly discovered American territories.

Source: Edwards, *Ferdinand and Isabella*, p. 168.

Extract B

Well before the death of Ferdinand, America began to create conflicts and pose problems. The enslavement of Indians, begun by Columbus, was firmly opposed by Isabella, who encouraged the formation of encomiendas and the payment of wages for labour. Abuses in the system, however, led the Dominican friars on their arrival in Hispaniola in 1510 to campaign for the abolition of the encomienda, thereby initiating a great debate on both sides of the Atlantic about the nature of human freedom.

Souce: Kamen, *Spain*, p. 60.

Further reading

There is a good and accessible overview of Ferdinand and Isabella's reign in Colin Pendrill's *Spain, 1471–1700* (Heinemann, 2002). The biographies of *Isabel the Queen* by P.K. Liss (University of Pennsylvania Press, 2004), and of *Ferdinand & Isabella* by Felipe Fernández-Armesto (Weidenfeld & Nicolson, 1975) and John Edwards (Longman, 2005) provide a more detailed insight; the latter forms part of the excellent series of historical biographies, *Profiles in Power*. It is also worth looking at histories of late medieval and early modern Spain, notably those written by Henry Kamen and John Lynch, as listed in the end notes to this chapter, as well as John Edwards's *The Spain of the Catholic Monarchs, 1474–1520* (Oxford, 2000), J.H. Elliott's *Imperial Spain, 1469–1716* (Penguin, 2002) and C. Mulgan's *The Renaissance Monarchies, 1469–1558* (Cambridge University Press, 2002).

Chapter summary

By the end of this chapter you should understand:

- the nature of the Iberian peninsula inherited by Ferdinand and Isabella
- the ways in which Ferdinand and Isabella restored royal authority at home, especially focusing on religious, economic and political factors
- the effect of Ferdinand and Isabella's policies abroad, including their diplomacy and military campaigns
- how far Ferdinand and Isabella established royal authority by 1516.

A/AS Level History for AQA: **Spain in the Age of Discovery, 1469–1598**

Speak like a historian

Felipe Fernández-Armesto and John Lynch

Read these statements by the historians Felipe Fernández-Armesto and John Lynch, and use your knowledge of Ferdinand and Isabella's reign to answer the questions below:

Inheriting distinct and mutually hostile kingdoms, shattered by social and political strife, Ferdinand and Isabella left to their Habsburg successors the makings of a nation state, united, peaceful, and powerful beyond any in Europe.[21] (Lynch)

Castile remained essentially an agrarian, pastoral and feudal country as it had been in the Middle Ages and the Catholic monarchs never even began to undertake the admittedly formidable task of integrating the various regions of Spain into an economic whole.[22] (Lynch)

The containment and, if possible, reversal of these two centrifugal [French/Ottoman] monarchies was the aim of the foreign and dynastic policy of the Catholic monarchs.[23] (Fernández-Armesto)

In the fullness of time, it has become apparent that the greatest achievement of the Catholic monarchs' reign was the discovery and colonisation of America.[24] (Fernández-Armesto)

Discussion points:
1. How successful were Ferdinand and Isabella in the pursuit of their domestic and foreign policy objectives?
2. What was Ferdinand and Isabella's greatest achievement?
3. Have their contributions to the development of early modern Spain been exaggerated?

End notes

[1] Henry Kamen, *Spain, 1469–1714: A Society of Conflict*. Harlow: Longman, 2005, p. 17.
[2] Cited in Felipe Fernández-Armesto, *Ferdinand & Isabella*. London: Weidenfeld & Nicolson, 1975, p. 47.
[3] Cited in Kamen, *Spain*, p. 24.
[4] Cited in Armesto, *Ferdinand & Isabella*, p. 108.
[5] Kamen, *Spain*, p. 34.
[6] John Lynch, *Spain under the Habsburgs: Volume I, Empire and Absolutism, 1516–1598*. Oxford: Basil Blackwell, 1981, p. 10.
[7] Lynch, *Spain*, p. 3.
[8] Cited in Armesto, *Ferdinand & Isabella*, p. 169.
[9] Cited in Armesto, *Ferdinand & Isabella*, p. 95.
[10] Cited in Armesto, *Ferdinand & Isabella*, p. 95.
[11] Cited in Armesto, *Ferdinand & Isabella*, p. 96.
[12] Cited in Jon Cowans (ed.), *Early Modern Spain: A Documentary History*. Philadelphia: University of Pennsylvania Press, 2003, pp. 15–19.
[13] John Edwards, *Ferdinand and Isabella*. Harlow: Longman, 2005, pp. ix–x.
[14] Cited in Kamen, *Spain*, p. 40.
[15] Lynch, *Spain*, pp. 16–17.
[16] Kamen, *Spain*, p. 9.
[17] Cited in Armesto, *Ferdinand & Isabella*, p. 149.
[18] Lynch, *Spain*, p. 4.
[19] Kamen, *Spain*, p. 18.
[20] Lynch, *Spain*, pp. 3–4.
[21] Lynch, *Spain*, p. 1.
[22] Lynch, *Spain*, p. 19.
[23] Armesto, *Ferdinand & Isabella*, p. 127.
[24] Armesto, *Ferdinand & Isabella*, p. 144.

2 The drive to 'Great Power' status, 1516–56

In this section, we will examine how Charles V established his authority in Spain and how far his broader dynastic objectives affected its domestic and foreign affairs.

Specification points:

- Charles V's inheritance; opposition and consolidation; revolts of the *Comuneros* and *Germanía*
- the workings of empire: ideas and image; conciliar government; individuals and domestic policy
- foreign relations within Europe; campaigns against the Turks
- religious policies and the Church in Spain
- the expansion of empire: the conquistadores; economic and social impact of the New World on Spain
- the political, economic, social and religious condition of Spain in 1556.

Charles V's inheritance

When Ferdinand of Aragon died in 1516, the kingdom his grandson Charles inherited was undoubtedly stronger than the political legacy that was left to the newly crowned Ferdinand and Isabella. However, the monarchical system that he took over still remained more medieval than modern. The Iberian Peninsula lacked a centralised and unifying political institution. The Habsburgs did not inherit 'a monolithic regime but a variegated and decentralised one, a personal union of independent states'.[1]

Figure 2.1: Titian's portrait of Holy Roman Emperor Charles V, also known as Charles I of Spain.

Unlike his Castilian and Aragonese predecessors, Charles I of Spain inherited an empire of which Spain formed only a part; he is better known across Europe by his title as Holy Roman Emperor, Charles V. In January 1515, he became ruler of the Netherlands, which stemmed from the Habsburgs' Burgundian inheritance. This included not only the territories of Luxembourg, Brabant, Flanders, Holland, Zeeland, Hainault and Artois, but also Franche-Comté and even a claim to the French-controlled duchy of Burgundy. As Emperor Maximilian I's grandson, Charles was also the heir to the Habsburg hereditary lands: Austria, Tyrol and parts of southern Germany. Charles's election as Holy Roman Emperor in 1519 gave some credibility to the declaration by **Mercurino Gattinara** (Charles's chancellor) that Charles was 'on the path to universal monarchy [and would] unite all Christendom under one sceptre'.[2]

Figure 2.2: Charles V's empire.

For all the apparent strength that these vast territories symbolised, the power of Charles's empire was deceptive. Interestingly, contemporaries did not use the word 'imperial' to describe his policies. Although there may have been some imperialists at court, such as Gattinara himself, Charles lacked the means to create and maintain a strong, unified empire. He would struggle to govern these dispersed territories, given that he could not be in more than one territory at a time. Charles was arguably doomed to fail, as Henry Kamen has implied; 'the one great obligation on him, to rule personally in each of his dominions, was of course impossible to fulfil'.[3]

It was highly likely that its association with a broader and more ambitious Habsburg imperialism would profoundly affect the government of Spain and the New World. Given the circumstances of his upbringing, combined with the nature of his massive inheritance, it would be difficult for Charles to establish his authority in Spain. In addition to the succession problems caused by Isabella's death in 1504 (particularly the tensions between Archduke Philip, Juana and Ferdinand of Aragon), there was further friction when Ferdinand died in 1516. Charles was born and had spent his entire childhood in the Netherlands, whereas his brother **Ferdinand** was raised in Castile. While Charles was proclaimed joint ruler of the Spanish kingdoms with Juana in 1516, the loyalty and submission of its inhabitants were far from guaranteed.

2 The drive to 'Great Power' status, 1516–56

Opposition and consolidation

Proclaimed regent until Charles's arrival in Spain, Cardinal Cisneros struggled to assert his authority. Cisneros's attempts to introduce a voluntary militia, raised from different regions and financed by the towns, were blocked by the aristocracy, who felt threatened. An inauspicious start was not greatly improved by Charles's arrival on Spanish shores. Having never visited Spain, Charles (who instantly dismissed the dying Cisneros) was overly reliant on his Flemish advisers, most notably his Grand Chamberlain, Guillaume de Croy, Lord of Chièvres, who monopolised access to the king. The royal household in Brussels contained few Spaniards and the Flemish counsellors who accompanied him immediately received various privileges, pensions and lucrative offices. The worst example of this Flemish favouritism was the appointment of Chièvres' 17-year-old nephew, Guillaume Jacques de Croy (already a cardinal and Bishop of Cambrai) as Archbishop of Toledo; Chièvres was also given the right to nominate all vacant posts in the New World. Laurent de Gorrevod, a Savoyard, received the whole of Yucatán and Cuba in August 1518 and was granted a licence to trade black slaves to the New World. These favours and privileges did not go unnoticed and in 1520 Charles's naming of his former tutor, **Adrian of Utrecht**, as regent during his absence from Spain would cause further resentment.

In 1518, Charles agreed to meet the Castilian *Cortes* at Valladolid, where he received a very cold reception. In keeping with his other pro-Burgundian appointments, Charles unwisely gave the presidency of the Castilian *Cortes* to a Walloon, Jean de Sauvage. The hostility to the new monarch was such that Juan de Zumel, a representative of the city of Burgos, publicly refused to recognise Charles as sovereign, claiming that his mother Juana was the real ruler of Castile. Other factions within the *Cortes* favoured his brother Ferdinand, on account of his Spanish upbringing. The *Cortes* presented more formal opposition when it officially demanded that Charles dismiss his Burgundian advisers and replace them with Spaniards. In an unconvincing response, Charles declared that his advisers were naturalised Spaniards. Charles was subsequently requested to learn Spanish and expected not only to adhere to Spanish laws and customs but also to be resident in Spain. In Salamanca, friars drew up a list of instructions for the *Cortes*, which insisted on the following: the '**Comunidades** must not be mis-governed, the king's duty is to govern them by his presence, not by his absence.'[4] In spite of their seemingly disrespectful, if not impertinent, requests, the *Cortes* voted 600 000 ducats for Charles without conditions for the next three years.

The response to Charles in Aragon was essentially similar. At first, the Aragonese *Cortes* hesitated to grant formal recognition to Charles's kingship during Juana's lifetime. However, in January 1519, the *Cortes* of Aragon acknowledged Charles as king conjointly with his mother, and also voted a grant of 200 000 ducats. While in Aragon, Charles heard of Emperor Maximilian I's death and declared himself a candidate to succeed him. The discussions with the Catalan *Cortes* were even more protracted than in Castile and Charles was in Barcelona for a whole year. It was there on 28 June 1519 that he heard that he had been elected Holy Roman Emperor; to achieve this he had spent close to one million gold florins on bribes. As a result, he was indebted to the Fuggers, arguably the most powerful merchant banking family in Europe, by more than 500 000 florins.

The *Comuneros* revolt

The *Comuneros* revolt of 1520–21 indicated just how vulnerable Charles's regime was in the early years. Toledo and Salamanca refused to send representatives to the 1520 *Cortes* in Santiago, which Charles summoned to ask for further funding prior to his departure for the Netherlands and Germany. Even before he had left, the *Corregidor* and other royal officials were expelled from Toledo, an example that was followed in numerous towns in central and northern Castile. In Segovia, the **procurador** was murdered and Adrian of Utrecht was unable to restore royal authority, partly owing to

---

ACTIVITY 2.1

Draw a spider diagram indicating the challenges facing Charles on his arrival in Spain. You may wish to consider his formative years and experience, as well as highlighting the potential political and financial problems.

Toledo's military assistance to that town. Popular opposition to Charles's government was responsible for much of the instability. The towns called for closer regulation of royal officials and the exclusion of foreigners from government. In addition, there were a number of economic and fiscal grievances, including demands for fiscal reforms and for the abolition of **subsidies** voted in the *Cortes*. They also requested the reduction of the *alcabala* to its 1499 levels, insisting that town officials rather than tax farmers should collect it. In some towns, there was a more radical agenda, daring to make demands on the monarch himself; Charles was expected to marry soon and to reduce his court expenses. The nature of opposition reflected deep-seated fears about Charles's priorities. As Lynch has argued, the 'gentry and townsmen of Castile revolted against a regime which they regarded as inimical to their interests, and which threatened to sacrifice Castile to an imperial or dynastic policy'.[5]

The revolt also stemmed from the different sectors within the textile industry. While wool exports from Burgos and Bilbao flourished, the manufacturers in the interior of Castile increasingly struggled. There is thus a direct economic correlation with the spread of the rebellion; for example, Segovia supported it and Burgos soon abandoned it. Many of the participants in the revolt were from the middle ranks of society and even the lower nobility. Having risen to prominence in local administration and government during the reign of Ferdinand and Isabella, they felt that Charles was now neglecting them. The revolt gained even greater momentum when Adrian of Utrecht's orders to punish Segovia accidentally led to a destructive fire in Medina del Campo, where Adrian had tried to seize the town's arsenal of weapons. This also served to radicalise the rebel movement, as Medina del Campo was Castile's financial and commercial centre. This government disaster accelerated the process of towns uniting under one central organisation, known as the *Santa Junta de Comunidad*, which met in Ávila. While the *Santa Junta* claimed to represent Spain's true government, only Salamanca, Segovia, Toro, Toledo and Ávila initially joined it. But by August 1520, 13 towns had become official members (including Valladolid). That autumn saw the zenith of the *Junta*'s success, which included the capture both of the Regent, Adrian of Utrecht, and Juana (who repeatedly refused to assert her leadership over the movement). The uprisings were certainly widespread, ranging from Zamora, Salamanca, Toro, Madrid, Guadalajara, Alcalá, Soria, Ávila and Murcia to Cuenca. In due course, the *Junta* represented 14 out of the 18 cities that were associated with the *Cortes*, with the notable absence of the four Andalusian cities (Seville, Granada, Córdoba and Jaen), and yet the revolt was certainly not restricted to the *Cortes* cities. At the peak of the revolt, the rebels were no longer soliciting reforms, but attempting to impose more rigorous restrictions on the king. At that point, the Bishop of Zamora joined the rebellion and seized Valladolid.

Ultimately, the *Comuneros* revolt failed. The radicalisation of the movement entailed increasingly outspoken criticisms of the nobility, so many grandees joined the royal army in order to defend their seigneurial privileges. In Valladolid, the *Junta* explicitly declared that 'the war was against grandees, **caballeros**, and other enemies of the realm, and against their properties and palaces to be waged with fire and sack and blood'.[6] This transformation from a political to a social movement brought crippling disunity to the rebel cause. The revolt also triggered peasant unrest as it moved from urban to rural areas. Perhaps inevitably, the aristocracy rallied to Charles's cause, even though they bemoaned his absence. Clear rifts emerged between reformers and revolutionaries. The *Junta* declared that the kingdom stood above the king and that the *Junta* represented the kingdom, thereby alienating any moderates, especially those in Burgos and Valladolid who already felt under pressure from the nobility. While reformers sought the restoration of good government, the radicals deliberated upon the creation of sovereign republics, modelled on the Italian city states.

The revolt was also hindered by the serious obstacle that every late medieval and early modern rebellion encountered, namely the strong sense of regionalism. The movement was undermined by the 'intense localism and particularism of Spanish towns' and found no support across the frontier in Aragon.[8] In early November 1520, Burgos withdrew from the *Junta* and on 5 December Charles's supporters seized and sacked Tordesillas (the headquarters of the *Junta*), and secured the person of the queen. The revolt was now apparently doomed, though it took until 24 April 1521 for the main rebel army of Juan de Padilla to be defeated at the battle of Villalar. Royal forces were led by the constable of Castile, Don Íñigo Fernández de Velasco, and Charles's victory culminated in the death of only 200 rebels and 20 royalists. A small number of rebel leaders, including Juan de Padilla, Juan Bravo and Pedro Maldonado, were executed. Although this marked the official end of the revolt, Toledo held out for a further 10 months, commanded by Maria Pacheco and Antonio de Acuña, the bishop of Zamora. Charles's own contribution to the defeat of the *Comuneros* revolt was not insignificant on account of his timely appointment of Constable Velasco and the hereditary Admiral of Castile, Fadrique Enríquez de Cabrera, as co-regents with Adrian. This served to defuse opposition to the Regent but also helped to convert any wavering nobles to the royal cause. Ultimately, the nobility could not ignore the political realities within the peninsula. Their power was inseparably linked to that of the monarchy. With aristocratic backing, royalist troops were mostly of a far higher quality, particularly the **hidalgos**, the lesser nobles, and the military retainers of the greater nobles, whose superior cavalry was decisive. When the Regent promised that Charles would return and marry a Spanish princess, most nobles were won over. In October 1521, Toledo surrendered and the Bishop of Zamora was executed for treason.

The *Germanía* revolt

The *Comuneros* revolt was not the only uprising that Charles faced. There was a simultaneous uprising, the **Germanía**, in Valencia. In August 1519, armed mobs attacked the Inquisition in the city of Valencia for being too lenient. There was an atmosphere of heightened security because they feared an attack by Muslim pirates from the Mediterranean. The Valencian guilds were well equipped with weapons for that very reason. The grievances were also social in motivation as the masses resented noble protection of the Moors, who cultivated their lands and who allegedly threatened the livelihood of Christian peasants by working for lower wages. Yet the protests were spontaneous, and the various grievances were never transformed into a proper political programme, though they asked for municipal representation. By undertaking an armed uprising, the rebels defied the city governor and viceroy, the Count of Melito, and claimed the right, as a *Germanía* (a holy brotherhood), to bear arms. In so doing, they were also exploiting the particular political circumstances; an outbreak of plague had emptied the town of its nobles and governor. A local weaver, Juan Llorenz, exploited the political vacuum, chose a governing committee of 13 and seized the city. The committee planned to remodel Valencia's constitution along the lines of the Venetian Republic, a proposal that was not entirely dissimilar to the more radical elements of the *Comuneros* revolt. The *Germanía* then sent a deputation to Charles in Catalonia, asking him to confirm their rights. Charles naively acquiesced, thinking that it would prevent him from having to summon the Valencian *Cortes*; Charles had repeatedly postponed meeting the Valencian *Cortes* and this combination of factors left its members profoundly disgruntled. The growth in opposition stemmed partly from noble and monarchical weaknesses. While Charles's mistakes had acted as a catalyst, the longer term pre-existing problems within Valencian society were more important. Unlike the *Comuneros*, the *Germanías* were driven by class conflict between urban groups and the aristocracy. This led to a more widespread revolt against nobles and government officials. In addition to targeting the Moors, the rebels overwhelmed the governor of Valencia's army at Gandía in 1521.

Timeline: The *Comuneros* and *Germanía* revolts

Year	Event
August 1519	Armed mobs attacked Inquisition in Valencia
1520	Toledo and Salamanca refused to send representatives to the Santiago *Cortes, Corregidor* expelled from Toledo, Adrian of Utrecht unable to restore royal authority in Segovia
August 1520	13 towns are members of *Santa Junta de Comunidad*
Autumn 1520	*Junta* captured Adrian of Utrecht and Juana
November 1520	Burgos withdrew from *Junta*
December 1520	Charles's supporters sacked Tordesillas
1521	Rebels overwhelmed governor of Valencia's army at Gandía
24 April 1521	Juan de Padilla defeated at the battle of Villalar
October 1521	Toledo surrendered and Bishop of Zamora executed; *Comuneros* revolt ended; Diego Hurtado de Mendoza destroyed *Germanía*'s forces
March 1522	*Germanía* revolt ended
1523	Germaine de Foix appointed Viceroy of Valencia

The *Germanía* revolt was eventually quashed. The *Germanía* represented too many interest groups (peasants, artisans and labourers), all of which lacked any meaningful power and influence. They were further weakened by their inability to find common cause with the *Comuneros*, owing to the divisive particularism in Spain. After Llorenz's death, the movement lost its direction and became increasingly violent. The rebels overplayed their hand when Vincente Peris, the revolt's new leader, attacked the Moors in the south and left Valencia unguarded. The Marquis of Zenete retook Valencia and Peris was defeated and executed. In October 1521, the viceroy, Diego **Hurtado de Mendoza**, destroyed the *Germanía*'s forces and 800 rebels were executed. By March 1522, the revolt had come to an end. The following year, Charles appointed Ferdinand of Aragon's second wife Germaine de Foix as viceroy of Valencia, and she later published a general pardon in December 1524. Ultimately, as with the *Comuneros* revolt, the aristocracy and higher clergy gave their unconditional support to Charles.

The aftermath of the revolts

The *Comuneros* revolt paralysed much of Castile for over 12 months. Government repression was noticeably harsh until Charles's return to Spain in July 1522. Accompanied by his new advisers, Mercurino Gattinara and **Francisco de los Cobos**, Charles undertook a royal progress, accompanied by 4000 German soldiers (and the latest artillery) through the rebel towns, but only an additional 22 agitators were tried and executed. Another 290 were excluded from the general pardon, though most were exonerated again on the payment of a fine. This was a defining moment for the Crown as royal authority was re-established and the *corregidores* returned to their positions.

The failure of the *Comuneros* revolt dealt an enduring blow to the political autonomy of the cities, especially because the government refused to undertake any significant reforms. While the social status and the privileges of the leading nobles remained secure, their political influence did not increase significantly. The real winner was Charles himself, as Lynch has indicated, 'if, in crushing the *comuneros*, Charles V received the collaboration of the grandees and nobles, he did not subsequently satisfy their ambitions or give them the power they wanted'. He concludes that 'it was a victory of the aristocracy over the townsmen, but the prize was taken by the king'.[9]

The aftermath of the *Germanía* had similar consequences. While the aristocracy partly benefited from the restoration of royal control, the Moors suffered as an edict was decreed in 1525 declaring that no Muslim was allowed to practise the Islamic faith in Spain. The *Germanía* had been prompted by a gradual decline in the kingdom of Valencia. This was largely the result of Ottoman and Barbary corsairs disrupting local trade, often assisted by *Moriscos* who lived on the coast. However, it was to Charles's great credit that there were no more serious revolts in Spain. He remained in situ for just under a decade, learnt Castilian and started to appoint Castilians to government positions. Charles came to realise the importance of accepting and protecting regional liberties.

The workings of empire: government and administration

One ruler, independent lands

Charles's inheritance did not consist of an empire in the traditional sense of lands acquired by territorial conquest. Spaniards, and especially Castilians, favoured the term 'monarchy', which allowed the possibility of independent lands being symbolically unified by their allegiance to the same ruler. A central administrative organisation was impractical, given the diverse lands and customs under his control. Even so, this was attempted with Gattinara's introduction in 1526 of a new Council of State for governing Spain and the German lands. In theory, this represented a central institution for Charles's empire, composed of leading Burgundian, Italian and German officials. In practice, Charles rarely used it and preferred to work through **Antoine Perrenot de Granvelle** and Cobos in order to draw up policies. After Gattinara's death in 1530, Charles let the office of Chancellor lapse and divided any major responsibilities between Cobos and Granvelle.

The *Comuneros* and *Germanía* revolts were a stark reminder that monarchs would endanger their own position if they ignored the privileges and threatened the autonomy of different states. For that reason, provincial leaders would have approved of the fact that Charles's imperial administration had no official capital. The imperial court followed the Emperor, though Castile remained a crucial political centre. During the course of his reign, Charles spent 11 years in Castile and only five years in Aragon. The Castilians contributed enormously to the administration of the monarchy. While the administrators worked in Valladolid, the councils tended to move with the king. Each individual part of his empire had a separate political, judicial and fiscal system, and no part was considered constitutionally subordinate to another. The Spanish jurist, Juan de Solórzano, indicated how sensitive and pragmatic Charles's approach to administering the empire needed to be: 'the kingdoms have to be ruled and governed as if the king who keeps them together were only the king of each [of] them'.[10]

In keeping with family strategy, Charles controlled the empire as the head of a dynastic organisation. A regent or viceroy represented him in each state and he tended to appoint family members to the more important states: Germaine de Foix became viceroy of Valencia; from 1521, his brother Ferdinand was put in charge of the Habsburg lands; in the Netherlands, his aunt Margaret of Austria (1518–30) and sister Mary of Hungary (1531–55) were successive governors. In theory, the system seemed to have every chance of working; however, it did not take long to realise that the Emperor's presence or absence had a profound impact on the judgement and effectiveness of his rule. Each territory's inhabitants expected Charles to be resident for a decent period of time, and this would be impossible for him to achieve. The Admiral of Castile reflected on this problem in 1531: 'Your Majesty's protracted absence

> **ACTIVITY 2.2**
>
> How effectively was royal authority restored in the aftermath of the *Comuneros* and *Germanía* revolts? Create a table to answer this question, using a SWOT analysis: Strengths, Weaknesses, Opportunities and Threats.

from your Spanish kingdoms is a thing to which your Spanish subjects can hardly reconcile themselves.'[11] While his Spanish subjects were arguably more sympathetic if his absence resulted from the Emperor's persecution of Lutheran heretics, they were unwilling to tolerate a lengthy absence.

Conciliar government

The Castilian government was closely intertwined with the royal court. Although Spanish officials replaced most of the Flemish advisers, Charles insisted on a Burgundian-style court, with elaborate, complex and luxurious ceremonies. By the 1550s, the court included over 750 members, and was costing approximately 200 000 ducats per annum. After a rather imperfect start, Charles showed himself to be a quick learner and made a concerted effort to adapt his policies. The language of the court

The Inheritance of Charles V

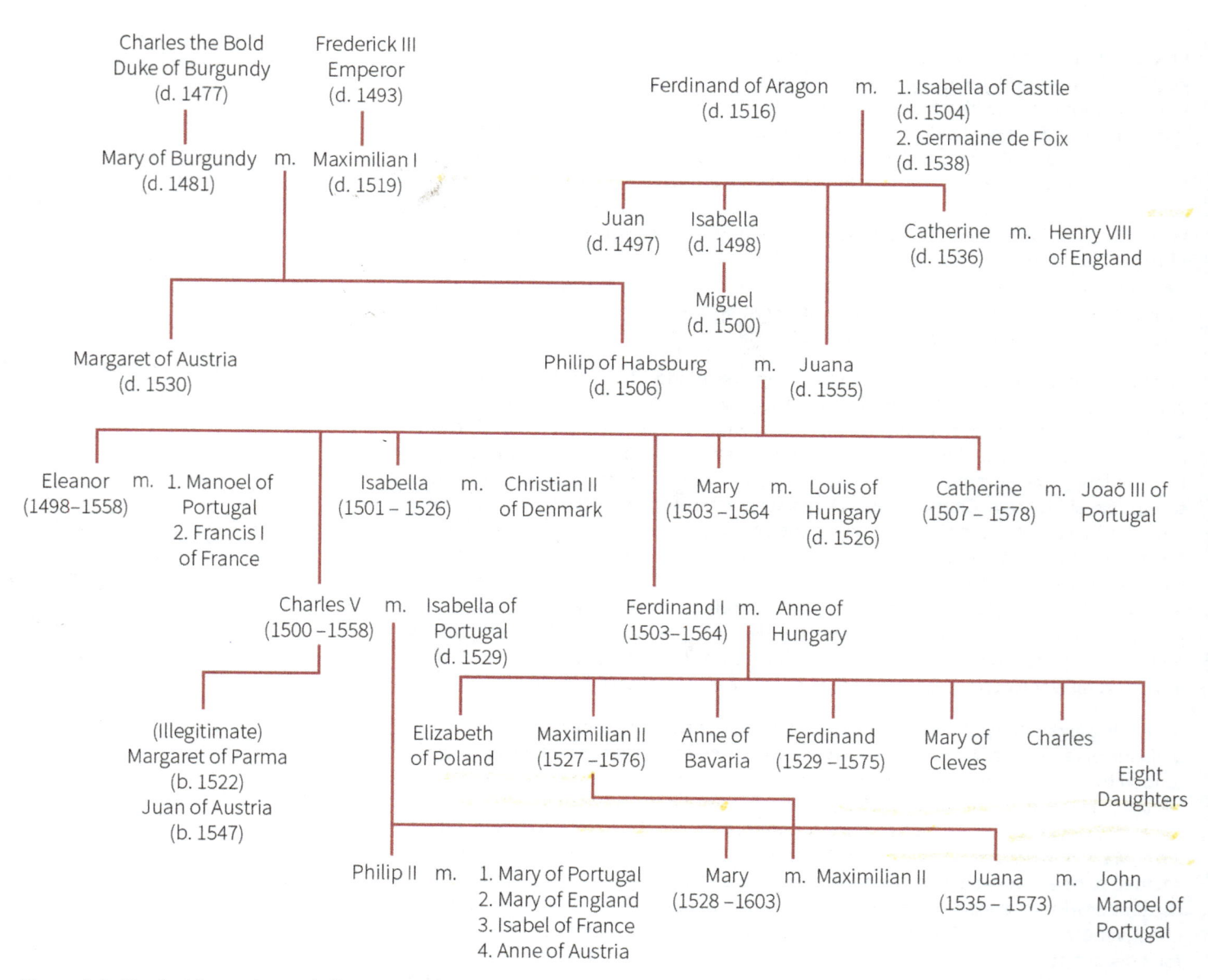

```
Charles the Bold        Frederick III
Duke of Burgundy        Emperor
(d. 1477)               (d. 1493)                    Ferdinand of Aragon    m.    1. Isabella of Castile
                                                     (d. 1516)                     (d. 1504)
                                                                                   2. Germaine de Foix
Mary of Burgundy  m.  Maximilian I                                                 (d. 1538)
(d. 1481)             (d. 1519)
                                              Juan         Isabella              Catherine  m.  Henry VIII
                                              (d. 1497)    (d. 1498)             (d. 1536)      of England
                                                      Miguel
                                                      (d. 1500)
Margaret of Austria                    Philip of Habsburg   m.   Juana
(d. 1530)                              (d. 1506)                 (d. 1555)

Eleanor    m. 1. Manoel of    Isabella    m.  Christian II    Mary       m. Louis of    Catherine   m.  Joaõ III of
(1498–1558)   Portugal        (1501–1526)     of Denmark      (1503–1564)   Hungary     (1507–1578)     Portugal
              2. Francis I                                                  (d. 1526)
              of France

              Charles V    m.  Isabella of           Ferdinand I   m. Anne of
              (1500–1558)     Portugal               (1503–1564)      Hungary
                              (d. 1529)

(Illegitimate)         Elizabeth   Maximilian II   Anne of    Ferdinand     Mary of    Charles
Margaret of Parma      of Poland   (1527–1576)     Bavaria    (1529–1575)   Cleves
(b. 1522)                                                                              Eight
Juan of Austria                                                                        Daughters
(b. 1547)
              Philip II  m.  1. Mary of Portugal    Mary      m. Maximilian II   Juana       m.  John
                             2. Mary of England     (1528–1603)                  (1535–1573)     Manoel of
                             3. Isabel of France                                                 Portugal
                             4. Anne of Austria
```

Figure 2.3: Charles V's matrimonial alliances and family tree.

became Castilian, in which Charles developed an impressive degree of fluency within a short space of time. In 1526 the Castilian aristocracy particularly welcomed Charles's marriage to his cousin Isabella (the King of Portugal's sister), who was to act as regent during his absences from Spain. The following year, the political elites celebrated the birth of a son, Philip, on 21 May 1527. As his reign progressed, Spaniards increasingly dominated not only Castilian offices, but also the more important roles elsewhere in the empire. With these significant changes, his Spanish subjects became more sympathetic to the extent and nature of Charles's responsibilities.

In terms of administration, Charles extended the system of conciliar government that he inherited from Ferdinand and Isabella. This was the only practical option because Spain itself still lacked political unity. Charles was King of Castile and King of Aragon, not King of Spain, and his power varied in each territory. For that reason, he built on the tradition of councils, and decided to create new ones to deal with specific issues. The most important council was the royal council of Castile, which comprised 12 members, all of whom were lawyers. It also acted as a supreme court, to which the high courts (**audiencias**) could appeal. A Council of War was established from 1522 to devise the monarch's military policies. This was followed by the Council of Finance (1523), the Council of the Indies (1524) and the Council for Italy (1555, by which time Charles had added the duchy of Milan to the kingdom of Naples). The councils were responsible for preparing and discussing their respective agendas. In turn, secretaries were to liaise with the King himself. These new councils were not innovations and represented a natural extension of Ferdinand and Isabella's policies. Like the Council of Castile, the other councils were not dominated by the aristocracy and were staffed largely by lawyers (**letrados**). The Council of Finance was directed by Cobos and by 1525 all members were Spaniards. Its main function was supposed to be the preparation of budgets and the balancing of income and expenditure in Spain, though it became preoccupied with imperial expenditure as well. In general, conciliar government was not especially efficient and rather cumbersome.

Figure 2.4: Portrait of Empress Isabella by Titian.

Individuals and domestic policy

Bureaucracy versus nobility

Charles established a good working relationship with the Castilian *Cortes* after 1522. He convened the *Cortes* regularly thereafter, every three years or so (meeting 15 times during the reign), conveying the impression that he was prepared to listen to their grievances. The meetings of the *Cortes* often coincided with Charles's return to Spain from his foreign ventures. The *Cortes* was convened mainly to vote subsidies and their response was invariably generous. This was not dependent on Charles meeting particular demands. Charles undoubtedly saw it that way, as he himself acknowledged; 'Yesterday I asked you for funds; today I want your advice.'[13] The legacy of Ferdinand and Isabella's reign was equally significant where the Aragonese *Cortes* was concerned. The General *Cortes* of the Crown of Aragon met six times during Charles's reign, whereas the individual *Cortes* of Aragon, Catalonia and Valencia rarely met. Like his predecessors, Charles realised that his authority was restricted in part by the fiscal and judicial powers of each *Cortes*. He became increasingly aware that it was not worth challenging their influence, such was the limited potential of their respective economies.

A far more politically influential force was represented by Charles's secretaries, who became increasingly powerful as his reign progressed. Royal secretaries represented the primary medium of communication between the king and the council. They dominated the agenda for most council meetings and drafted the majority of royal documents. Secretaries were also vital in controlling incoming correspondence. They made the decision as to whether it should be passed on directly to the king or whether it should be handed to the relevant council. Charles rarely communicated with his

> ### Speak like a historian
>
> ### William Maltby
>
> Read the following account by William Maltby:
>
> In Castile, Charles therefore possessed a realm whose financial, ecclesiastical, and legal systems were as firmly under his control as anything could be at a time when poor communications, inadequate information, and established privilege limited the effectiveness of all governments. It also had the best army in Europe. Officers and men trained in the Italian wars under the guidance of Gonzalo de Córdoba and his disciples made up the fighting core of Charles's multinational armies. Like Castile's administration, the army, improved and reorganised in the course of the reign, became a bulwark of the Emperor's power. In terms of usable finance, manpower, and organisation, Castile was therefore the most valuable of Charles's possessions. After 1519, its acquisition of a vast new empire in America would further increase its importance.[12]
>
> #### Discussion points:
> 1. According to Maltby, what are the strengths and weaknesses of Castile?
> 2. Using this chapter and your own research, do you agree with Maltby's interpretation?

councils, but was reliant on his secretaries to keep him informed. The councils would have barely functioned at all without the vital input provided by the secretaries.

Unsurprisingly, secretaries were greatly sought after, given their immediate access to the corridors of power. Being close to the key source of patronage, the ever-growing administration 'became a vested interest and grew to parasitic proportions'.[14] The most influential secretary was Francisco de los Cobos. As an Andalusian of humble origins, Cobos served a 15-year apprenticeship before his appointment as royal secretary in 1516. He became the Emperor's chief secretary and was directly involved in the 1523 reforms. He was the dominant figure in the new Council of Finance, and later promoted to the Council of State in 1529. After Gattinara's death in 1530, Granvelle and Cobos were the king's chief counsellors. During 1530–38 Cobos accompanied Charles on his travels. While Granvelle was put in charge of foreign affairs and northern Europe, Cobos was exclusively focused on Spanish affairs from 1539. He excelled in that role by laying the foundations for an increasingly intricate and professional bureaucracy, helped by some highly competent senior advisers such as **Juan Vazquéz de Molina** and **Gonzalo Pérez**. The pre-eminence of Cobos and Granvelle was not lost on contemporaries. The Venetian ambassador wrote in 1546 that 'Cobos and Granvelle transact all the business of all his states'.[15]

Political stability could not be secured without the support, or at least the control, of the nobility. Charles's regime was vulnerable in its early years and the nobles did not hesitate to communicate their disaffection. Nobles were understandably outraged by his appointment of pro-Flemish advisers and some leading grandees, such as the hereditary Admiral Enríquez and Constable Velasco, expressed open dissent. Ultimately, the course of the *Comuneros* and *Germanía* revolts in a more radical, and anti-seigneurial direction meant that serious noble opposition never really materialised. In any case, the aristocracy remained divided by family rivalries and always found it too difficult to unite. These inter-family tensions were also mirrored in some cities; the major centres in Castile (Burgos, Córdoba and Seville) were split into factions associated with rival nobles.

The aristocracy was expected to perform military service, hold public office and serve the state in law, finance and trade. Some nobles, such as the Duke of Alba, were given honorary positions in the Council of State, but the majority of officials were not part of the hereditary aristocracy. As a result, the grandees were critical of the new political elite of lawyers and merchants. The opportunities in the New World posed a further threat to the pre-eminence of the aristocracy. The sheer scale of wealth that came from the Seville trade was a vital source of social advancement. For all these apparent problems and threats, the nobility continued to dominate the towns and the countryside. The former were especially dominated by the *hidalgos*, who had risen to prominence in the aftermath of the revolts. Municipal offices, such as mayor, chief of police and of the militia, previously closed to the nobility, were now open to them. *Hidalgos* had every reason to be loyal to the Crown in order to maintain the status quo and their influential position. The countryside was controlled by a combination of the aristocracy and the Church. While the aristocracy might refuse to pay taxes for foreign campaigns that were unrelated to Spanish interests, it did not prevent other nobles from seeking political and social advancement abroad. In the longer term, the absence of aristocratic unrest can be attributed to the determination of nobles to protect their interests. Noble careers were guided by lucrative opportunities in the rapidly expanding court and bureaucracy of a worldwide monarchy.

Figure 2.5: Portrait of the influential secretary, Francisco de los Cobos, painted by Jan Gossaert.

The economy: trading and royal revenues

The emergence of Spain as a great power impacted upon its finances and economy in contrasting ways. Undoubtedly benefiting from a long period of internal peace that followed the early revolts, the Castilian economy was in a better position to exploit the stimulation of trade and industry resulting from the conquests in the New World. The numbers employed in the silk and cloth industries continued to rise (from 10 000 to 50 000 between the years 1525 and 1550), while there was very successful iron and steel production in the Basque provinces of Guipúzcoa and Álava. Medina del Campo retained its prominence in controlling financial transactions as well as maintaining influential links with European trade. Seville's population grew substantially and it secured a virtual monopoly of American trade that was sufficient to energise Castilian industry for a generation. In 1523, the Exchequer was reorganised and the Council of Finance was established to regulate all income and expenditure. Count **Henry of Nassau** was appointed chief of finances, as he had gained experience in a similar role in the Netherlands. Cobos soon dominated that Council.

The dominance of the *hidalgo* class in the *Cortes* caused some longer-term economic problems, especially given their disregard for Spanish industry. In 1548, the *Cortes* demanded the importation of cheaper cloth from abroad on the grounds that the poor could not afford Spanish cloth. This was motivated by their wish to pressurise Castilian manufacturers into producing cheaper cloth. The same *Cortes* called for the prohibition of numerous imports from the Indies, including cloth, silk, leather, iron and steel in order to make commodities cheaper at home. The detrimental impact of the *hidalgos* on local industry was replicated in the countryside. A 1525 decree had ordered that all pasture land should be brought under tillage in the first eight years of Charles's reign to be placed at the disposal of sheep farmers. There was a similar decree in 1552, which focused on the previous 12 years. From the *Comuneros* revolt onwards, northern Castile lived almost exclusively on imported wheat. This required a far-reaching export trade, which would be difficult to achieve, given the policies of the *Cortes*. The majority of Castile's wool production went abroad because her domestic manufacturers were too weak to compete for it, thereby preventing the development of a formidable domestic textile industry.

A/AS Level History for AQA: **Spain in the Age of Discovery, 1469–1598**

ACTIVITY 2.3

Francisco de los Cobos was one of Charles's most influential secretaries. Conduct some further research on los Cobos and produce a short biography. This should include a brief timeline, as well as a section explaining the reasons for his political significance. You may wish to assess this in relation to Charles himself, in addition to the nobility, conciliar government and the Castilian *Cortes*.

ACTIVITY 2.4

How was Charles able not only to contain but also harness the power of the nobility? Use this section and your wider reading.

ACTIVITY 2.5

Define the following terms and explain their significance: *alcabala, subsidio, juros, cruzada*.

The burden of paying for wars against the French, the Lutherans and Ottomans fell increasingly on Castile. The province was able to support Charles's foreign campaigns because its *Cortes* presented so little constitutional resistance to higher taxation. In contrast, Aragon was already in economic decline and provided minimal sums. From six meetings of the *Cortes* (1528, 1533, 1537, 1542, 1547 and 1552), Aragon provided approximately 500 000 ducats for each five-year period. Further afield, the Netherlands economy was exhausted by the 1530s and 1540s, having previously been a major and influential centre for trade and industry. Naples was relatively poor, even though it did provide the hardly insignificant sum of 1.75 million ducats between 1525 and 1529 in taxes.

Charles's regime was partly dependent on ordinary revenue in order to fund his military campaigns and the extravagance of his household expenses (costing a tenth of national income). The most lucrative indirect tax remained the *alcabala*, though wheat and bread, which were imported by sea, were exempt. At the Madrid *Cortes* of 1534, Charles granted the principle of **encabezamiento**, which allowed towns to convert the *alcabala* into a fixed sum. Despite noble exemptions, the *alcabala* amounted to 75 per cent of Crown revenues by 1550. For all its importance, the value of the *alcabala* declined in real terms, as Charles's ordinary revenues failed to keep pace with inflation. Between the years 1536–53, the yield from the *alcabala* rose by 21 per cent, while prices rose by a third.

Charles derived considerable wealth from the Church. Although they were also exempt from the *alcabala*, the clergy were heavily taxed in other ways, most notably via the *terciareales* (representing a third of tithes), the *subsidio* (500 000 ducats in 1551 alone), and the *cruzada* (121 000 ducats per annum between 1523 and 1554). In 1523, Pope Adrian, Charles's former tutor, confirmed royal possession of the properties and revenues from the three great military orders of Santiago, Alcántara and Calatrava, which were administered by the Fuggers from 1525. The sale of royal lands, formerly owned by the military orders, produced 1.7 million ducats between 1537 and 1551. The Crown sought numerous alternative methods of raising revenues, many of which were extra-parliamentary, thereby reducing its reliance on the *Cortes*. Some taxes emerged as a direct response to military pressures. For example, in 1538, the German, North African and French campaigns necessitated the imposition of a new tax, the *sisa*, which was a tax on foodstuffs (not imposed on the aristocracy). With Castile bearing such a heavy burden for imperial campaigns, the Crown inevitably resorted to borrowing, especially from foreign bankers, most notably the Fuggers and the Welsers. Their role cannot be overestimated. For the imperial election alone, the Fuggers and Welsers had supplied 543 000 and 143 000 florins respectively out of the total 850 000 florins spent by Charles. He continued with the pre-existing system of **juros** or bonds to pay for loans; *juros* were annuities that repaid loans out of ordinary revenues. As early as 1522, the repayment of loans consumed 36 per cent of normal revenue; by 1543, this figure had risen to a staggering 65 per cent.

During Charles's reign, borrowing came close to 30 million ducats and interest payments on loans stood at 10 million ducats. Much of this borrowing resulted from his military campaigns. In 1552, he borrowed 4 million ducats to finance his war against France, where the unsuccessful campaign at Metz cost 2.5 million ducats. As the financial situation deteriorated, interest charges paid by the Crown rose from 18 per cent of annual revenues in the 1520s to 49 per cent in the 1550s. This increased the influence and control of foreign financiers on the Spanish treasury. They secured a sufficient stranglehold on the country's finances that they were allowed to buy offices, lands and *juros*; they were invited to administer the three military orders and to control the mercury mines at Almadén. Between the years 1524–38, Charles also rewarded foreign bankers by giving them permits to trade directly to America; the Welsers, for example, started to colonise Venezuela.

> **2 The drive to 'Great Power' status, 1516–56**

Charles experienced mixed fortunes when he convoked the Castilian *Cortes*. For example, in 1527 he summoned nobles and clergy to the *Cortes* at Valladolid in order to strengthen his brother Ferdinand's Hungarian campaign against the Ottomans, but came away with nothing. While the nobility and clergy tended to be far more hesitant, this does not mean that the *Cortes* refused to vote subsidies. During the 1520s, Charles's regime collected approximately 130 000 ducats per annum from the *Cortes*, and this had increased to 410 000 by the 1550s. The move from indirect to direct taxation imposed a greater fiscal burden on ordinary taxpayers. Revenues from the New World, which amounted to 270 000 ducats per annum and represented 20 per cent of the Crown's ordinary revenue, boosted Castile's financial contributions. Revenues were raised by a variety of means, including taxes, sales of monopolies on trade and production, tribute from native Indians and the receipt of the royal fifth (representing a 20 per cent tax on precious metals mined in the New World).

Charles's regime undoubtedly encountered some major economic problems, in particular, unprecedented inflation. Between 1511 and 1559, the price of wheat doubled and the price of oil tripled in Andalusia. While most landowners and merchants prospered, the numbers of poor increased. Inflation inevitably led to a fall in living standards, as salaries could not match the price rises. In Valladolid, for example, wages rose by 30 per cent between 1511 and 1550, yet the prices of wheat and wine increased by 44 per cent and 64 per cent respectively. Worse still, some land rents between the years 1530–55 rose by 86 per cent. The inflation was partly caused by the introduction of bullion, which greatly undermined the export trade; in simple terms, it was a bad market to buy from and a good one to sell to. The situation was sufficiently desperate in 1534 that the government had spent most of its revenues for the next six years. With numerous campaigns in North Africa, France and the Holy Roman Empire in the 1540s, it became the norm that ordinary revenue was always completely exhausted for several years in advance. This was exacerbated by the fact that between 1542 and 1547, there was a temporary reduction in the number of shipments of American treasure. In 1546, most of the Crown's income had been sold or pledged up to the end of 1549 and even part of 1550. Cobos and his Council of Finance adopted desperate measures in the 1540s, such as confiscating all treasure from the Indies and seizing all coins in Spain in order to finance Charles's victory at Mühlberg. The military victory was short-lived, and the battle left a devastating economic legacy in Spain. By the end of Charles's reign, the kingdom was virtually bankrupt. When his son acceded to the throne, it was not long before the new regime realised that it was paralysed by a lack of money and the inability to borrow, and there was no choice but to sue for peace with France in 1559.

Foreign relations

Relations within Europe

One is tempted to agree with Henry Kamen that Charles's policies reflected neither the pursuit nor the existence of an 'imperial idea'.[16] Rather than pursuing a premeditated plan or blueprint, Charles's foreign policy was more haphazard and influenced by the immediate circumstances that he faced. Yet for Charles to dictate terms to his enemies, he obviously required a well-drilled army. The Spanish territories were in a position to supply a quality army because they had already gained battle experience in the Granada campaign. The Italian wars would serve to improve the professionalism and efficiency of the Spanish troops through the introduction of military reforms, including the addition of **pikes** and **arquebuses**. They also introduced *tercios* in 1534, which became the standard regimental unit. Gonzalo de Córdoba masterminded the key changes. The royal treasury also made contracts with reputable captains, whose responsibility it was to raise a sufficient number of troops, including the younger sons of the aristocracy. Although Spanish troops formed an integral part of Charles's army,

---

ACTIVITY 2.6

How effective was the management of royal finances during the period 1516–56? Answer this question by researching the key components of income and expenditure.

the number and regularity of his campaigns forced him to depend on German and Walloon mercenaries.

The French Valois dynasty remained a constant rival throughout Charles's reign. This was consistent with Aragonese foreign policy, which had been anti-French. Spain had recently gained Cerdagne, Roussillon and the kingdom of Navarre (see Chapter 1). Future rivalries focused partly on Navarre, but mainly on the old duchy of Burgundy (secured by France in 1477) and the Italian city-states. Some of Charles's imperial policies were undertaken to protect Spanish interests. For instance, Francis I of France attacked Spanish Navarre in 1521 in order to exploit the internal instability caused by the *Comuneros* revolt. Although he succeeded in capturing Pamplona (a battle in which the young Ignatius of Loyola was wounded), Francis invaded the Iberian peninsula as the *Comuneros* revolt was petering out. In fact, some of the *Comuneros* rebels joined royal forces to drive out Francis's army. Six thousand Frenchmen were killed, much French artillery was seized, and thousands were taken prisoner, including the French commander L'Esparre. Henceforth, both the French and the Spanish considered the Pyrenees a suitable border. In 1522, a year later, Charles secured an alliance with Henry VIII, known as the Treaty of Windsor, in which the two rulers ambitiously agreed on a complete conquest of France. The terms of the treaty stipulated that Henry would be given the French Crown and the western provinces, while Charles would recover the former Burgundian lands, in addition to Languedoc, Provence and the Rhône valley. The plan was hopelessly unrealistic and greatly underestimated French strength. In truth, it is doubtful that Charles genuinely sought to fulfil these objectives. He was surely more pragmatic than this, and exploited the opportunity to gain a useful ally.

Figures 2.6 and 2.7: Pikemen and arquebusiers were key components of the Spanish *tercios*.

2 The drive to 'Great Power' status, 1516–56

Figure 2.8: The Italian city-states, 1520.

The Spanish also encountered the French on the Italian peninsula. The Spanish had consolidated their position in Naples by 1516, making it difficult for the French to challenge Spanish supremacy. France tried to secure Naples during various campaigns in the late 1520s, but its troops were defeated at the battle of Landriano in 1529. The French defeat was followed by the one-sided Peace of Cambrai, signed in August 1529, which left Charles in virtual control of Italy. In 1542, a sizeable French army of 40 000 soldiers attacked Spain's northern frontier. Strong Spanish resistance at the city of Perpignan delayed the French advance, allowing time for Fernando Álvarez de Toledo, **the third Duke of Alba** to bring reinforcements of 2000 experienced soldiers, veterans from a North African campaign.

> **ACTIVITY 2.7**
>
> Compose a set of linked timelines, indicating Habsburg and Valois territorial and diplomatic gains and losses.

> **ACTIVITY 2.8**
>
> As you read through this section, make a list of the problems that Charles V encountered in the Holy Roman Empire. What was the greatest threat to his authority?

The extension of Franco–Spanish rivalry to northern Europe and the duchy of Milan represented a departure from Spanish interests. At its essence, the wars between the Spanish and French were part of a broader dynastic conflict. Habsburg interests and priorities led Charles to embark on major campaigns in northern Italy, arguably the principal theatre of war. Although Francis I had secured the duchy of Milan following the battle of Marignano in 1516, Charles managed to reconquer it in 1524. Worse was to come for the French. In February 1525, Charles secured a decisive victory at the battle of Pavia. Charles's generals Pescara, Leyva and Lannoy routed the French, and Francis himself was captured. Although Spanish soldiers represented a minority in the imperial army, they did bear the brunt of the fighting. In the subsequent Treaty of Madrid, signed in 1526, Francis undertook not only to renounce his claims to Italy and Flanders, but also to hand over Burgundy to the Emperor, in return for his own freedom. Following his release in 1526, Francis realised that the Treaty of Madrid was unenforceable and soon established the League of Cognac with the Pope, Venice and Florence. The Habsburg–Valois wars were constantly affected by the various unstable and inconsistent alliances that were established. The Italian city-states refused to commit to any permanent alliances. They were quite content to vacillate between the Habsburg and Valois dynasties as dictated by the circumstances. They were determined to prevent any one power from securing a military and political ascendancy in the Italian peninsula.

The duchy of Milan continued to be an important source of conflict throughout Charles's reign. It was of strategic importance because it linked the Holy Roman Empire and the Netherlands to Spain and the Italian city-states (via the Valtelline and the Tyrol). The French triggered another set of wars in 1536 when they invaded the duchy of Savoy, with the ultimate goal of conquering Milan. By 1538, they had failed in their objective, though Charles's disastrous campaign in Provence (during the summer of 1536), driven by his desire to relieve pressure on Milan, left him deeply indebted. An apparent stalemate had been reached, but it certainly seemed that the odds favoured the Emperor when, in 1540, he conferred the duchy of Milan on his son Philip and those lands came to be associated with the Spanish Crown.

Foreign relations in Europe also diverted Charles's attention away from Spain because his dynasty had ruled the Holy Roman Empire ever since Frederick III's accession in 1440. Yet the power that this position symbolised was illusory. In truth, Charles had little power in the German lands because the Holy Roman Empire was so fragmented. This political decentralisation was characterised by a strong sense of particularism, which was driven by a determination to uphold and safeguard local traditions and privileges (especially regarding laws and taxation). This strong sense of regionalism both weakened the emperors and empowered local princes and towns.

Confessional divisions in the Holy Roman Empire

The vulnerability and fragility of Charles's political position was accentuated by the emergence of Luther's revolt. In the same year that Charles arrived in Spain, Luther posted his 95 theses on the castle church door in Wittenberg. On his return to the Holy Roman Empire in 1521, Charles was faced with an ever-growing religious crisis, which he underestimated. At the Diet of Worms that same year, Luther was put under an imperial ban (known as the Edict of Worms), but he was not arrested because the most important German prince in the Empire, **Elector** Frederick the Wise of Saxony, continued to protect him. Charles's brother Ferdinand, appointed in 1522 as Charles's permanent representative in the Holy Roman Empire and given the Austrian hereditary lands, was unable to do much about it. He could not wield the same political authority as his brother. Charles underestimated both the theological differences between Luther and the Catholic Church and the nature of the threat posed by Luther. This meant that he refused to commit himself to any decisive action, allowing Luther's ideas to develop into a powerful force. He thereby lost the only opportunity he could

2 The drive to 'Great Power' status, 1516–56

have had to suppress Luther and his burgeoning movement. Given his actions in the Netherlands, it is curious that he was not more proactive against Lutheranism in the Holy Roman Empire (see section 'Revolt in the Netherlands'). An Inquisition was introduced as early as 1522, and there was a succession of harsh edicts decreed against Lutherans and Anabaptists in 1525. Intriguingly, Charles's letter to Mary of Hungary suggests that the Emperor knew what he was doing in the Holy Roman Empire: 'What is tolerated in Germany must never be suffered in the Netherlands.'[17]

Charles's absence from the Holy Roman Empire meant that the fate of Luther and Lutheranism would be controlled by the Imperial Diets. In Charles's absence, the princely and urban representatives at the Diets were allowed to procrastinate and Luther's movement was able to grow unimpeded. In the Imperial Diet at Nuremberg (1524), the political authorities were called on to suppress Lutheranism, unless such actions provoked social and political instability. The contrasting decisions at the two Diets of Speyer (1526 and 1529) illustrated that the political tide was changing. Lutheranism was given breathing space in the early years because the majority of princes were unwilling to commit either to support or suppress Lutheranism. By the end of the 1520s and early 1530s, Lutheranism had firm roots as an urban movement and was beginning to acquire vital princely support. At the second Diet of Speyer in 1529, this political support protested in defence of Lutheranism and by 1531 they had formed a defensive, military alliance, known as the Schmalkaldic League. This organisation was greatly empowered by its urban support, as well as by its princely leadership, including John Frederick, Elector of Saxony, and Philip, the **landgrave** of Hesse.

Ultimately, there were two ways in which the religious problems could be confronted. The first, and Charles's favoured option, was through negotiation. Charles certainly supported the meeting of Catholic and Lutheran theologians at Regensburg (or Ratisbon) in 1541. Although the participants agreed on a doctrine of double justification of faith (which was quickly rejected by both the papacy and Luther himself), the religious discussions broke down over the Eucharist, as they had done over a decade before between rival Protestant leaders (Luther and Zwingli at the Marburg Colloquy in 1529). The subsequent Declaration of Ratisbon (July 1541) secured the following significant concessions to Lutherans: the safety of any adherents to the Augsburg Confession (a statement of Lutheran beliefs drafted in 1530) was assured; the secularisation of Church property was sanctioned; Lutheran princes were given the right to reform monasteries and other religious institutions; and finally, Lutherans were given greater prominence in imperial institutions. The Pope condemned this declaration and while Charles gained nothing, the Lutheran princes and cities exploited it to the full.

The second approach to the Lutheran problem represented the last resort, namely suppressing the movement by force. This would be difficult to achieve while Charles had so many other priorities outside the Holy Roman Empire. During the period 1542–44, Charles was faced with, and had to repel, a French invasion of the Netherlands. At the same time, he sought to consolidate, as well as expand his territories there; he had gained Tournai in 1521, while Artois, Utrecht, Groningen and Gelderland were added in 1543. This led the Habsburgs to reorganise their territories in the Netherlands into one administrative unit in 1548. Yet once war with France had come to a temporary halt, marked by the Peace of Crépy, Charles was in a position to take on the Lutherans. Given the devout Catholicism of the Spanish elites (Luther was reviled as a dangerous heretic), it was with Spain's blessing that Charles turned to the suppression of Lutheranism in the mid-1540s. This decision also happened to coincide with the opening of the Catholic Council of Trent in December 1545. Pope **Paul III** had published a bull in June 1542 to convene a council that November, but the council was continually postponed until peace between the Emperor and Francis I was in place. Once Charles had secured the support of Duke Maurice of Saxony (who betrayed his Lutheran allies and joined Charles to target the electorship of Saxony) and of the

> **Key term**
>
> **Imperial Diets:** The Holy Roman Empire was politically fragmented, composed of diverse princely states and imperial cities. Leading secular and ecclesiastical princes, as well as urban representatives, were invited to discuss policies at the Imperial Diets. Its members often struggled to reach consensus and took full advantage of Charles's frequent absences from the Empire to advance their agenda.

Bavarian **Wittelsbachs**, he mobilised an army of 25 000 commanded by the Duke of Alba and defeated the Lutherans at Mühlberg.

Apparently decisive though this defeat seemed for the Lutherans, Charles's victory actually served to increase dissensions within the Catholic camp. Even the Catholic Church became fearful of Charles's power. The religious settlement that followed on 30 June 1548 (known as the Augsburg Interim) appeared to satisfy nobody. Lutherans detested it because it was too Catholic; the Interim preserved key Catholic doctrines and upheld papal authority. Despite this, the Catholics also disapproved because the Interim showed a degree of sympathy with Lutheranism, which they denounced as heresy; there were some concessions to Lutheran views on Church discipline and worship. The Interim was certainly criticised in Spanish quarters, most noticeably by the Jesuit Nicolás Bobadilla.

And then France fatefully intervened at an inopportune time for the Emperor. The French King, Henry II, promised military and financial assistance to the Schmalkaldic League, formalised by the treaties of Friedwald (October 1551) and Chambord (January 1552), in exchange for the cities of Metz, Toul and Verdun (which were part of the Holy Roman Empire). France had also persuaded the Ottomans to break their truce with the Habsburgs, which they did by seizing Tripoli in August 1551. Charles's military gains at Mühlberg were then reversed in the Second Schmalkaldic War, as a combined French and German Protestant army forced Charles to sue for peace. Charles's attempt to regain Metz from the French was unsuccessful. The Treaty of Passau, signed on 15 August 1552 and negotiated by Ferdinand and Maurice of Saxony, was later ratified by Charles, and foreshadowed the Peace of Augsburg of 1555. The latter treaty, negotiated by Ferdinand, represented much of what Charles had spent his career trying to avoid. Lutheranism was given legal and official recognition within the Empire, and individual princes were allowed to dictate the religion of their inhabitants (*cuiusregio, eiusreligio*). Charles was even more disillusioned owing to the opposition (from within his own family, as well as within the Empire) to his son's succession as Emperor. Catholic and Lutheran princes would only accept a German prince as his successor. Added to this, the Cardinal of Augsburg protested against the intolerable presence of Spaniards within the Empire. Charles's woes were compounded when the anti-Spanish Neapolitan Cardinal Caraffa was elected Pope Paul IV.

Campaigns against the Turks

The Emperor was unable to give Lutheranism his undivided attention because the Habsburgs also had to contend with the threat in central Europe from the Ottoman armies of **Suleiman** the Magnificent. On 29 August 1526, his **janissaries** defeated the last king of the Jagiellon dynasty, Louis II of Hungary, at the battle of Mohács and several days later the Ottomans were in Buda, within striking distance of Austria's eastern frontier. Although eager to provide military and financial support against the Ottomans in the Mediterranean, Charles's Spanish subjects were noticeably reluctant to assist the Habsburg dynasty in a part of Europe that did not concern them. This may partly explain Charles's limited contribution to the defence of the Hungarian lands. Despite his apparent reluctance, the gravity of the threat symbolised by the siege of Vienna in 1529 was sufficient for Charles to mobilise an army (albeit several years later in 1532), commanded by his best generals, including Antonio de Leyva and the marquis of Vasto. As many as 6000 Spaniards accompanied Charles to the Danube for the 1532 campaign. The evidence suggests that Charles was willing to defend Austria, but that he did not have enough financial and military resources to protect the Hungarian lands from Ottoman expansion. The immediacy of the Ottoman threat forced Charles to make a compromise with the German Lutherans in May 1532 known as the Peace of Nuremberg. A general peace was to be established within the Empire, whereby Lutherans would not be condemned for their religious beliefs until a religious council was convened.

2 The drive to 'Great Power' status, 1516–56

The Ottoman Empire was an equally potent threat in the Mediterranean, especially given its naval superiority. Although the Ottoman fleet could not reach Spain directly, they secured strong links with the North African corsairs and there was plenty of potential for the *Moriscos* to assist Suleiman on Spanish soil. In 1516, **Hayreddin Barbarossa** and his brother Oruc founded a pirate commonwealth, with Algiers as their headquarters. Algiers became a credible Mediterranean power and the Barbarossas sought to drive all Christian garrisons out of North Africa. In 1518, the people of Algiers placed themselves under the Sultan's protection and Algiers became the administrative centre for an Ottoman province in 1525. In due course, Suleiman secured a formal alliance with its leader Barbarossa. In contrast, Charles lacked a sufficient number of trained sailors, as well as having a shortage of naval stores. In the first decade or so, Charles was only able to establish his navy by securing contracts with private ship owners because he did not possess a permanent navy. In July 1528, however, the Genoese naval commander **Andrea Doria** defected from the French and transferred his fleet to the Emperor. The Peace of Cambrai in 1529 gave Charles almost seven years of peace with France, allowing him to focus on the Ottoman threat. With the establishment of the Knights of St John on Malta in 1530 and greater security for his communications and trade, Charles was in a stronger position to reverse Ottoman gains and challenge their increasing stranglehold on the Mediterranean. The Spanish were also more willing to support a Mediterranean war against the Ottomans.

Charles was spurred into action by two events in 1529: there were Muslim raids on the Valencian coast, and Barbarossa seized Peñón de Vélez and defeated a Spanish fleet of eight galleys off Ibiza. In due course, Charles responded in 1532 by sending Andrea Doria with 44 galleys and over 10 000 men to the eastern Mediterranean. Doria seized Patras and then garrisoned and held Coron in the southern Peloponnese for two years. Although both Patras and Coron were only temporary gains, they served to relieve pressure on the Habsburgs in central Europe.

In 1534, Barbarossa seized Tunis and La Goleta, the fortress that guarded it, from Spain's Moorish ally, Mulay Hassan. This was of strategic significance because Tunis and La Goleta commanded the narrow seas between Sicily and Africa. The following year, thanks to peace with France and the support of 10 000 Spaniards, 82 galleys and 300 transport vessels, Doria led another expedition, which successfully retook Tunis and expelled Barbarossa. The expedition benefited from a revolt by Christian slaves in Tunis itself and was largely financed by bullion that Hernando Pizarro had brought from Peru. Mulay Hassan was restored to his previous position and Charles's forces regained control over the straits of Sicily, though the overall balance of power in the Mediterranean had barely altered. One might criticise Charles's commanders for not pursuing Barbarossa. R. Trevor Davies claimed that 'Barbarossa's escape made the success more apparent than real'.[18] Yet although Barbarossa fled to Constantinople, where he was appointed commander of naval operations in the eastern Mediterranean, Charles's fleet could not pursue him because it was late in the campaigning season and his troops were sick and exhausted. In any case, Charles's successful African campaign of 1535 could not be followed up mainly because he was forced to redirect his attention back to France.

Figure 2.9: Andrea Doria, Charles V's Genoese naval commander.

In 1538, a new Holy League against the Ottomans was established as a response to a Venetian call for assistance. The subsequent naval battle at Preveza in the eastern Mediterranean achieved little. Barbarossa fought very effectively, so that the imperial navy, although numerically superior, was brought to a standstill, and in 1539 he went on to sack Gibraltar. In 1541, Charles amassed a powerful fleet of 65 galleys, 450 other ships, and 24 000 troops, half of which were Spanish, with the Duke of Alba and even **Hernán Cortés** (see section 'The *Conquistadores*') in attendance. They reached the North African coast by October, but disaster struck when the fleet was destroyed by a storm before it could besiege Algiers. As it happens, Andrea Doria had advised against the offensive on the rather simple grounds that it was too late in the year, especially for landing on an open beach. Heavy rain had also rendered muskets and cannon useless.

> **ACTIVITY 2.9**
>
> Use this section and your own research to assess Charles's foreign policy. For each theatre of war (divide into the French, the Ottomans, and the Holy Roman Empire), outline Charles's principal objectives and identify the strengths and weaknesses of both his diplomacy and military campaigns. Was he largely successful? How far was his foreign policy undertaken to the detriment of the Spanish kingdoms?

Historians are united on the negative implications of this campaign. While Lynch has described it as 'one of the greatest catastrophes of the Emperor's career',[19] A.W. Lovett has commented on how the 'Tunisian triumph had turned into an Algerian disaster' (with the loss of up to 12 000 troops and 150 ships).[20]

It was to be the last of Charles's major naval battles because thereafter he became preoccupied with fighting German Protestants and the French. It left the western Mediterranean at the mercy of Barbary corsairs. During the winter of 1543–44, Barbarossa wintered his fleet in Marseilles, allowing him to disrupt Spanish trade and communications between Genoa and Barcelona. Barbarossa's death in 1546 did not relieve pressure on the Spanish, as he was replaced by his equally competent successor **Dragut**. The corsairs persisted with the original policy of targeting Spanish fortresses on the North African coast and they had considerable success in the 1550s. The Spanish lost Tripoli in 1551, Peñón de Vélez in 1554 and Bougie in 1555. By 1556, Spain had only four outposts left on the North African coast. Fortunately for Charles and his young successor Philip, the Sultan was distracted by war with Persia and, for all the Ottoman Empire's strengths, never achieved naval supremacy in the western Mediterranean. Finally, it is interesting to note that the creation of a Council of Italy (1555) was a sign that Mediterranean policy was ceasing to be imperial and becoming part of Spanish foreign policy.

Religious policies and the Church in Spain

Charles had considerable control over the Spanish Church. He undoubtedly benefited from the firm foundations laid by his predecessors Ferdinand and Isabella. His former tutor, Pope Adrian VI, whose 1523 bull empowered him to appoint every major ecclesiastical office in Spain, helped Charles enormously. Building on Ferdinand and Isabella's legacy, Charles rendered the Church's power almost entirely subordinate to royal authority. Yet Charles was not politically motivated in this and he was certainly dedicated to promoting a reform programme. He understood that episcopal reform was vital to the Church's future success. In Juan Pardo de Tavera (1472–1545), Archbishop of Santiago then Toledo, Castile had its very own equivalent of the renowned reforming bishop of Verona, Gian Matteo Giberti. The Instructions and Constitutions of Tavera's diocesan synods were considered to be exemplary, a model for other Spanish bishops to follow. Key clerical leaders, such as Hernando de Talavera, Archbishop of Granada, enforced the religious reforms on a local level. Consistent with his predecessors' intentions, Charles was keen that the Crown, independently of Rome, should direct Church reform in Spain. The Popes were acutely conscious of Habsburg power in Europe and most of them were keen to maintain a balance of power between the Habsburg and Valois dynasties. Although Adrian VI was an ally, he died in September 1523 and his successors would not be quite as supportive.

Humanism was another important characteristic of the Spanish Church during Charles's reign, for which Ferdinand and Isabella's reign again laid the foundations. Cardinal Cisneros remains a central figure in this regard, given his responsibility for the foundation of Alcalá University. Its first chancellor was Pedro de Lerma, who was joined by leading humanists, including Juan and Francisco de Vergara, and Antonio de Nebrija. Cisneros established an excellent library and he employed the distinguished printer Arnao Guillén de Brocar, granting him the most important commissions. Supported by the Archbishop of Toledo, **Alfonso de Fonseca**, and the Inquisitor General Alonso Manrique de Lara, the University of Alcalá became one of the leading centres of learning in Europe. The role of Christian humanism in the service of Spanish reform is illustrated by biblical scholarship, which was well established in Spain before Luther's revolt. Cisneros commissioned a critical edition of the Bible, which brought together a collection of different biblical texts. Commissioned in the previous reign, the project was completed in 1517 and the first edition was published in 1522. The result was the extraordinary Polyglot Bible, consisting of five volumes printed in the original languages with the Latin version (the Vulgate) in parallel columns.

The second key example of Christian humanism was the circulation of Erasmus's works. **Erasmus** was well received in Spain on account of his biblical studies, as well as his critique of monastic abuses and indiscipline. At the court of Charles V, Erasmus's influential supporters included the Emperor's Latin secretary Alfonso de Valdés, Juan de Vergara, secretary to Archbishop Fonseca, and Alfonso Manrique, Archbishop of Seville and Inquisitor General. Between the years 1522 and 1525, the Erasmian movement was successfully established in Spain, as evidenced by the many Spanish translations of his works. For example, a Castilian edition of his *Handbook of a Christian Soldier* was published in 1526. Erasmus's works were especially well received at the court. Cisneros even invited Erasmus to Spain in 1516 after the publication of the latter's New Testament, though Erasmus did not accept his offer.

However, the Spanish Church was threatened by the rise of heterodox ideas, as evidenced by the **alumbrados** (or illuminists), and the circulation of Lutheran ideas (albeit in a rather diluted form). There were various groups of *alumbrados* (including the circles around Isabel de la Cruz, Pedro Ruiz de Alcaraz, the Bishop Juan de Cazalla, and Francisca Hernandez), some of which emerged as early as 1512 in Guadalajara and Salamanca. Although essentially Catholic in their theology, they believed in the necessity of abdicating one's will to God. The illuminists asserted that, as and when they communed with God through ecstasy, they were incapable of committing sin and that good works were useless. In the early 1520s, there was a flourishing group of illuminists in Toledo, which was largely confined to nuns and friars. From 1525 onwards, the authorities started to arrest members of the *alumbrados* and the Inquisition targeted them. A royal edict of 23 September 1525 condemned illuminist teachings. Even Ignatius of Loyola, later founder of the Jesuits, was jailed in 1527 and submitted to three examinations for suspected illuminist leanings.

Lynch believed that 'Spanish illuminism served to pave the way for the entry of Protestantism into Spain', but in reality there was no indigenous movement in Spain, no native heretical movement on which Lutheran ideas could build.[21] At an early stage, in April 1521, Adrian of Utrecht issued the first ban on Lutheran books. Only two years later, the Inquisition tribunal of Mallorca executed Gonsalvo the Painter for adhering to suspected Lutheran ideas. The region most vulnerable to heresy was Seville, a centre of international trade. There was another circle of Protestants in northern Castile, which included the Italian Carlos de Seso and the eminent convert Dr Agustin Cazalla, former chaplain to Charles V. By 1558, there had been only 105 cases of Lutheranism in Spain, of which 66 were foreigners. Lutheran ideas enjoyed little success in Spain because of the alertness of the Inquisition. The integrity of the 16th-century Spanish Church was protected by the existence of a national institution dedicated to the persecution of heresy.

From the late 1520s onwards, the main target of the Inquisition was Erasmus. From an early stage, the mendicant friars, whom he had criticised, despised Erasmus. The monastic orders accused Erasmus of heresy. Between 1527 and 1528, the Erasmian Alfonso de Valdés wrote two popular dialogues in Spanish attacking clerical, and particularly monastic, abuses. Yet when his brother Juan de Valdés published a book, the *Dialogue of Christian Doctrine*, it was put on the **Church's Index of Forbidden Books** because it was tainted with heretical ideas. Soon afterwards, the works and ideas of Erasmus became associated with heterodoxy. Francisca Hernandez and Bernardino de Tovar were arrested in 1529 for their Erasmian sympathies. That same year, Charles left Spain for the Italian city-states, taking his court and many of its influential Erasmians with him. The Erasmians who stayed behind were vulnerable to attack. In 1533, Vergara was arrested, which was significant given that he was secretary to Cisneros and later to Fonseca, a professor at Alcalá and friend of Erasmus. Alonso de Virués (Charles V's chaplain) was arrested in 1533, though he was eventually released

> **Key term**
>
> **Fifth column:** A group or faction with a common identity (i.e. the *Moriscos*) who seek to undermine from within a larger group with different principles (i.e. Old Christians throughout Spain) on behalf of an external enemy. Fifth columnists tend to adopt varying methods (open or secretive, violent or more passive) in order to fulfil their subversive objectives.

ACTIVITY 2.10

Define the following terms: humanism, *alumbrados*, *Moriscos*. Did these groups pose a serious threat to the Church?

and appointed Bishop of the distant Canary Islands. By Charles's return in 1533, the Inquisition had successfully associated the writings of Erasmus with Lutheran heresy: Juan de Vergara was in prison; the leading Erasmians at Alcalá University, such as the librarian Miguel de Eguía, the former rector Mateo Pascual and the chancellor Pedro de Lerma were under investigation and de Lerma was subsequently jailed in 1537. The death of Inquisitor General Manrique in 1538 removed the last remaining Erasmian from a position of ecclesiastical authority in Spain. As Kamen neatly summarised, 'the influence of Erasmus was successfully extirpated and Protestantism in the peninsula was strangled at birth'.[22]

Another potential religious threat was presented by the existence of numerous *Moriscos* in Spain. Following the conquest of Granada in 1492, and the forced conversion of Castilian Moors in 1502, Spain contained a large alien minority. Although nominally Christian, the *Moriscos* had never been properly assimilated into Christian culture and were continually perceived to represent a fifth column who could, and would, ally themselves with Ottomans and corsairs in the Mediterranean. The suppression of the *Germanía* revolt in Valencia convinced Charles's regime to decree an edict in 1525, which forced the Moors to convert or go into exile, thereby extending the Castilian decree of 1502 to Aragon and Valencia. This provoked an armed revolt in Sierra de Espadán in 1526 and the problem was further intensified in 1529 when Barbarossa's corsairs undertook a sacking expedition of the Valencian coast. Charles planned to eradicate Moorish customs, but an offer of 80 000 ducats from the *Moriscos* persuaded him to withdraw the edict. Another attempt in 1530, this time by the Empress Isabella acting as regent, was also bought off by *Morisco* money. The use of Moorish language and dress was permitted in exchange for a regular tax (known as the *farda*), which produced 20 000 ducats per annum.

The expansion of empire

The Spanish undertook their voyages of exploration and discovery for a variety of reasons. They were partly motivated by their rivalry with the Portuguese, who were technologically advanced and experienced. Bartolomeu Dias's voyage round the Cape of Good Hope in 1486, and Vasco da Gama's landing in southern India twelve years later suggests that they were reasonably successful. The Spanish conquerors, the *conquistadores*, were clearly determined by self-interest; they sought glory and wealth in the form of land, slaves and gold, among other commodities. Cortés was, at least, honest about his intentions: 'I came here to get gold, not to till the soil like a peasant.'[23] These materialistic concerns can be attributed to the fact that the early pioneers were not nobles, but poorer Spaniards, including soldiers, sailors and simple labourers. Rural poverty presented a convincing reason to emigrate. The pioneers were not exclusively guided by financial incentives. Some were firmly committed to spreading Christianity, as illustrated by the Dominicans in Hispaniola and the Franciscans in Mexico. Militant Catholicism, consistent with the ideology of a *Reconquista* Spain, deeply influenced the conquests in the New World. While every expedition had its priest, one of the intended objectives was to civilise and convert the natives. Bernal Díaz's contemporary view reveals that these varying motives were perceived to be complementary; 'We came to serve God and His Majesty, and also to get rich.'[24] With so many reasons to explore, it is scarcely surprising that many Spaniards dared to take the risk. By 1550, 150 000 Spaniards had already crossed to America. Approximately 35 per cent of all emigrants to the New World were from Andalusia, and over 50 per cent from Extremadura.

The *conquistadores*

Christopher Columbus left a reasonably strong legacy for the *conquistadores* who followed him. While the town that he founded, San Domingo, became the capital of the Spanish Indies, his third expedition had also discovered the coast of South America in 1498. One of his most notable successors was Hernán Cortés (1485–1547). Cortés was mainly responsible for the Spanish conquest of Central America, for which he showed tremendous courage, inspired leadership and excellent organisation. He was appointed commander of the expedition that was sent in 1519 by Diego Velázquez, governor of Cuba; he was accompanied by 600 men, 16 horses and some artillery. Cortés later repudiated Velázquez's authority and sought to establish an independent kingdom. He was highly successful in securing allies from other Indian tribes, especially the Totonacs and the Tlaxcalans who paid regular tribute to the Aztecs. Crucially, they supported his successful siege of Tenochtitlan in 1521; the Aztecs had a population of 1.5 million (with 200 000 in Tenochtitlan itself) and ruled over an empire of 5 million. Cortés undoubtedly benefited from the spread of smallpox, which decimated the Aztec population.

The success of the Spanish *conquistadores* owed much to the weaknesses of the Aztecs, especially their rudimentary military organisation and weapons, and the disaffection of their subjects and allies. The fall of Tenochtitlan had a profound impact because it gave the Spanish control over the entire Mexican valley. Cortés called his territorial conquests New Spain, then returned to Spain in 1529. By that stage, the Spanish government had (from 1527) already established an *audiencia* in New Spain and a civil government. In 1535, Antonio de Mendoza was appointed Viceroy.

The second influential *conquistador* was Francisco Pizarro (1476–1541). From 1524 and on behalf of the Spanish regime, Pizarro undertook several expeditions southwards from the Pacific port of Panama. In 1528 he went to Spain and managed to secure a licence for conquest from the Crown that named him governor of Peru, where he had found gold in 1527. The Peruvian Inca Empire was geographically larger, more centralised and more populous than the Aztec Empire. Pizarro arrived in 1530 with 180 men and 27 horses, and took full advantage of an Inca civil war that was being fought over a disputed succession. He launched a successful surprise attack against Emperor Atahualpa, who was eventually executed. Having sacked the capital Cusco in 1533, he founded a new capital in 1535 near the coast at Lima. He managed to overcome a major Indian rising in 1537. However, when Pizarro had Diego de Almagro, an old friend, executed in 1538, he was himself murdered by Almagro's embittered son in 1541. It was not until 1548 that Pedro de la Gasca (1493–1567) established royal authority in Peru, even though Indian resistance continued. There were three further expeditions to the Chibcha kingdoms (now Colombia), and Pedro de Valdivia invaded Chile in 1541 (founding Santiago).

Economic and social impact of the New World in Spain

There were obvious benefits to the Spanish conquests in the New World. Although the amounts of gold and silver found were relatively small up to 1530, thereafter the quantities were considerable. The transportation and receipt of gold and silver produced 324 000 ducats per annum between 1536 and 1540, and the annual revenue from these sources had increased to 871 000 ducats per annum during the years 1551–55. During the course of Charles's reign, silver and gold produced in the region of 11 million ducats in total. Charles's regime also managed to obtain a further 3.5 million from seizures of contraband bullion. The increasing wealth was also partly the result of what could be cultivated from the fertile lands of the New World, particularly given the abundance of a ruthlessly exploited Indian labour force. The speed and success with which the Spaniards expanded their empire gave them enormous self-confidence and a sense of imperial destiny.

However much the *conquistadores* thought that they were undertaking a civilising mission and benefiting the local inhabitants, millions of Native Americans died, mainly due to forced labour and their lack of immunity to European diseases. The reduction in the population of the Aztec and Incan empires was staggering: from 25 million to 3 million between 1520 and 1556 in Mexico; and from 9 million to 600 000 in the period

1530–1620 in Peru. The New World economy was dependent on forced labour, firstly by native Indians under the **encomienda** system then by African slaves. From 1518 onwards, licences were issued for the importation of black slaves and their numbers later increased considerably in order to compensate for the large numbers of Indians who had died. By the 1560s, they outnumbered whites in Spanish America.

Since the *conquistadores* generally acted independently of Spanish government, the colonisers essentially pursued their own policies. They relied heavily on forced labour because it helped them to maximise their profits, and the designation of Indians as savages justified their brutal treatment. One beneficiary of this system, Bartolomé de las Casas, gave up his position, joined the Dominicans and subsequently fought for the liberation of the Indians. His enormous influence at the Spanish court contributed to the New Laws of 1542, which proclaimed the abolition of the *encomienda* and Indian slavery. However, it took time to enforce this on the ground.

Figure 2.10: The Native American empires conquered by the Spanish *conquistadores* in the New World.

The importation of gold and silver led to high inflation. The total currency within Europe was so small in proportion to the American bullion imports that prices were bound to be affected. This had a detrimental impact on the poorer ranks in society. While Spanish culture made its mark on language, religion, architecture and the economy of the New World, the impact of America on Spain was limited. The New World was 'important less for its direct than its indirect impact: it brought wealth, it stimulated enquiry and it promoted social mobility'.[25]

The political, economic, social and religious condition of Spain in 1556

During the four decades that Charles reigned, he spent most of his time in Spain, though his absence from the Iberian Peninsula in his final years (1543–56) was pronounced. Although repeated absences from any territory provoked discontent, Charles was relatively quick to secure the trust of his Spanish subjects. After all, there was no major unrest after the early revolts. In preparation for his son's succession, he wrote two instructions (one that was 'Confidential' outlining his personal and political ideals, and one that was 'Private' as a report concerning principal advisers). Charles advised his son to assert his authority over chief advisers. This required him to balance the interests of Tavera and Cobos, the councillors that he was about to inherit. Charles had allowed royal secretaries to dominate conciliar government, a political change that served and would continue to enhance royal authority. Castile continued to dominate Spanish politics, though Charles, understandably, had not felt the need to challenge Aragonese particularism.

Despite its apparent pre-eminence on the Iberian Peninsula, Castile's economy lacked the power to sustain a world empire. The significant influx of silver had its limitations, as well as its strengths. New World silver was essential in supporting Charles's numerous military campaigns, though the domestic consequences were problematic. The rise in inflation, combined with the fiscal pressures of major taxes such as the *alcabala*, pressurised the poorest ranks in society. Towards the end of his reign, every conceivable source of revenue in Castile was pledged to one banker or another as security for debt. By 1556, the Spanish government owed the Fuggers as much as 5 million ducats.

For all its economic woes, Spain had become part of a major empire that extended beyond the European continent, and Charles now dominated Italian affairs. The pursuit of an active foreign policy was facilitated by the existence of domestic stability.

A religious crisis on the Iberian Peninsula was averted by the continuation of religious reforms, as well as the persecution of heresy. Although the *Moriscos* rebelled in Philip's reign, Spain would not experience the same religious crisis as the French in the second half of the 16th century.

Practice essay questions

1. To what extent was Charles personally responsible for the strengthening of royal authority in Spain?
2. 'Charles's domestic achievements outweighed the failures.' Explain why you agree or disagree with this view.
3. 'Charles's Spanish interests were always subordinate to broader dynastic objectives.' Assess the validity of this view.
4. With reference to these extracts and your understanding of the historical context, which of these two extracts provides the more convincing interpretation of the impact of the *Comuneros* and *Germanía* revolts?

ACTIVITY 2.11

You are the Venetian Ambassador to Castile. Fearing the ever-growing Ottoman threat in the Mediterranean, the *Doge* (ruler in Venice) is eager to strengthen relations between the Spanish Empire and the Venetian Republic, and has requested you to compile an accurate impression of the state of the Iberian Peninsula in 1556. Divide your analysis into political, economic, social, religious and foreign affairs. For each theme, note down any achievements and limitations.

Extract A

The bitter divisions of Castile's civil war did not extend much beyond the emperor's return to the kingdom in 1522. Loyalists and rebels were never totally at odds, because they had some common goals, such as inducing their sovereign to make a proper marriage. For his part, Charles did not object to the fact that many towns sent former rebels as procuradores to the Cortes, because he needed the towns as a counterweight to certain of the great nobles who had grown even more powerful as a result of their role in suppressing the revolt.

Source: James Tracy, *Emperor Charles V, Impresario of War: Campaign Strategy, International Finance, and Domestic Politics*. Cambridge: Cambridge University Press, 2002, p. 289.

Extract B

The collapse of the Germanía on the mainland, and also on the Balearic Islands where it pursued an even more violent course, brought lasting political change. The urban guilds were punished severely for their part in the recent events; and the towns were saddled with indemnities which were still being paid off in the reign of Philip II. The drain on municipal resources made their economic recovery all the more uncertain. But for the aristocracy which had restored order without help from Charles V the rewards of loyalty (or opportunism) were substantial. The agrarian character of the Valencian kingdom became even more pronounced, the noble dominance of government and society unassailable.

Source: Lovett, *Early Habsburg*, p. 39.

Further reading

There are helpful summaries of Charles's reign in Colin Pendrill's *Spain, 1471–1700* (Heinemann, 2002) and the aforementioned textbooks on Early Modern Spain by Henry Kamen, John Lynch, A.W. Lovett and J.H. Elliott. Owing to Charles's other European possessions, many biographies, textbooks and academic monographs do not focus exclusively on his governance of the Spanish kingdoms. For the conduct of war and its financial implications, see James Tracy's *Emperor Charles V, Impresario of War: Campaign Strategy, International Finance and Domestic Politics* (Cambridge University Press, 2002). On Spanish imperialism, see William Maltby's *The Rise and Fall of the Spanish Empire* (Palgrave Macmillan, 2009). See also William Maltby's *The Reign of Charles V* (Palgrave, 2002); Henry Kamen's *The Spanish Inquisition* (Phoenix Press, 1997); Martin Rady's *The Emperor Charles V* (Longman, 1988) and Hugh Thomas's *The Golden Empire, Spain, Charles V and the Creation of America* (Random House, 2011).

2 The drive to 'Great Power' status, 1516–56

> **Chapter summary**
>
> By the end of this chapter you should understand:
>
> - the nature of Charles's inheritance and how the new regime dealt with the *Comuneros* and *Germanía* revolts
> - the workings of Spain's domestic policies, especially religious and economic
> - the nature of Spain's relationship with the wider world, particularly the Mediterranean and the New World
> - how far Charles managed to strengthen the monarchy in Spain.

End notes

1. John Lynch, *Spain Under the Habsburgs: Volume I, Empire and Absolutism, 1516–1598*. Oxford: Basil Blackwell, 1981, p. 7.
2. Cited in Jean Bérenger, *A History of the Habsburg Empire, 1273–1700*. London and New York: Longman, 1994, p. 144.
3. Henry Kamen, *Spain, 1469–1714: A Society of Conflict*. Harlow: Longman, 2005, p. 71.
4. Kamen, *Spain*, p. 79.
5. Lynch, *Spain*, p. 42.
6. R. Trevor Davies, *The Golden Century of Spain, 1501–1621*. London: Macmillan, 1967, p. 47.
7. Cited in Jon Cowans (ed.), *Early Modern Spain: A Documentary History*. Philadelphia: University of Pennsylvania Press, 2003, pp. 46–48.
8. Kamen, *Spain*, p. 81.
9. Lynch, *Spain*, p. 46.
10. Cited in Lynch, *Spain*, p. 52.
11. Cited in Kamen, *Spain*, p. 64.
12. William Maltby, *The Rise and Fall of the Spanish Empire*. Basingstoke: Palgrave Macmillan, 2009, pp. 41–42.
13. Cited in Lynch, *Spain*, p. 50.
14. Lynch, *Spain*, p. 58.
15. Cited in Kamen, *Spain*, p. 72.
16. Kamen, *Spain*, p. 71.
17. Cited in Kamen, *Spain*, p. 76.
18. Trevor Davies, *Golden Century*, p. 97.
19. Lynch, *Spain*, p. 97
20. A.W. Lovett, *Early Habsburg Spain, 1517–1598*. Oxford: Oxford University Press, 1986, p. 133.
21. Lynch, *Spain*, p. 69.
22. Kamen, *Spain*, p. 127.
23. Cited in Kamen, *Spain*, p. 97.
24. Cited in Kamen, *Spain*, p. 97.
25. Kamen, *Spain*, p. 101.
26. Cited in Cowans, *Spain*, pp. 58–63.
27. Cited in Cowans, *Spain*, pp. 64–68.

PART 2: PHILIP II'S SPAIN, 1556–98

3 The 'Golden Age', 1556–98

In this section, we will examine Philip's domestic policies and assess how effectively Spain was governed. Attention will be drawn to political, religious, socio-economic and cultural factors, in addition to analysing the internal rebellions that occurred during his reign.

Specification points:

- Philip II as ruler: character, inheritance, change and continuity in government, administration and policy
- opposition of individuals and groups: faction and curbing internal rebellions
- religion and society: the Jesuits, Inquisition and relations with the papacy
- economic developments: royal finances, policies and impact of overseas empire
- social and cultural developments of the 'Golden Age': impact of new ideas and intellectual movements
- the condition of Spain by 1598: political, economic and social strengths and weaknesses.

Philip II as ruler

Philip's character

Consideration of Philip II's character is essential to any assessment of his reign. His disciplined upbringing and education, under the supervision of Juan de Zúñiga, nurtured a man of considerable integrity. Philip felt inspired by a sense of divine mission and the belief that he was accountable to God for the welfare of his subjects. He was more interested in the practicalities of governing than courtly ritual. Relative to contemporary kings, Philip's reign did not produce a triumphalist cult of monarchy and there was less emphasis on ceremonialism. He was, accordingly, serious-minded and insisted on seeing every paper himself. He had an excellent memory and paid considerable attention to detail. The sheer scale of his output was well known to contemporaries; in 1574, a Venetian diplomat wrote that 'the King works with such diligence, without any recreation, that there is no minister in the world, however diligent he may be, who is as involved in his work as His Majesty'.[1] Philip seldom made decisions without consulting one of his ministers and he encouraged differences of opinion. Yet his ministers never dominated him; he was guided by his father's confidential instructions to trust nobody ('Depend on none but yourself').[2] Like his Spanish predecessors, he preferred Castilians and ministers of lesser rank. His Castilian subjects found his fluency in Castilian and incompetence in other languages an endearing trait. This would make the task of ruling outside Castile more problematic.

While his work ethic cannot be faulted, historians and contemporaries have criticised Philip for his lack of political vision and for being a slow thinker. He apparently struggled to distinguish between important and trivial matters. For example, while Spain was busily preparing for the Armada, Philip was debating the state of clerical dress with the Pope. Lovett was damning about Philip's character: 'emotionally stunted and intellectually limited, only the physical and mental shortcomings of his descendants made Philip appear of kingly timber'.[3] Philip was undoubtedly overcome by the sheer volume of correspondence and paperwork, which was self-inflicted in Geoffrey Parker's view: 'Philip's insistence on acquiring ever more data, feeding his illusion that this enabled – entitled – him to micromanage both policy and operations, paradoxically slowed down his ship of state and thus diminished his control.'[4] He had a tendency to read daily **despatches** and his advisers' comments without taking a clear stance. Even Pope Pius V drew attention to the consequences of his indecision: 'Your Majesty spends so long considering your undertakings that when the moment to perform them comes, the occasion has passed.'[5] This was surely the result of the innumerable problems that he encountered. Some policies, such as the response to the Dutch Revolt, were so fervently debated that it would have been difficult to be decisive.

Although he often demonstrated caution, Philip never tolerated rebellion. He could be irresolute at times, but he could also be very decisive and even ruthless on occasions. This was particularly evident in the treatment of his increasingly unpredictable son, **Don Carlos**. Having promised the governorship of the Netherlands to Don Carlos, who had already attended the meetings of the Council of State, Philip gave the post to the Duke of Alba. The boy's grandfather, Charles V, was appalled by Don Carlos's appearance and temperament, and he refused to host him at Yuste, where Charles had retired. His conduct became increasingly erratic, and his fellow councillors were often targeted. Don Carlos's volatility and uncontrollable temper explains why father and son fell out in the 1560s: Don Carlos drew a knife on the Duke of Alba; on at least six occasions he tried to murder somebody who resisted him and he **defenestrated** a page who annoyed him. He was increasingly critical of his father and sought to gain assistance from various leading nobles, such as the **Count of Egmont**, the **Prince of Eboli** and the Baron de Montigny. While Carlos asked Eboli to give him 200 000 ducats to escape to the Netherlands, he demanded that **Don John** of Austria take him to Italy,

Figure 3.1: Philip II, a portrait by Alonzo Sanchez Coello.

> ### Speak like a historian
>
> ### Geoffrey Parker
>
> How do historians approach the writing of biographies? What are the potential pitfalls? Read the following extract from Geoffrey Parker's recent biography of Philip II.
>
> The extent of his Monarchy, combined with the long duration of his reign, present Philip's biographers with the first of four major interpretive obstacles: an excess of data. On one occasion, the king claimed he had signed 400 letters in a single morning and on some days, 2,000 documents passed across the royal desk. The second major interpretive obstacle seems to contradict the first. Even if a diligent historian managed to consult all the relevant papers that survive, many of the king's decisions would remain impenetrable. Although Philip committed more of his thoughts and decisions to paper than almost any other ruler, he deliberately left others in obscurity, and at all times urged his ministers to proceed 'with secrecy and dissimulation'. Sometimes he tried to destroy all written evidence specifically to conceal what he had done and why. A third interpretive obstacle is memorably described by Voltaire: 'To understand Philip II, one cannot state too often that we must mistrust the descriptions of contemporaries, who were almost always motivated by either flattery or hatred'. But one important exception exists: the dispatches of the dozen foreign ambassadors who resided at the court of Spain. The final obstacle to understanding Philip is the hardest to overcome: his exalted status. Biographers must not implicitly trust their subjects; on the contrary, we must be ready for them (whether living or dead) to mislead us, both deliberately (through the falsification or destruction of compromising documents) and inadvertently (through our own limited ability to comprehend their world, or by considering future developments that the protagonists could not have known).[6]
>
> #### Discussion points:
> 1. What features are essential for writing a historical biography?
> 2. Why are biographies invaluable?
> 3. What are their limitations?

promising him Naples and Milan when his cause triumphed. On both occasions, Philip was informed, but as Lynch points out, Carlos's plans did not represent a real threat: 'even his schemes for escaping Spain – all of them pathetically lacking in secrecy – must be considered as the outpourings of a disordered mind rather than a calculated plot to subvert the monarchy, of which he was palpably incapable'.[7]

It became increasingly evident that Don Carlos was unfit to rule and his father took the courageous and decisive step of imprisoning him. This was justified on the basis that Don Carlos could no longer be held responsible for his actions. Philip was aware of this several years before the prince's arrest. One of his advisers, Ruy Gomez, informed the French ambassador that 'it is more than three years since the king fully realised that the prince's brain was even more deformed than his body and that he would never have the necessary judgment' to govern.[8]

Don Carlos was seized in January 1568 and his household was disbanded. One can get an accurate insight into Philip's motives from a private letter addressed to his aunt Catherine, Queen Dowager of Portugal, dated 20 January 1568: 'the prince's condition has deteriorated so far that, I could not avoid arresting and imprisoning him'.[9] Philip's resolve and decisiveness are obvious, given that he was not only depriving himself of a successor (which was not resolved for another decade) but also imprisoning his own son. Tragically, his son died shortly afterwards. The most likely reason for his death on 25 July 1568 was due to his various excesses in confinement, including a hunger strike, a bout of gluttony, and a massive consumption of ice.

Far more sinister is the high probability that Philip was aware of, and may have condoned, the murder of several key figures during his reign. Judicial murder was a standard technique in 16th-century statecraft. Geoffrey Parker believes in Philip's connivance in Juan de Escobedo's murder in 1578. Philip had allowed Antonio Pérez to persuade him that Don John and his secretary Escobedo were traitors and that murdering the latter would enable him to assert his authority. It is likely that Pérez wanted Escobedo murdered because the latter could prove that the former had accepted bribes and it is possible that Pérez and Escobedo had conspired, perhaps with Don John, to deceive Philip himself. Philip must have been aware of other murders committed during his reign, such as that of the Baron de Montigny, the brother of the **Count of Hornes**, in October 1570, who was executed secretly in the castle of Simancas. Philip's letter to the Duke of Alba, dated 3 November 1570, provides irrefutable proof: 'The affair went so well that till now everyone has believed that he died of illness. And this must be given out there too, by discreetly showing round two letters coming from here.'[10] This might lead historians to criticise Philip's integrity and sense of virtue, a tradition that had its roots in William of Orange's *Apologia*, published in 1581, as well as the *Relaciones* of Philip's treacherous secretary, Antonio Pérez, published in 1594. Philip has also been lambasted because the French, Dutch and English incorporated hatred of Philip and Spain as part of their respective national traditions. While Protestant authors detested his Catholicism, 19th-century liberals targeted both his bigotry and his autocracy. Much attention was drawn to the alleged torture and murder of his own son, Don Carlos.

Philip's apparent support for judicial murders is not entirely representative of his character. This is particularly true if we contrast it with the profound affection for his daughters Isabella and Catherine, as evidenced by his letters from Portugal between 1581 and 1583. Successive Venetian ambassadors were extremely complimentary about his generosity of spirit. Giovanni Michaeli noted that 'there is no one, however lowly he may be, who does not find him easily approachable and a patient listener. He is generous; for he grants more than he leads one to hope.'[11] Similarly, Michele Soriano wrote that 'he has always shown such humanity as no prince could surpass, he preserves his royal dignity and gravity in all his doings, and they only serve to enhance the courtesy with which he treats everyone'.[12] As these ambassadors were reporting back to the Doge (ruler) in Venice, there is no obvious reason to suppose that their judgements were misplaced.

These contrasting portrayals of Philip represent the norm for histories of his reign. But John Lynch is right to steer a different course that is less judgemental; 'Apologists have seen him as a Catholic crusader, critics as a reactionary bigot. Neither view is realistic; one ignores his concern for national interests, the second implies that he was wrong not to be a democrat and a Protestant.'[13] For all his deficiencies, Philip's task as monarch was inhibited by his difficult inheritance. The political, economic, legal and linguistic aspects of his Empire were too incoherent to be sustainable and neither Philip nor any other ruler could have governed it effectively.

ACTIVITY 3.1

Compose a biographical timeline of Don Carlos's life, draw up a chart of the identities of his parents, grandparents and great-grandparents. Explain why Philip was hesitant to given him a major political office. Should Philip II be criticised for the way in which he dealt with his own son?

ACTIVITY 3.2

The Black Legend: myth or reality?

Using this section and your broader reading, identify the strengths and flaws in Philip's character and policies, and assess whether the negative portrayals of Philip are justified or exaggerated. In particular, research William of Orange's *Apologia*, and Antonio Pérez's *Relaciones*. Explain their motives and the ways in which these may have influenced their writings.

Define what you understand by the 'Black Legend'. What are its roots and main characteristics, and does it represent a valid interpretation of Philip's character and reign?

Philip's inheritance

Philip's territorial inheritance was substantial and the diverse territories still lacked any significant political unity. Although essential to imperial administration, communication between the different parts of the Empire was invariably slow, with disastrous consequences. The governance of the Empire was obviously hampered by distance; it took approximately two weeks for letters to reach Brussels and two months to get to Mexico. On numerous occasions, the problems in communications were exacerbated by Philip's own indecision and caution. Too often he refused to delegate trivial matters, when the serious and important demands of his vast and unwieldy empire demanded instant decisions. Philip had to rely on the various governors and viceroys in the regional capitals, such as Brussels and Naples.

Even in Spain, Philip inherited a dynastic union, rather than a unified country. Lacking a centralised political body, Philip could neither undermine nor challenge provincial liberties. Each territory was autonomous, and only shared a common king. Some parts of the Iberian Peninsula suffered a significant lack of royal control. Only 35 per cent of land in Salamanca and 73 out of 300 towns in Valencia were under royal authority. Like his predecessors, Philip was faced with rigorous independent and active parliamentary systems in Aragon and Navarre. As the central and most powerful province, Castile's population was still too small and her economy too underdeveloped to operate an empire based on its own resources.

Change and continuity in government

In theory, Philip proceeded with a similar approach to government as his father. The person and presence of the monarch remained central, as did the King's use of political institutions. During the first decade of his reign, Philip went abroad, spending some time in the Netherlands. Thereafter, he stayed on the Iberian Peninsula, which allowed him to pay closer attention to the governmental process. Although he travelled extensively within Spain, he stayed for lengthy periods at the great palace he built at Escorial.

Within Spain, only in Castile was there a degree of political centralisation, but even here effective government depended on the cooperation of the local elites. Like his father, Philip partly relied on the numerous councils (increasingly situated in Madrid), which were divided according to territories and governmental departments. These included the councils of Aragon, of the Indies, of Flanders, of the Inquisition, of the *cruzada* tax, and from 1582, of Portugal. As before, these councils acted as advisory bodies, which discussed and drafted papers for the King. Lawyers dominated the councils, which fulfilled both executive and legislative roles. The Council of Castile was the most important, and functioned as a supreme court of law. Following the retirement of Luis Hurtado de Mendoza (the second Marquis of Mondéjar) as President of the Council in 1563, the next six occupants of that position, excepting the Count of Barajas, were all either jurists or clerics. Yet even the Council of Castile was a purely consultative body and entirely dependent on the King's will. The King appointed its members, and rarely attended its meetings. His absence allowed councillors the freedom to express their own opinions. In his presence, advisers would seldom object and often refused to commit themselves in case they backed the wrong proposal. The Council of Castile never developed into the influential equivalent of the Tudor Privy Council, and lost a degree of authority following the Pérez disgrace. Even the Count of Barajas, President of the Council of Castile from 1583 to 1592, complained of its deficiencies, 'which render intolerable the office of president of this Council'.[14]

THE KING AT WORK

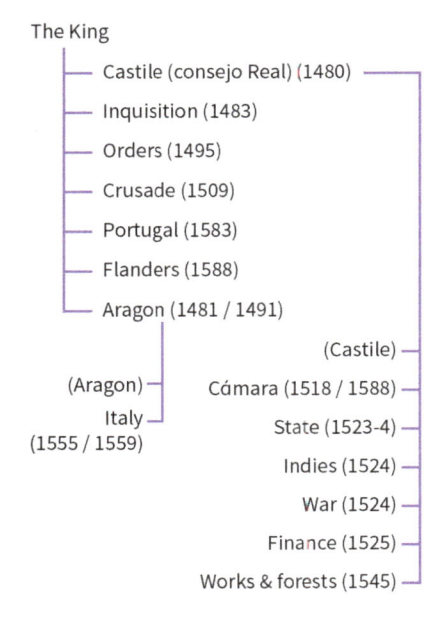

The King
- Castile (consejo Real) (1480)
- Inquisition (1483)
- Orders (1495)
- Crusade (1509)
- Portugal (1583)
- Flanders (1588)
- Aragon (1481 / 1491)
  - (Aragon)
  - Italy (1555 / 1559)
    - (Castile)
    - Cámara (1518 / 1588)
    - State (1523-4)
    - Indies (1524)
    - War (1524)
    - Finance (1525)
    - Works & forests (1545)

Figure 3.2: The conciliar system under Philip II.

Administration and policy

From the early 1570s, informal committees or *juntas* emerged, sometimes taking the place of, and performing similar functions to, the councils. The *juntas* were also divided into different departments (such as Castile, Aragon, Italy, Foreign Affairs and Finance). On 1 April 1573, **Mateo Vázquez** took his oath as the royal secretary and coordinated the informal *juntas*, which had been created by Diego de Espinosa. As with the councils, the King dictated the membership of the *juntas*. They were composed of bureaucrats, mainly taken from the lower nobility, and few had any experience outside of Spain. Philip liaised with Vázquez in order to determine the times of meetings and the contents of their agendas. Although apparently informal, the *juntas* met on a daily basis and flourished (at least until 1588) because they contributed much to the formulation of royal policies. Their particular value lay in the flexibility of their membership, as genuine experts were frequently co-opted to deal with specific problems. For that reason, *juntas* were called as and when they were needed. For example, the *Junta Grande* was convened from 1586 to organise the logistics for the Armada. Most importantly, the *juntas* included an inner group comprising **Cristóbal de Moura, Juan de Idiáquez**, the **Count of Chinchón** and Vázquez himself, who advised on major governmental strategies. They came to be known as the *Junta de Noche*, which rose to prominence in the aftermath of the Armada fiasco. At that point, Philip delegated increasing authority to its key members, particularly Moura, Idiáquez, Chinchón and Vázquez.

The various councils and *juntas* served the government of Spain and the broader Empire. Of greater significance than these organisations was the succession of key individuals, who were empowered by Philip himself. This is in spite of his father's secret instructions, in which Charles had warned his son not to allow himself to be controlled by powerful councillors. This may explain Philip's profound distrust of prominent councillors, such as the Duke of Alba, the Marquis of **Santa Cruz**, Don John of Austria and **Alexander Farnese**. A single chief minister never dominated Philip and he much preferred to confide in lesser personalities, such as Ruy Gomez, the Prince

> **Key term**
>
> *Junta de Noche:* The committee of the *Junta de Noche* included a number of key secretaries, including Cristóbal de Moura, Juan de Idiáquez and the Count of Chinchón. Its members dealt with a broad range of domestic and foreign policies, and they had a considerable impact on the decision-making process.

> **ACTIVITY 3.3**
>
> Based on this section and your broader reading, how far did the nature and structures of Spain's government allow Philip to maintain political control?

of Eboli, and his secretary Mateo Vázquez. Philip's closest councillors were only given access to limited areas of policy, so that the King alone could understand the broader context for all state affairs. The status of royal secretaries was enhanced by the vast correspondence and extraordinary growth of government paperwork. While ordinary secretaries dealt with routine matters of government, the King coordinated major decisions with his private secretary.

Royal secretaries, who attended council meetings, were the vital links between the monarch and his councils and *juntas*, and they were primarily responsible for drawing up the **consultas** (memoranda and reports). In simple terms, they had direct and constant access to the King, which was invaluable given how Philip operated. They shared government secrets with the monarch, and were instructed either to pass on information or to withhold it from the councils. Secretaries also selected the letters and papers the King should read in full, those that he would see merely in summary, and occasionally those that he would not see at all. The implications of this are striking. For example, Don Juan de Idiáquez intercepted and withheld a letter addressed to the King by the seventh Duke of Medina Sidonia, declining his appointment to command the Spanish Armada and expressing serious doubts about the wisdom of the enterprise itself. Idiáquez was clearly aware that Philip would not accept Medina Sidonia's opinions on the matter and realised that the King was determined that Medina Sidonia should lead the expedition.

Successive secretaries played a formidable political role in Philip's government. Gonzalo Pérez started as a royal secretary under Philip's father in 1541 and continued to work for Philip for 10 years until 1566. An archdeacon of Sepúlveda, he was supremely intelligent and a superb secretary, taking charge of foreign correspondence. His son, Antonio Pérez, was also extremely able. While his duties were partly restricted to northern affairs, his secretaryship of the Council of Castile gave him control of domestic correspondence. For over 10 years, he was a leading figure at Philip's court. He was on familiar terms with anybody who mattered and even the aristocracy were obliged to recognise him because he was sufficiently powerful to help them: one such beneficiary was **Cardinal Quiroga**, who was promoted to the see of Toledo.

While Pérez's rise to power was unequalled in 16th-century Spain, this did not prevent his dramatic fall. In the late 1570s he was accused of double-dealing, and charged with not only accepting bribes but also betraying state secrets, for which he was arrested in 1585. Philip's suspicions towards Pérez had emerged in the previous decade, which explains why he appointed Mateo Vázquez to the secretariat in 1573. Vázquez held that position until his death in 1591, on account of his unswerving loyalty, as well as his willingness to inform on others. Following Pérez's fall from power in 1579, to which Vázquez had contributed, Vázquez became chief secretary and the most important state business came through him.

Philip asserted his authority over the Castilian *Cortes*, though by the time of his accession it had lost almost all its rights. Philip's stance, articulated as early as 1555, was unambiguous. 'If it be my pleasure, I shall annul, without the *Cortes*, the laws made in the *Cortes*; I shall legislate by edicts and I shall abolish laws by edicts.'[15] In an attempt to regulate the affairs of the *Cortes*, Philip focused his attention on the **poderes**, the instructions given by towns to their deputies. Philip's authority undoubtedly benefited from the existence of royal officials in urban centres. In the Castilian towns, there were at least 66 *corregidores*, who were granted judicial and administrative functions, and some dominated the town councils as a result.

For all his apparent disregard for the Castilian *Cortes*, Philip continued to summon it for a variety of reasons. He was eager to be seen to respect the technicalities of the law and the deliberations of the *Cortes* kept him informed of regional interests and concerns. The Castilian *Cortes* was never likely to pose a real threat to his authority because its members were devoted principally to local affairs, though many of these admittedly had broader ramifications – such as the state of the economy, the flow of foreign trade, the strength of coastal defences, the threats from Moorish and English corsairs and privateers, the *Morisco* problem and the excesses of the Inquisition.

Outside Castile, Philip remained receptive to Aragonese concerns. He had inherited an Aragonese kingdom that strongly upheld its traditions and privileges, and it would have been foolish to challenge the status quo. Philip's sensitivity can partly be explained by the question of security, for the proximity of France meant that any disturbance in eastern Spain could be exploited. In reality, much like his father, Philip rarely visited his eastern kingdoms and summoned few meetings of the *Cortes*. Three meetings of the Aragonese *Cortes* were held in 1563, 1585 and 1592, the first two to discuss relatively trivial matters. In the final one, on the occasion of the Aragonese revolt, Philip was understandably more assertive. Fortunately, though not surprisingly, the Crown never faced unified opposition from the eastern kingdoms, owing to their separate and distinctive traditions. Philip tended to communicate with each one separately. While the loyalty of the Catalans was never questioned, Philip found it a difficult region to govern owing to their social and economic problems. Ultimately, he took less interest in the eastern provinces and did not bother to threaten their various privileges because their taxable capacity was far less than in Castile. It was not worth exerting significant political pressure when the financial benefits were negligible.

Another important feature of Philip's political consolidation in Spain was to secure the succession. In 1543, he married his first wife, Mary of Portugal, who gave birth to Don Carlos and then died two years later. In 1554, he married Mary Tudor, who bore him no children. In 1559, a year after Mary's death, he married a Valois princess, Elizabeth, who gave birth to two daughters, Isabella Clara Eugenia then Catherine. His fourth marriage (in November 1570, two years after Elizabeth's death) was to Anne of Austria; although she produced four sons and one daughter, only one son, Philip III, survived.

Opposition: faction and internal rebellions

Factions

Philip willingly promoted, rather than suppressed, faction at court and within the government. His political dominance was assured and he felt sufficiently confident to encourage debate. Philip 'took deliberate care to select the personnel in such a way that it would be sharply divided into two violently opposed parties of equal strength … by this means he made sure that its advice could never be unanimous'.[16] If Philip supported one faction regarding a particular policy, he would later counterbalance it by favouring the opposite faction on a different issue. This prevented him from being challenged by a united group of councillors. Factional rivalry was both creative and constructive because different and competing opinions would evaluate in detail the possible implications of a particular policy. Philip's absence from Council of State meetings allowed him to remain largely immune to factional pressures. In practice, loyalty to the Crown overrode these rivalries, so factions should be interpreted as interest groups rather than political blocks. Policies were the **prerogative** of the Crown and councillors were expected to provide counsel, which the King could either accept or dismiss.

The two key factions were associated with Ruy Gómez da Silva (the Prince of Eboli) and the Duke of Alba respectively. A Venetian report conveys a foreign observer's perceptions of these factions; 'Alba and Eboli are the two columns which support the great machine: on their advice depends the fate of half the world.'[17] The Eboli faction attracted a sizeable group of nobles, including the Marquis of los Vélez, the Duke of Sessa, members of the Mendoza family, Cardinal Quiroga and especially Antonio Pérez. Pérez became a central figure and took over the leadership of this faction after Eboli's death in 1573. Alba's faction included his own extensive household, a number of important secretaries including Vázquez, Gabriel de Zayas, Idiáquez and Moura,

ACTIVITY 3.4

Write brief biographies for each of Philip's wives and focus on the precise timing and broader context for each marriage alliance. What were the motives (especially regarding foreign policy and diplomacy) behind the choice of each wife?

A/AS Level History for AQA: Spain in the Age of Discovery, 1469–1598

ACTIVITY 3.5

Class discussion: faction

- What is faction?
- What were the advantages and disadvantages of factional rivalry?
- Was Philip II really in control of competing factions?
- Did factional rivalry serve to destabilise or to reinforce the Spanish regime?

the King's confessor Fr. Diego de Chaves, in addition to the counts of Barajas and Chinchón (treasurer general of Aragon and Italy). The rivalry between these two key factions focused on numerous issues, including whether Philip's territories should be administered on a federal basis (Eboli) or a more centralist, Castilian system (Alba). The Eboli faction tended to be more moderate in its foreign policy, whereas the Alba faction led the war party.

Yet the opinions of these groups were rarely consistent and could easily change according to time and circumstances. For example, while Alba intended to suppress the Dutch Revolt by force, he had no desire to invade England, where he encouraged restraint. Eboli advocated peace in the Low Countries, but was eager to wage war on England. The lack of consistency in policy and approach can largely be explained by the determination of each faction to disagree on most issues. At its worst, factionalism could spiral out of control. Pérez encouraged Escobedo's murder in 1578. The subsequent factional struggles between Vázquez and Pérez in Madrid in the late 1570s virtually paralysed government. In the end, Pérez overreached himself by interfering in the affairs of the Low Countries and Portugal without royal authorisation. In so doing, he contributed to his own demise. But Philip's personal authority remained unchallenged throughout these various bouts of factional strife.

Philip tended to treat the Spanish grandees with suspicion. He rarely employed nobles in Spain's domestic politics, as illustrated by the membership of the various councils. Grandees were used abroad in war, diplomacy and government. Philip was willing to give them greater responsibilities abroad because it took them away from their own centres of power (their estates and their tenants) and from political affairs in Spain. The nobles who remained on the Iberian Peninsula were encouraged to reside at court, where they could be more easily controlled. Even the few who were given enormous political power were prevented from posing a threat to the King. For example, the Duke of Alba was banished to his own estates in 1578 over a trivial matter.

Figure 3.3: *Morisco* and Aragon revolts.

3 The 'Golden Age', 1556–98

Curbing internal rebellions

The *Morisco* revolt

The first significant domestic revolt which Philip's regime encountered came from the *Moriscos*. As an isolated minority, the *Moriscos* could be tolerated but as potential allies of Ottomans and North African corsairs they became a security risk. Although they were Muslim converts to Christianity, the sincerity of their conversion was doubted. They were accused of only attending Mass to escape punishment, of working behind closed doors on feast days, and of observing Fridays more carefully than Sundays. The Crown and Church were partly to blame for not supplying sufficient funds to pay for their education and to train Arabic-speaking priests.

In simple numerical terms, they were a force to be reckoned with; there were over 400 000 in 1556, representing 6 per cent of the Spanish population and over 50 per cent of the Granadan population. In Granada, there were more *Moriscos* than Old Christians (150 000 to 125 000); the former were keenly aware of their recently lost independence. From the 1550s onwards, the *Moriscos* increased in number much faster than the Old Christians. The *Moriscos* were resented because some were wealthy landowners, benefiting from the lucrative silk industry. In contrast, the large *Morisco* peasant population in Valencia was subject to Christian landowners, many of whom came to their defence. The greatest fear came from their potential links with the North African Barbary states and with the Ottomans. Many *Moriscos* had emigrated and it was common knowledge that collaboration with Barbary corsairs was on the increase in the mid-1560s. This included the flow of refugees from Spain to the Mediterranean and the smuggling of weapons and ammunition to the Iberian Peninsula, where some *Moriscos* acted as a fifth column. It was virtually impossible for the Spanish authorities to patrol the southern and eastern coasts and the growing tensions made the Crown increasingly paranoid about the possibility of civil war.

The *Morisco* revolt against the Crown was partly provoked by govrnment legislation. In 1560, over 85 per cent of those punished by the Inquisition were *Moriscos*, so from an early stage they were a marked enemy. Three years later, a government edict targeted any *Moriscos* who could not prove their ownership of the land, which led to mass confiscations. The edict also decreed that the *Moriscos* were not allowed to possess weapons, and worse still, it targeted their prize possession, the silk industry. They were subjected to heavy taxes, exports were banned, and cheap silk imports from the rest of Spain were introduced and favoured, with disastrous results. Several years later in 1565, news came from the Mediterranean of the Ottoman siege of Malta. Although unsuccessful, the siege reminded the Spanish Christians that it would not take much for the Ottomans to secure a stranglehold in the western Mediterranean. Closer to home, there were corsair raids in August 1565, which penetrated as far as Órgiva in the kingdom of Granada. It was suggested that these raids had been planned with *Morisco* collaboration. The 1567 Edict against the *Moriscos*, proclaimed by Pedro de Deza, President of the *Audiencia* of Granada, decreed that all the most characteristic *Morisco* customs would be forbidden, including their distinctive costumes, surnames and ceremonies. The Arabic language was to be prohibited after three years, by which time *Moriscos* were expected to have learnt Spanish. These new laws simultaneously targeted the identity and economic foundations of the *Moriscos*. Added to these socio-economic and cultural pressures, there was a harvest failure and economic crisis between the years 1567 and 1568.

The revolt started in December 1568 and 4000 rebels had joined it by January 1569. By the time Don John of Austria launched a full-scale campaign in January 1570, the rebel numbers had increased to 30 000, with their stronghold in the Alpujarra Mountains. The Andalusian militia was replaced by Don John's regular troops from Italy and eastern Spain and there were numerous atrocities on both sides. When the *Moriscos* conquered Serón, they killed 150 and reduced 80 to slavery. In February 1569,

Francisco de Córdoba led a force of 800 against Inox (near Almería), and killed 400 men, reducing 2700 women and children to slavery. Most strikingly of all, the Marquis of Mondéjar raised a small force and captured the fort of Guájar and killed everybody inside. Don John's troops eventually defeated the rebel forces, and by October 1570 the government had secured sufficient control to issue orders for the evacuation of all *Moriscos* from Granada, regardless of whether they had rebelled or not. In total, up to 90 000 *Moriscos* were redistributed across Castile and over 30 per cent of them perished en-route.

In 1573, a scheme was launched to establish a network of parishes in areas of high *Morisco* settlement in order to strengthen their allegiance to Christianity. The government sought to restrict *Morisco* access to the maritime districts in Andalusia (from 1579) and Valencia (from 1586) in order to distance them from their Muslim supporters. Despite the redistribution, there were still approximately 10 000 *Moriscos* in Granada as late as 1587. By that time, there was a growing political consensus that the expulsion of the *Moriscos* was the only solution to the problem. No action was taken while Spain remained at war and it took several decades before this policy was implemented between 1609 and 1611.

In some ways, the government mishandled the revolt. In the first instance, it had largely provoked the rebellion. The Duke of Alba had advised Philip not to enforce the edicts, insisting that they would be counter-productive. Bizarrely, the captain-general of Granada, the Marquis of Mondéjar, had not been consulted, though this could be attributed to his relative sympathy for the *Moriscos*. With large landed estates in Granada, he was, unsurprisingly, hesitant to adopt extreme measures and was desperate to avoid a civil war. On a more practical level, Mondéjar warned the government that he lacked sufficient troops and munitions; southern Spain had sent the majority of its regular troops to serve in Alba's army in the Low Countries. While the government was unprepared militarily, the inaccessible terrain and geography of Granada worked to the advantage of the *Moriscos*. During the early stages of the revolt, government forces were paralysed by indecision over methods of campaigning, in particular how to deal with the terrain and the inability to blockade the long coastline of rebel territory.

Although the *Morisco* revolt was suppressed, the government was fortunate that the rebels were not joined by the *Moriscos* in Aragon, Valencia and the richer inhabitants in Granada itself – the old Moorish quarter of the city, the **Albaicín**, refused to rebel. Don John also benefited from the debilitating internal divisions within the *Morisco* community. Hernando de Válor, who was proclaimed their king, was deposed by his own guards, while his successor was murdered in 1571. The *Moriscos* were further weakened by the minimal intervention from North African Muslims and from the Ottomans. While the latter were involved in the conquest of Cyprus, the former only sent a small detachment of volunteers. The Ottoman grand vizier, Mohammed Sokolli, had wanted to intervene. Despite the apparently limited external support, as many as 60 000 Spaniards were killed during the revolt. R. Trevor Davies emphasises the gravity of the revolt: 'in fighting the Moriscos of Granada, it is not too much to say that the Spanish Empire was fighting for its very life. It was good fortune rather than anything else that saved it.'[18] The actions of Old Christians (such as Deza, President of the *Audiencia* in Granada, and the Marquis of los Vélez, captain-general of neighbouring Murcia), particularly their mistreatment of *Moriscos*, served to prolong the rebellion, though at least they supported Mondéjar's suppression of the revolt.

In the aftermath of the revolt, it was clear that while the *Morisco* problem was less intense, the redistribution only aggravated it, by extending it across the whole Iberian Peninsula. The *Moriscos* were replaced in Granada by Christian families from the north. Approximately 12 500 families arrived in Granada, occupying 270 out of the 400 villages, yet the lands offered were of poor quality so many new settlers did not stay. Further afield, the revolt gave confidence to other Spanish foes, especially in the

Netherlands. The exiled William of Orange wrote to his brother early in 1570, only a few years after the outbreak of the Dutch Revolt: 'if the Moors are able to resist for so long, even though they are people of no more substance than a flock of sheep, what might the people of the Low Countries be able to do?'[19]

Timeline: The *Morisco* revolt

Year	Event
1560	Over 85 per cent of those targeted by the Inquisition were *Moriscos*
1565	Siege of Malta
1567	Royal Edict against the *Moriscos*
1567–68	Harvest failures and economic crisis
December 1568	*Morisco* revolt started
January 1569	4000 rebels involved (later increasing to 30 000)
October 1570	Government in control
1587	10 000 *Moriscos* still in Granada
1609–11	Expulsion of *Moriscos* from Iberian peninsula

Setting aside the obvious limitations of its response, the regime was largely successful in dealing with the *Morisco* revolt. Although the government had contributed to the outbreak of the revolt, their pre-emptive strike arguably prevented a far worse crisis. The revolt was successfully put down, which was even more impressive given the Crown's preoccupation with the Dutch Revolt at that same time. Key features were Mondéjar's decisive assault on Guájar during the early months of 1569, the forces commanded by Don John of Austria in support of Mondéjar (*tercios* were brought across from distant Naples) and the Italian galleys that patrolled the southern Spanish coast. In due course, the whole region of the Alpujarra Mountains was subdued. The suppression of the revolt owed much to the pursuit of a successful policy of pardoning those who submitted immediately and showing inflexible severity to any who resisted. In the longer term, the economic and military power of the *Moriscos* was greatly weakened. Their redistribution throughout Spain definitely ensured that they posed less of a threat. It was also driven by the government's view that the separation of *Morisco* communities into smaller units would facilitate their integration into Christian society. The enforcement of this transportation policy was strict: any male *Morisco* over the age of 16 found within 10 leagues of Granada would be put to death; any female over the age of nine would be reduced to slavery. In due course, 80 000 *Moriscos* were expelled from Granada. At the same time, over 80 forts were constructed within the kingdom of Granada in order to encourage the resettlement of Old Christians and to consolidate their position.

The Aragonese revolt

Another notable political crisis in 16th-century Spain was the Aragonese revolt in 1591. Philip was nominally King of Aragon, but he preferred to rule from a distance. He rarely visited the province and appointed a viceroy in his absence. In addition to encouraging intermarriage between Castilian and Aragonese nobles, he largely respected Aragonese rights and privileges. The president and five councillors of the Council of Aragon were expected to be Aragonese, Catalans and Valencians. While the Council of Aragon was meant to be the supreme court of justice for Valencia, Sardinia and the Balearics, it did not serve the same role for Aragon or Catalonia, whose *fueros* demanded that justice be administered within each kingdom. Aragonese laws were enforced by the *Audiencia* of Zaragoza and by the Court of the *Justiciar*. For the latter, the Crown and the Aragonese *Cortes* nominated 5 and 16 members respectively, chaired by a magistrate, the *Justiciar* of Aragon. The only tribunal against which the *fueros* of Aragon had no validity was the Inquisition. The Aragonese *Cortes* was determined to uphold Aragonese privileges, but there was not a single assembly during the period 1563–85, even though Castile's *Cortes* was summoned no fewer than six times in the same period and the Navarrese *Cortes* met even more frequently.

From 1578 onwards, the growing lawlessness in Aragon was sufficiently serious that civil war was a distinct possibility. In the 1580s, there were considerable tensions between the poor and their lords. A genuine fear of a corsair invasion led Castile to send troops in 1582 in order to defend Valencia. The heightened sense of insecurity was also the result of skirmishes between a large *Morisco* population and Old Christians in the county of Ribagorza. To make matters *worse*, in 1588 Philip unwisely decided to appoint a non-native viceroy, the Marquis of Almenara. This was interpreted as a potentially serious threat to the *fueros*. The following year saw significant disturbances in Aragon, especially Zaragoza, where the viceroy resided. The royalist cause was not helped by Almenara's tactlessness and arrogance; he had also befriended the unpopular treasurer general of Aragon, the Count of Chinchón.

By 1590, Zaragoza was in open defiance, triggering the creation of a Council of War by the government. Most nobles and towns refused to join it, Almenara was himself fatally wounded and Philip's other supporters were expelled. At this point, Antonio Pérez, who had been found guilty of selling royal favours and of divulging state secrets, escaped from his Castilian jail and returned to his home province of Aragon. In April 1590, he claimed protective custody from the *Justiciar*, Juan de Lanuza, realising that his execution for murdering Escobedo was imminent. Although a Madrid court had sentenced Pérez to death in July 1590, the *Justiciar*'s court prevented his extradition. Pérez had been both fortunate and astute with his timing. The protection of Aragonese *fueros* dominated the whole province's attention and gave apparent legitimacy to an anti-royalist cause. In response, the Castilian authorities changed tack and accused Pérez of heresy. They followed this up by sending 14 000 soldiers and 3000 cavalry in October and November 1591; the province of Aragon was quickly overcome. Following Pérez's escape from the country, there was a general amnesty in 1592 in which Philip swore to observe the laws and traditions of Aragon and attended the final session of the Aragonese *Cortes*. Despite his willingness to compromise, Philip also acted ruthlessly; the *Justiciar* and approximately 150 ringleaders were executed.

Timeline: The Aragonese revolt

1578	Growing lawlessness in kingdom of Aragon
1582	Castilian troops move to Aragon to defend against suspected *corsair* invasion
1588	Philip II appointed non-native viceroy, Marquis of Almenara
1590	Aragon in open defiance, leading to the creation of the Council of War
April 1590	Antonio Pérez fled Castile and sought protective custody in Aragon
October/November 1591	14 000 soldiers and 3000 Castilian cavalry arrive in Aragon
1592	General amnesty
June 1592	Philip addressed the Aragonese *Cortes*

3 The 'Golden Age', 1556–98

The Aragonese Revolt represented one of the biggest challenges of Philip's reign. The substantial military response was expensive and used up precious resources required elsewhere, in the Netherlands and France. Zaragoza was in open defiance for much of the time, and Philip's viceroy was killed in the process. The severity used to restore royal authority, such as the execution of the *Justiciar* and various ringleaders, indicates the gravity of the situation. The timing of the revolt further hampered Philip's government; it coincided with unrest in several cities in Castile, including Madrid and Toledo, as well as a taxation revolt in Sicily. When Pérez became embroiled in the affair, it made a bad problem far worse. Pérez had numerous supporters, including magnates such as the Duke of Villahermosa and the Count of Aranda, and among the lower ranks of the nobility including Diego de Heredia, Martin de Lanuza and Juan de Luna. While some nobles fought to defend their rights in the face of ever-increasing royal authority, others resisted owing to their exclusion from office. It was even suggested that some individuals in the Pérez camp sought to separate Aragon from the Spanish crown in order to transform it into a republic, possibly under the protection of the Prince of Béarn. The *Morisco* problem added a racial flavour to the crisis, which had the potential to snowball with corsair assistance. The very fact that Philip decided to visit Aragon shows how seriously he perceived it. Had he in fact neglected Aragon?

Despite the evident resistance to the regime, the Aragon revolt did not pose a serious threat to the Crown nor did it represent a constitutional crisis. While the Aragonese resented the appointment of Almenara, it did not stop Philip from appointing non-native viceroys. Philip did promise to support Aragonese *fueros* but that did not prevent the execution of the *Justiciar* without a trial. During his visit to Aragon, Philip summoned the *Cortes* to Tarazona in June 1592 and enforced some significant changes to the constitution. The Aragonese accepted the clause that a fugitive from justice, who sought sanctuary in Aragon from another Habsburg territory, would be extradited. The office of *Justiciar* was changed from a life appointment to one dictated purely by the king, who was also responsible for the selection of the *Justiciar's* lieutenants. The king was given a greater voice in the promotion of senior judges so that they were less vulnerable to aristocratic pressure. The **Diputación del Reyno**, a permanent committee of the Cortes, lost much of its control over Aragonese revenues and over the regional guard, and was forced to give up its right to call together representatives of the kingdom's cities.

Philip also took the opportunity to strengthen the Aragonese Inquisition, which was located in the newly fortified palace of the *Aljafería* in December 1593 and protected by a royal garrison. Nor did the revolt pose a serious military threat. It was barely a contest, 'a military promenade' in the words of A. Lovett, and far less threatening than the earlier *Morisco* revolt.[20] Philip had acted decisively and assembled an army of 12 000 under Alonso de Vargas, an experienced commander and veteran of the Low Countries. The severity of the royal response can be credited to Philip's hatred of rebellion rather than the gravity of threat. Resistance within Zaragoza disintegrated and, despite his impressive support, Pérez took flight to Béarn. Some of the great nobles who had supported the revolt, the Duke of Villahermosa and Count of Aranda, were imprisoned.

Outside Zaragoza, there were no significant uprisings in defence of the *fueros*; Catalonia and the rest of Aragon, while arguably sympathetic, did not stir. The timing of the Aragon revolt was inopportune, but the problems elsewhere were to be expected and scarcely surprising. They formed part of a much broader European economic crisis. In response, Philip's decision to visit Aragon was not borne out of desperation, but was timely and advisable. Moreover, the harsh suppression of the revolt gave way to a relatively moderate political settlement. Aragon's institutions were not tampered with, but remodelled to meet the requirements of royal power. Philip felt sufficiently confident to nominate another non-native viceroy, even though this had contributed to the unrest in the first instance.

ACTIVITY 3.6

Identify the relative strengths and weaknesses of Philip's policies and actions in the province of Aragon. Did he neglect Aragon or do you think that his remoteness was deliberate and advisable?

> **ACTIVITY 3.7**
>
> Using the section 'Religion and society' and your broader reading, research the nature of Philip II's Catholicism. With what terms and phrases would you describe his Catholicism? Devout, fanatical, extremist, loyal to Rome?

Religion and society

The Iberian Peninsula has traditionally been perceived to be at the vanguard of the Counter-Reformation. The Spanish Church had its own Inquisition, Spaniards figured prominently among the key early members of the Jesuit order and numerous Spanish clerics contributed to the formulation of Tridentine decrees (see section 'Relations with the papacy'). Yet in reality the Spanish crown maintained an uneasy relationship with Rome and the Spanish Inquisition predated the emergence of Lutheranism. Nor did the defence and promotion of Catholicism exclusively drive Spanish foreign policy.

Philip undeniably took a personal interest and care in the Catholic Church. He attended daily Mass and heard sermons at least once a week, as well as spending much time engaged in private devotions. His own valet, Jehan Lhermite, observed that there was not 'a corner of his bedroom where one did not see a pious image of some saint or a crucifix, and he always kept his eyes fixed and absorbed on these images, and his spirit lifted to the heavens'.[21] It is hardly coincidental that the Escorial palace included a monastery of Jeronimite monks – another powerful reminder of his Catholic devotion. The Escorial also included a seminary, a hospital and its church had 44 altars. Philip's support for monasticism was well known to contemporaries. **St Teresa of Ávila** remarked that 'Don Philip is very well disposed to religious [i.e. monks and nuns] who are known to keep their Rule, and will always help them.'[22] Philip frequently confided in his confessors and theologians, and religion permeated many different aspects of his rule. He even consulted his religious advisers when making political decisions.

Philip inherited a Spanish Church with ecclesiastical independence. While his predecessors had been its architects, Philip now became the Church's chief administrator. He played an active role in its supervision, devoting energy to the careful selection and appointment of bishops, and he was determined to set high clerical standards. He intervened to such a degree that Trevor Davies argued that 'in the domestic affairs of the Spanish Church, Philip was as Erastian [i.e equally convinced that the church was subordinate to the state] as Henry VIII'.[23] He was equally eager that papal authority should be carefully handled and contained; no papal bull was published without royal approval. Spanish Catholicism was protected from any foreign interference or threats. In November 1559, a royal edict recalled all Spaniards attending foreign universities, insisting that future study abroad would be permitted only under special authorisation. Similarly, Philip endeavoured to dissolve the links that bound religious orders that were of foreign origin from their motherhouses beyond Spain's borders. For example, in 1561, Philip secured the separation of the Spanish province of the Cistercian Order from the jurisdiction of Cîteaux in France. Philip's regime naturally took full advantage of the Church's financial potential, collecting as much as 50 per cent of its revenues. As in previous reigns, the *cruzada and subsidio* remained lucrative taxes.

The Jesuits

Philip's relations with the papacy were also affected by the emergence of the Jesuits. The Society of Jesus quickly developed into one of the most important Catholic orders in the 16th century. From an early stage, Spaniards dominated the movement, particularly its founder **Ignatius of Loyola** (died in 1556) and his two successors as General, Diego Laínez and Francis Borja. Of the first six followers of Ignatius, four were Spaniards and one was Portuguese. However, the Jesuits' special vow of obedience to the Pope caused friction with the Spanish Church, since they were sometimes seen as papal agents. In the first six decades of its existence (1540 to Philip's death in 1598), national rivalries appeared within the order, as individual Jesuits sought to gain political support from their own countries. During Philip's reign, and with his blessing, a group of Spanish Jesuits attempted to resist the centralising tendencies of the Jesuit order. While the foreign Everard Mercurian and Claudio Aquaviva were Generals, some

Spanish Jesuits railed against the authority of the Jesuit General in Rome. Philip ultimately failed in his attempt to nationalise the Jesuits and bring them under the control of the Spanish Inquisition. Yet this did not mean that they had a detrimental impact on the Spanish Church. Jesuit colleges, preaching and missions were found in every important town on the Iberian Peninsula and contributed enormously to the revival of Spanish Catholicism.

Relations with the papacy

There was some conflict between Spain and almost every pope with whom Philip dealt during his reign, though the tensions should not be exaggerated. Some popes lamented the secular motives of Philip's foreign policy. For example, in 1589, Sixtus V argued that 'the preservation of the Catholic religion, which is the principal aim of the Pope, is only a pretext for His Majesty whose principal aim is the security and aggrandisement of his dominions'.[24] This was especially noticeable in Philip's foreign policy towards England. For some time, Philip refused to align himself with the papacy and was guided by political considerations. On two occasions, he managed to thwart the excommunication of Elizabeth I. This helps to explain the cordial relations between Spain and England for much of their respective reigns and the lack of substantial Spanish support for Mary Queen of Scots, Elizabeth's potential Catholic replacement; this was also due to her links with France.

Popes during Philip II's reign

Paul IV	1555–59
Pius IV	1559–65
Pius V	1566–72
Gregory XIII	1572–85
Sixtus V	1585–90
Urban VII	1590
Gregory XIV	1590–91
Innocent IX	1591
Clement VIII	1592–1605

As regards the Iberian Peninsula, popes were undoubtedly frustrated that no papal decree was published in Spain unless first examined by the Council of Castile. In November 1567, Pius V's edict against bullfighting was completely ignored. Five years later in 1572, it was decreed that all papal briefs secured for cases before the ecclesiastical courts should be disregarded. In the same year, the Council of Castile declared null and void papal briefs that cited Spaniards in foreign ecclesiastical courts. In 1582, the papacy still objected, in vain, to Philip's sending royal officials to the synod of Toledo. The Crown controlled ecclesiastical tribunals through the Council of Castile, which regarded itself as an ecclesiastical court of appeal and consistently opposed appeals to Rome. There were also tensions concerning the investigation and prosecution of heresy cases. The Carranza investigation for heresy provides a case in point. Carranza was a leading Spanish cleric who had powerful enemies within the Iberian Peninsula (see section 'The Spanish Inquisition'). His works were closely scrutinised. By 1566, the Carranza case had become a struggle for ecclesiastical power between the Pope and Philip II. The former demanded that Carranza be tried in Rome, and eventually Philip did yield. A report from one of Philip's ministers, Requesens, points towards non-religious motives; 'there is no *cruzada* yet, but no doubt there will be when the Pope gets satisfaction over Carranza'.[25]

Philip encountered particular difficulties with a number of individual popes. While Paul IV (1555–59) was intensely anti-Spanish, with similar consequences, Clement VIII (1592–1605) was pro-French. Despite these various tensions, Philip never overstepped the mark, for at various points he needed the financial, as well as the moral, support of the popes. As supreme head of the Church, the Pope disposed indirectly of Church revenues (notably the *cruzada*), on which Philip relied. Philip's foreign policy often complemented that of the papacy, especially in the Mediterranean and in the Low Countries. Regarding the latter, both despised Calvinism, even though the popes were keen to emphasise the religious character of the conflict, whereas the Spanish interpreted it as the suppression of a rebellion.

The **Council of Trent** also helped to strengthen Catholicism in Spain. Although Philip was anxious about the implications of a papal-led council for his power over the Spanish Church, he generally welcomed the **Tridentine** decrees. In fact, there was a strong Spanish presence in the Council's final session (1562–63), estimated at 130 Spaniards. Spanish representatives at the Council were the earliest and most persistent advocates of episcopal residence. Spanish participation in the Council was also marked by the quality of its representatives, including Cardinal Pacheco, the Dominicans Melchor Cano and Domingo de Soto, and the Jesuits Diego Laínez and Alfonso Salmerón. Laínez is generally regarded as one of the most influential theologians at Trent, especially for his views on justification by faith.

The papacy undoubtedly benefited from the Spanish contribution, though papal and Spanish views did not always complement each other. The prerogatives of the Crown would clash with papal interests and authority. This was particularly the case regarding episcopal jurisdiction; for Spanish theologians and bishops, ecclesiastical reform was more likely to be promoted by native bishops than by agents of the **Roman Curia**. Despite this, the Tridentine decrees were accepted almost immediately in Spain and served to revolutionise the Church. Although the decrees were published in Spain, Philip was hesitant at first. Following their ratification by Pius IV on 26 January 1564, he feared that the decrees might threaten the rights and privileges of the Spanish Crown. This highlights an obvious weakness of the Council, namely its significant dependence on the cooperation of secular rulers.

In Spain, the Tridentine decrees were certainly implemented, but at a speed dictated by the Crown. There was a strong emphasis on increasing the power and efficiency of bishops, focused on the summoning of diocesan synods and directing of visitations. The Crown took this opportunity to establish six new bishoprics in Aragon, and the Castilian bishopric in Burgos was upgraded to an archbishopric. One of the Spanish bishops who attended the final session of the Council, **Guillem Cassador**, bishop of Barcelona (1561–70), returned to his diocese determined to implement Tridentine reforms. In addition to undertaking visitations, he also founded a seminary to train the clergy within his diocese. Gaspar de Quiroga was another key figure within the Spanish ecclesiastical and political hierarchy. His various jobs and responsibilities included: from 1558, inspector of monasteries in Sicily and Naples; President of the Council of Italy in 1567; Bishop of Cuenca in 1572 and Inquisitor General the following year; Archbishop of Toledo and primate of Spain in 1577; he was appointed a cardinal in 1578. Quiroga was a resident bishop, setting an example by his own frugal living. The revenues created from within his diocese financed the religious reforms, particularly the promotion of education. He worked closely with the Augustinian and Jesuit orders, as well as being a patron of the arts (including the artist El Greco). At no point did he question papal supremacy in spiritual matters.

> **Key term**
>
> **Council of Trent:** The reforming Council of the Roman Catholic Church opened in 1545 and concluded in 1563. Trent's decrees represented the Church's response to Protestant teachings, as well as a serious attempt to reform the abuses and corruption within the Church. The Tridentine decrees were met with mixed responses throughout Europe; successful implementation was largely dependent on local factors.

> **Key term**
>
> **Roman Curia:** The Roman Curia represents the government and organisation of the Roman Catholic Church, on which successive popes were dependent for the effective administration of all Church affairs.

Figure 3.4: The burial of the Count of Orgaz, El Greco.

The Spanish Inquisition

The Spanish Inquisition was another important feature of Philip's church. The Inquisition was supervised by **Hernando de Valdes**, Archbishop of Seville and Inquisitor General from 1547 to 1566, and advised by the Dominican theologian Melchor Cano. As in the previous reign, the Council of Inquisition was based in Madrid, and comprised over 15 tribunals. The papacy greatly empowered the Spanish Inquisition by introducing a papal bull in 1559 that allowed the Inquisition to take the revenue from a canonry and prebend from every cathedral or collegiate Church in Spain and the Canary Islands. In the early years, the Inquisition was particularly severe, and Philip was largely responsible. While still in the Netherlands in 1558, he heard that there were Protestant congregations in Valladolid and Seville, and he was determined to expel heresy from the kingdom. The Inquisition targeted the Valladolid group in two *autos da fé* in May and October 1559, with Cano preaching at the first, and Philip actually present at the second.

The focused and determined approach of the early years partly stemmed from the growing fear of Calvinism, especially given the apparent proximity of French Calvinists. As early as 1560, Philip ordered his viceroy of Catalonia, García de Toledo, to monitor the borders and assist the Inquisition in its investigations. From 1564, Philip ordered the new viceroy, Diego Hurtado de Mendoza, to improve the frontier fortifications. The threats were certainly real, as well as perceived. In 1565, his French ambassador warned him that Calvinist Geneva was planning to disseminate heretical books in Spain. Five years later, in 1570, a large Catalan force under Hurtado de Mendoza drove back a Huguenot (French Calvinist) attack on Perpignan.

Grand Inquisitor Valdes requested papal authorisation to go beyond Church law and condemn the guilty as circumstances dictated. The Inquisition tried over 800, many of them upper-class women. The policy of repression was sufficiently successful that it effectively quashed the existence of Protestantism in Spain. Strikingly, most cases were brought by individuals, not inquisitorial officials. In searching for heresy, much attention was devoted to the importation and circulation of books. A royal edict decreed that the importation of books without a royal licence was a crime punishable by death. This was reinforced by the appearance of Indexes of Forbidden Books. On 17 August 1559, Valdes brought out the first Spanish Index, in which 670 works were banned, only 170 of which were written in Castilian. Inquisitorial officials undertook intermittent checks of bookshops and ports. The most famous investigation concerns the high profile case of Archbishop Carranza of Toledo. Appointed Archbishop of Toledo in 1557, it did not take long for his powerful rivals (including Valdes and Cano) to accuse him of heresy, citing his *Commentaries on the Christian Catechism*. The trial lasted for 17 years due to Carranza's refusal to cooperate with Valdes. In 1567, the case was transferred to Rome and further delayed by the death of Pius V in 1572. When Gregory XIII eventually reinvestigated the case, a decision was made to suspend Carranza from his diocese and he retired to a monastery.

One cannot discuss Spanish Catholicism without making reference to **Christian mysticism**. Religious reform was driven by the secular clergy, but also benefited enormously from individual monks and nuns. St Teresa of Ávila (1515–82) has become one of the most eminent female authors in Spain. She wrote various devotional and mystical works, including her autobiography, *The Way of Perfection and Interior Castle*. She masterminded the reform of the Carmelite order to which she belonged and this led to a notable increase in new communities. Equally significant was the influence of **St John of the Cross** (1542–91), who was a disciple of St Teresa and became a Discalced Carmelite. He also wrote numerous mystical works, including *Ascent of Mount Carmel* and *Dark Night of the Soul*. While St Teresa frequently wrote to train novices in the spiritual life, St John's writings focused more on the higher planes of mystical experiences. These two reformers were joined by Fray Luis Ponce de León (1527–91), who is described as one of the last great mystics of Golden Age Spain. He wrote during the period of his incarceration, with his greatest work being *The Names of Christ*.

> **Key term**
>
> **Christian mysticism:** The aspect of Christian belief and practice that prepares the individual believer for a direct spiritual encounter with God.

Economic developments

Philip's financial inheritance

Charles V left an unstable financial legacy, which stemmed from his expansive foreign policy. Philip inherited external debt of approximately 20 million ducats, in addition to the liability of *juros*, estimated at 50 million ducats. It left Spain in a state of virtual bankruptcy in 1557 and the government was forced to suspend payments to creditors and substitute them with *juros* bearing five per cent interest. The financial crisis partly explains Philip's return to Spain from the Netherlands. As before, the financial burden for the Spanish Empire was carried by Castile. Sicily, Naples, the duchy of Milan and the Low Countries were unwilling to contribute to the defence of the Empire when their own interests were not involved. In the Mediterranean, Spanish imperial policies did occasionally dovetail with those of Naples and Sicily, though the latter had no interest in northern Europe. Philip was not especially sympathetic to this sense of provincialism, as he told the Council of Italy in 1589: 'And since God has entrusted me with so many [kingdoms], since all are in my charge, and since in the defence of one all are preserved, it is just that all should help me.'[26]

Despite the size and power of the Empire, the Castilian financial administration struggled to cope with the responsibilities. The Council of Finance tended to be rather backward in its approach and lacked expertise. Philip was further debilitated by the fact that his country lacked a state bank, and was consequently reliant on private bankers. The transfer of money was central to the administration of a large empire, making the Spanish all the more dependent on the leading banking families. These powerful financiers provided money and generated government revenue before it was due. In exchange, the Genoese had a monopoly over the sale of playing cards in Spain and control of salt works in Andalusia. Similarly, the Fuggers were put in charge of the mercury mines of Almadén and silver mines of Guadalcanal in southern Spain, and were granted the property of the military orders.

Securing the movement of money

The Spanish regime was further hindered by the logistical difficulties of transferring money throughout the Empire. It was particularly problematic getting funds to the Low Countries, especially following the rise of English privateering. In 1568, the Duke of Alba's pay ships were seized and there were further threats from the Dutch **Sea Beggars** from 1572 onwards. Between the years 1566 and 1581, one of the objectives of Spanish diplomacy was to secure the transport of money across France; in 1572 alone, 500 000 ducats reached the Duke of Alba via the kingdom of France. After 1578, an alternative route was established across the western Mediterranean from Barcelona to Genoa. Substantial sums of money reached Alexander Farnese via Milan in 1584, 1586 and 1588.

Economic growth in Spain did not keep pace with Spain's rise to great power status. There was sustained demographic growth in the early part of Philip's reign, including an increase in agricultural production. Yet this was not matched by an increase in efficiency, much land remained infertile and birth rates fell after 1580. Wool represented the single most important export and the *Mesta* continued to dominate proceedings. Sheep provided Castile with its main source of foreign income and the wool trade affected every aspect of the Spanish economy. With so little land being cultivated, there was an ever-increasing reliance on imported grain.

Crown income

The income of the Spanish crown increased significantly during the course of Philip's reign. From 1559 to the 1590s, royal income tripled from 3 million ducats to 10 million. Castile's inhabitants were pressurised by increased taxation and by the imposition of new duties or the modification of old ones. Taxation was increased by 50 per cent during the years 1556–70, and by 90 per cent between 1570 and 1600. The sums received by the Spanish navy and army from Castile were impressive: between 1571 and 1577, 7 million ducats were received by the Mediterranean fleet; in the same time period, 11.7 million ducats were received by the army of Flanders. The *alcabala* continued to be the most important tax, still levied mainly in Castile, though other territories provided limited contributions. While the revenues from the *alcabala* rose by 14 per cent, customs duties tripled in Spain and quadrupled in Seville. Philip continued to make the most of church revenues, including the *subsidio* tax on church rents, lands and clerical incomes (including bishops), which was made permanent from 1561. The Bishop of Toledo, Don Sancho Busto, denounced the Spanish regime's meddling in the Church's finances, declaring in 1574 that Spain was setting a worse example than its Lutheran counterparts in the Holy Roman Empire. Thanks to the

3 The 'Golden Age', 1556–98

ACTIVITY 3.8

St Teresa of Ávila and St John of the Cross

Using this section and your own research, compose a biographical timeline for both saints, and explain their significance in Spain and beyond.

Figure 3.5: Bernini's Sculpture of St Teresa of Ávila in ecstasy.

> **ACTIVITY 3.9**
>
> Read through section 'Economic developments'. Make a list of the economic problems that were out of Philip's direct control. Was Philip largely to blame for the Empire's financial problems?

> **ACTIVITY 3.10**
>
> Draw up a timeline of key military campaigns and commitments during Philip's reign at home and abroad. What was their financial impact?

quadrupling of the *cruzada* and the exploitation of Carranza's vacant see, church revenues amounted to 20 per cent of Crown revenues by the 1590s.

Like his father, Philip was also reliant on government borrowing, which increased substantially during his reign. In the lead-up to the Spanish Armada, there were a number of enormous *asientos*, or loan contracts, several amounting to more than 1 million ducats. Bankers demanded substantial interest rates for their loans and the *asientos* became the largest financial transactions in Europe during the period 1580–96. In addition to borrowing, Philip's regime benefited from several new taxes. In 1567, Pope Pius V allowed Philip to introduce the **excusado**, a tax on the property of each parish, which generated more revenues for the Duke of Alba's army in the Low Countries. The Castilian *Cortes* agreed to a new tax (the **millones**) in 1589, voted in the aftermath of the Spanish Armada. As a result, all of Castile's inhabitants (the wealthy and poor, the laity and clergy) were taxed on meat, wine, oil and vinegar; 8 million ducats were collected within 10 years. Although intended as an exceptional measure, the *millones* became a permanent tax.

Crown expenditure

With so many commitments at home and abroad, the Spanish crown's expenditure was substantial. It was rising much faster than income, and the number of state bankruptcies (1557, 1560, 1576 and the most serious in 1596) was unprecedented and indicative of the scale of Philip's commitments. By declaring a decree of bankruptcy, Philip's government sought to convert short-term debt at high interest into long-term debt at low interest. Rather than refusing to pay debts, the regime merely rescheduled them. The interest from debts absorbed half of the Crown's income (5.5 million ducats per annum), and the government was 85 million in debt by the time of Philip's death in 1598.

Warfare remained the largest source of expenditure. Although the regime endeavoured to make each theatre of war self-financing, this was never realised. By the 1570s, Spain's military campaigns were costing the government 700 000 ducats per month. In 1571 alone, Castile paid 18.5 million ducats for the Dutch and Mediterranean campaigns. The Treasury was under sustained pressure during the 1580s. In the period 1587–90, the French Catholic League received up to 3 million ducats from the Spanish government. This coincided with the Armada campaign, which cost 900 000 ducats per month. Towards the end of Philip's reign, while the Prince of Parma was governor, the Spanish spent 21 million in the Low Countries. In the final decade of his reign, Philip's regime spent 30 million ducats in France.

Income from the New World

The Castilian crown was entitled to one-fifth of all the minerals mined in the New World and made the most of it through effective reorganisation of the governments and economies of its territories there. Revenue of 90 000 ducats per annum in the 1560s had tripled by the 1590s. During the course of Philip's reign, the New World generated 65 million ducats in gold and silver. Although American bullion never represented more than one-fifth of all state income, it provided hard cash for the regime. Without the assistance of the New World's bullion, Philip's regime would not have managed to intervene in as many conflicts. At critical moments, the influx of bullion even determined the timing of military campaigns. In 1566, the receipt of 1.5 million ducats funded the Duke of Alba's expedition to the Netherlands. New World silver largely explains why bankers continued to lend vast sums to the Spanish regime. Despite these considerable benefits, the importation of silver and gold did lead to price inflation. From 1530 to 1600, Spanish inhabitants could afford 20 per cent less goods. Although the Spanish government enjoyed significant gains, most of the bullion went to foreign merchants and ordinary Spaniards benefited little.

3 The 'Golden Age', 1556–98

Figure 3.6: The Atlantic routes of the Spanish treasure fleets, which departed via the Canary Islands and returned via the Azores.

Social and cultural developments in Spain's 'Golden Age'

The influence of the Inquisition

The Inquisition certainly had an impact on the social and cultural developments in Spain, but its role should not be exaggerated. The targeting of books put enormous pressure on authors. While some works were prohibited in their entirety, others were abridged only in certain sections. For example, a section (part ii, chapter 36) from Cervantes' *Don Quixote* was omitted on the grounds that it smacked of Luther's doctrine of *sola fide*: 'works of charity negligently performed are of no worth'.[27] Unlike elsewhere on the European continent, heretical books could be published on the condition that offending passages were removed. This has led historians such as R. Trevor Davies to challenge the harsh reputation of the Inquisition; 'the Spanish censorship of the press – contrary to usual opinion – [was] about the most liberal in Europe', and he remarks that 'what strikes one about the censorship of the Inquisition is not so much the books forbidden as the books allowed by it'.[28] The works of Giordano Bruno, Galileo, Copernicus and Hobbes's *Leviathan* all escaped the Index.

Universities, new ideas and intellectual movements

The establishment of new universities and the thriving of older ones contributed much to the development of new ideas and to the growth of intellectual movements. With new universities at Baeza (1565), Orihuela (1568) and Tarragona (1572), Spain gained intellectual pre-eminence in Europe in almost every branch of learning. This was matched by a prolific printing industry; the Spanish presses published 74 editions and 57 reprints of scientific treatises between 1561 and 1610. The Escorial library alone contained 14 000 volumes by 1598.

Figure 3.7: The royal library at the Escorial.

Individual authors and scientists secured European renown. First printed in 1589, José de Acosta's *Natural and Moral History of the Indies* was widely published in Spain and abroad. Rogete's construction of telescopes ensured that Spain became the principal market for astronomical instruments. Juan Lopez's observation of the eclipse of the sun in Spain and America during the 1570s influenced later astronomical methods. Deza de Valdes undertook ophthalmological work – research that contributed to the improvement of spectacles. Important works were published on tropical medicine, navigation, mineralogy, metallurgy and mining. Philip himself established a research centre in Madrid, and appointed three founding professors to a new academy of mathematics in Madrid. At court, Juan Bautista Lavaña, a Portuguese cartographer, received 400 ducats a year in order to undertake research on cosmography, geography, topography and mathematics. Spanish scholars excelled in a broad range of fields: Benito Arias Montano's publication of the Royal Antwerp edition of the Polyglot Bible; Francisco Lopez de Gomara's works on economics; and the work of the great orientalist, Juan Bautista Pérez. Felix Lope de Vega Carpio made the three-act play the regular form and completed as many as 1800 dramatic works. In scholarly and literary terms, this was undoubtedly a Golden Age.

The condition of Spain by 1598: what were its political, economic and social strengths and weaknesses?

The 1580s had seen the emergence of a Castilian, as distinct from a Habsburg, empire. For some time, Castile had remained a crucial political and economic centre on the Iberian Peninsula and beyond. This was further reinforced by Philip's reluctance to travel beyond Spanish borders during the latter decades of his reign.

In the pursuit of numerous military campaigns abroad, Castile inevitably bore the financial brunt. In the words of William Maltby, 'Spain was destroying itself to save its empire.'[29] The price of grain rose by more than 50 per cent in Castile and Andalusia within the short period 1595–99, by which point Spain had reached crisis point. At Philip's death, the Spanish treasury was not far from 100 million ducats in debt.

Despite these economic woes, Philip had chalked up considerable achievements on the domestic front. His own authority was never directly threatened and he imposed a rigorous hold on the numerous and varied political institutions and channels within the Iberian Peninsula. The problems that he faced were never insurmountable and he suppressed the Aragonese and *Morisco* revolts with relative ease. The nobility were kept in check throughout his reign. Shrewdly, he involved them in the broader affairs of the Spanish Empire, and sensibly, he did not empower them at home.

Central to Philip's own priorities was the role of the Church. Spain became a beacon of Catholic renewal and Counter-Reformation in many different ways: Tridentine decrees were welcomed and quickly enforced; the Spanish Inquisition continued its work, ensuring that Protestantism, and especially Calvinism, had no chance to establish itself; papal relations were tense but both the papacy and Philip gained much from their collaboration.

Philip was profoundly diligent in his approach to government and few early modern rulers matched his work ethic. If Philip had failings, they were primarily the result of the impossible task of governing the incoherent and fragmented Empire with which he was faced.

Practice essay questions

1. 'Spain was well governed under Philip II's reign.' Explain why you agree or disagree with this view.
2. 'Philip's reign represented a Golden Age.' Assess the validity of this view.
3. 'Philip's domestic achievements outweighed the limitations.' Explain why you agree or disagree with this view.
4. With reference to these extracts and your understanding of the historical context, which of these two extracts provides the more convincing interpretation of the workings of Philip's government?

Extract A

Beyond the scope of the king's councils, direct royal authority was tenuous. Spain, we have seen, was no centralised state. Its structure was much like that of France and most large European countries. There was no central administration, civil service, army or tax system. For all these things the crown relied on regional officials in the cities, provinces and lands controlled by the Church or nobility. It followed that the king was continually engaged in consultation with the officials and people over whom he ruled. Philip used the process of consultation for two purposes: to obtain information, and to secure consent.

Source: Henry Kamen, *Philip of Spain*. (Yale University Press, 1998), p. 212.

Extract B

Towards the end of his life, Philip seems to have conducted less business working alone with his papers and more in conference with his two chief ministers, Moura and Idiáquez. Both seem to have been soft-spoken and had made their mark in diplomacy, but neither was weak. Each had proved himself in an important situation, Idiáquez in Genoa during the financial crisis of 1573–1577, and Moura during the Portuguese succession struggle, 1578–1581.

Source: Peter Pierson, *Philip II of Spain*. (Thames and Hudson, London, 1975), p. 127.

Further reading

There are useful insights into Philip's domestic policies in the previously mentioned textbooks, especially Lynch, Kamen and Lovett. Students should also consider the numerous biographies of Philip II, especially those by Philip Pierson (London, 1975), Patrick Williams (London, 2001), Henry Kamen (Yale University Press, 1997), Geoffrey Woodward (Longman, 1997) and, most recently, by Geoffrey Parker (Yale University Press, 2014). For the Inquisition, see the books by John Edwards, Helen Rawlings and Henry Kamen, all entitled *The Spanish Inquisition* (Tempus Publishing, 1999; Blackwell, 2006; and Phoenix Press, 1997). See also the works of J.H. Elliott, including *Imperial Spain, 1469–1716* (Penguin, 1963) and *Spain and its World, 1500–1700* (Yale University Press, 1989), and Henry Kamen's *Spain's Road to Empire: The Making of a World Power, 1492–1763* (Penguin, 2009).

Chapter summary

By the end of this chapter you should understand:

- the workings of government and Philip's contribution to the political process
- the causes, motives and the relative challenges posed by internal rebellions
- the nature and effectiveness of domestic policies, especially relating to religious, social and economic factors
- the relative strengths and weaknesses of Spain by Philip's death in 1598.

End notes

1. Cited in Geoffrey Parker, *Imprudent King: A New Life of Philip II*. London and New Haven: Yale University Press, 2014, p. 61.
2. Cited in R. Trevor Davies, *The Golden Century of Spain, 1501–1621*. London: Macmillan, 1967, p. 121.
3. A. Lovett, *Early Habsburg Spain, 1515–1598*. Oxford University Press, 1986, p. 122.
4. Parker, *Imprudent King*, p. 300.
5. Cited in Henry Kamen, *Spain, 1469–1714*. Harlow: Longman, 2005, p. 153.
6. Parker, *Imprudent King*, pp. xv–xviii.
7. John Lynch, *Spain under the Habsburgs, Volume 1: Empire and Absolutism, 1516–1598*. Basil Blackwell, Oxford, 1981, pp. 188–89.
8. Cited in Parker, *Imprudent King*, p. 184.
9. Cited in Parker, *Imprudent King*, p. 178.
10. Cited in Lynch, *Spain*, p. 184.
11. Cited in Trevor Davies, *Golden Century*, p. 120.
12. Cited in Trevor Davies, *Golden Century*, p. 120.
13. Lynch, *Spain*, p. 181.
14. Cited in Lynch, *Spain*, p. 194.
15. Cited in Lynch, *Spain*, p. 207.
16. Trevor Davies, *Golden Century*, pp. 122–23.
17. Cited in Trevor Davies, *Golden Century*, p. 123.
18. Trevor Davies, *Golden Century*, p. 170.
19. Cited in Parker, *Imprudent King*, p. 208.
20. Lovett, *Early Habsburg*, p. 211.
21. Cited in Parker, *Imprudent King*, p. 81.
22. Cited in Lynch, *Spain*, p. 183.
23. Trevor Davies, *Golden Century*, p. 133.
24. Cited in Lynch, *Spain*, p. 273.
25. Cited in Lynch, *Spain*, p. 277.
26. Cited in Lynch, *Spain*, pp. 179–80.
27. Cited in Trevor Davies, *Golden Century*, p. 145.
28. Trevor Davies, *Golden Century*, pp. 145–46.
29. William Maltby, *The Rise and Fall of the Spanish Empire*. Basingstoke: Palgrave Macmillan, 2009, p. 117.

4 The 'Great Power', 1556–98

In this section, we will explore the motives and analyse the achievements and limitations of Philip II's foreign policies.

Specification points:

- Philip's inheritance and ambitions; ideas and pressures; the Spanish army and navy
- the eclipsing of French power; Italy; war and interference in France
- control of the Mediterranean: challenging the Turks; the conquest of and relationship with Portugal
- revolt in the Netherlands; relations with England: conflict in Europe and the Caribbean
- Spain in the New World: expansion, settlement and trade; the impact of empire
- Spain's international position by 1598: the extent of Spain's power; illusion or reality.

Philip's inheritance and ambitions; ideas and pressures

European territories and expansion

Philip's massive territorial inheritance was such that it made the Spanish Empire the leading European power of its time. With inherited possessions on the Italian peninsula and in the Mediterranean, Philip also had control of the Netherlands in northern Europe. When he acceded to the Spanish throne, furthermore, he was married to the queen of England, Mary Tudor. While the Habsburg–Valois wars had not ended, the conflict had reached its final phase, at least for the time being. With Portugal an unlikely foe, Spain was able to continue its territorial expansion in the New World.

Spain's priorities were focused on the promotion of its strategic and economic interests. The succession of a Protestant monarch in England did not discourage Philip from maintaining cordial relations. Trade between London and Antwerp was mutually beneficial, and the proximity of their respective coastlines meant that successful diplomacy was essential. Striking religious differences were underplayed and subordinated to political and economic objectives. In the Mediterranean, as before, the Spanish sought to protect their trade routes and maintain their lines of communication with their Italian possessions. Central to their strategy was the objective of containing and, where possible, reversing the growth of Ottoman naval power. Where Spanish interests coincided with those of the key powers in the Italian city-states, a united front would always have the greater chance of success against the superior naval and military forces of the Ottoman Empire. Although certainly not unchallenged, the Spanish Empire had achieved a dominant position in the New World. Further expansion was envisaged, but the priority was to consolidate existing territories and to take full advantage of the empire's wealth.

For all its strengths, the Spanish Empire was also vulnerable and under noticeable pressure. Charles V's abdication as king of Spain and Holy Roman Emperor left the Habsburg inheritance divided into Spanish and Austrian possessions. While Charles's brother Ferdinand was elected Holy Roman Emperor, Philip took over the Spanish territories, meaning that he would be likely to take a more Spanish-centred approach to diplomacy and foreign policy. Following his return from the Netherlands in September 1559, Philip would reside permanently on the Iberian Peninsula and events abroad were increasingly seen from a Spanish perspective. Philip's ability to control his empire was undermined by the considerable distance between his disparate lands, which hampered effective communication and government. Ottoman ambitions to secure a stranglehold in the western Mediterranean had a realistic chance of being fulfilled. The forces of Suleiman the Magnificent had taken Rhodes in the early 1520s. Towards the end of his sultanate, in 1565, the Ottoman attempt to take Malta would threaten all the lines of communication between the Spanish mainland and her Mediterranean possessions.

Even in the absence of conflict, the coordination of this fragmented empire was incredibly difficult. Of the 32 letters from Madrid received by the Spanish ambassador in Paris during 1578, the fastest took seven days, half of them took between 10 and 14 days, and one took 49 days. This hampered the regime's ability to hear about, and subsequently respond to, problems as they emerged. Frustratingly (and bizarrely) for Philip and his foreign officials, there was rarely a correlation between the importance of the letter and the speed of its arrival. In spite of these deficiencies, or perhaps because of them, the Spanish Crown developed the largest and best information services in Europe. Philip maintained permanent ambassadors in Rome, Venice, France, Genoa, Vienna, the Swiss Cantons and Savoy. He had no choice but to depend on his representatives abroad. His ambition was to take a personal and direct role in decision-making in his outlying territories, but in many affairs he was forced to rely on

> **Key term**
>
> **Ottoman Empire:** Unusually for the 16th century, the Ottoman Empire had a standing army, dominated by professional soldiers (janissaries) and cavalrymen (*sipahis*). In addition to provincial support, the participation of mercenaries meant that the Ottoman army numbered more than 100 000 men at full strength. Suleiman's sultanate represents the empire at its peak, though his death in 1566 did not greatly reduce the pressure exerted on the Spanish in the Mediterranean.

his viceroys and governors. This is most clearly illustrated in Spain's handling of the Dutch Revolt (see section 'Beyond the Mediterranean').

An additional pressure came in the form of the rise of Protestantism. Although relations with England were cordial at first, Elizabeth I's Protestantism had every chance of making them enemies. Of greater concern was the rise of Calvinism, which was becoming a potent force in Philip's early years as king. The Peace of Augsburg of 1555, which had granted legal and official recognition to Lutheranism within the Holy Roman Empire, had deliberately excluded Calvinism. Calvin had built firm foundations with his Genevan church, which became a powerful missionary organisation to any countries who were receptive. In different ways, the rise of Calvinism in France and in the Netherlands was of direct relevance to Spanish interests. The pressures were greatly increased as Calvinism gained noble adherents in both territories.

Timeline: Philip II in the early years

Year	Event
1555	Peace of Augsburg
1556	Philip II acceded to the Spanish throne and his father withdrew to Yuste in Spain
1557	Spanish inflicted heavy defeat on the French at the Battle of St Quentin
1558	English garrison surrendered as French successfully besieged Calais; Charles V died
April 1559	Peace of Câteau-Cambrésis between France and the Habsburgs
July 1559	Henry II of France died in a joust celebrating the end of the wars
September 1559	Philip II returned to Spain

The Spanish armed forces

The Spanish navy

As king of Spain, Philip inherited the advantages and problems that came with his interest in the Mediterranean. In particular, despite the importance of Andrea Doria's contribution during Charles I's reign, Philip inherited a naval force that could not compete with the Ottoman navy. By the late 1550s, Spain's Mediterranean fleet consisted of about 90 vessels, divided into four squadrons of galleys belonging to Spain, Naples, Sicily and Genoa. For that reason, and in response to several setbacks against the Ottomans in the early 1560s, the Spanish embarked on an extensive shipbuilding programme to increase the overall size of the fleet. The Castilian *Cortes* was summoned in 1562 in order to vote for an extraordinary subsidy to finance the new naval programme. By September 1564, García de Toledo, commander in chief of the Mediterranean fleet, supervised 100 Spanish-owned galleys between the coasts of Spain and North Africa. Even with that force, Spain had to combine its resources with the Italian city-states, especially Venice and the papacy, in order to compete with the Ottomans. This was considered to be a significant priority in the early part of his reign: 'for the first 20 years of his reign, the main concern of Spanish foreign policy was not the problem of Protestantism nor relations with northern Europe, but defence and counter-attack against Islam in the Mediterranean'.[1]

The Spanish army

In addition to the navy, Philip's sizeable inheritance also required a substantial army. On his accession, Philip had direct, centralised control of the machinery of war. As different pressures mounted, especially the extraordinary demands for soldiers, money and resources, the Spanish state became more heavily dependent on independent financiers, and also on regional governments. The production of weapons, the provisioning and recruitment of troops were delegated to provincial authorities because central government could no longer cope with the scale of the demands. The political consequence of this was a revival of noble power in the provinces. Seigneurial privileges were greatly strengthened, though this renewed noble power would not be wielded against royal authority.

Unit	Companies	Men
Infantry		
Tercio of Naples	19	1900
Tercio of Lombardy	10	1000
Tercio of Sicily	15	1500
Tercio of Flanders	10	1000
Tercio of Lombardy, presently in Italy	25	2500
German infantry at 300 men per company	86	25 800
Walloon infantry at 200 men per company	104	20 800
Total	**269**	**54 500**
Cavalry		
Scouts armed with light arquebuses	1	300
Men-at-arms	15	3000
Spanish, Italian and Albanian light cavalry	14	980
Mounted arquebusiers at 100 men per company	5	500
Total	**35**	**4780**

Source: Thomas F. Arnold, *The Renaissance at War*. London: Cassell, 2002, p. 72

Table 4.1: Philip II's Spanish Army used against the Dutch Revolt in the Netherlands

Castile continued to play a central role in assisting the military and financial preparations for the different conflicts. Yet other provinces also helped. In Catalonia, troops were raised by voluntary recruitment and even criminals were encouraged to participate in return for a royal pardon. The contributions were understandably more generous where Philip's imperial policies coincided with provincial interests. In Barcelona, galleys were constructed, equipped and manned in order to defend the Mediterranean against the Ottomans and corsairs. While the Catalans had a large contingent at the battle of Lepanto (see section 'Challenging the Turks'), they were poorly represented in the Spanish Armada campaign. As the century drew to a close, preparations for military encounters were certainly hampered by the inflation in Spain.

Relationships with European neighbours

During the early years of his reign, Philip enjoyed some significant foreign policy achievements. In 1557, the year after his accession, Spanish and imperial forces, with English assistance, inflicted a heavy defeat on the French at the battle of St

Quentin. The short-term consequence was the peace Treaty of Câteau-Cambrésis. Spanish ascendancy on the Italian peninsula was assured, though the balance of power between Spain and France remained delicately poised. Despite these apparent achievements, Spanish foreign policy and actions in France were not wholly successful. The peace of Câteau-Cambrésis allowed the French to consolidate their borders. Their defeat at St Quentin, in which the Constable of France, Anne de Montmorency, was captured, was counter-balanced by François de Guise's successful capture of Calais. Although this was an English defeat, the Spanish would not have failed to notice that the French now controlled a series of vital fortresses and towns on the borders of the Low Countries, including Calais, Metz, Toul and Verdun. This could potentially provide an obstacle to effective communications between the Spanish dominions of Franche-Comté and the Low Countries. Yet the apparent balance of power was undeniably affected by the accidental death of the Valois king, Henry II, which triggered a sequence of events that led France into a destructive civil war.

Figure 4.1: Illustration of Henry II being fatally wounded in 1559.

The eclipsing of French power

Although the 1559 peace of Câteau-Cambrésis did not leave any one dynasty in the ascendancy, French power was gradually eclipsed by Spain as France edged towards civil war in the early 1560s. With its origins in a monarchical crisis sparked by Henry II's death, French government was paralysed by the quick succession of two young and inexperienced kings, Francis II and Charles IX. Owing to his marriage to Mary Queen of Scots, Francis came to be dominated by the Guise family, to whom she was related, and this caused consternation among other distinguished noble families, most notably the **princes of the blood**. The conspiracy of Amboise, which represented a Calvinist attempt to take possession of the king in order to 'save' him from the manipulation of the Guises, ended in failure and served only to exacerbate the political situation. An escalation in the crisis was arguably prevented when the young king died in December 1560. While Francis II's death re-established greater balance between the noble factions at court and on the King's Council, the growing influence of Calvinism, particularly among the nobility, left the regent with a seemingly insurmountable problem. The monarchy was still in the hands of a young and inexperienced king, namely Charles IX, who had not yet reached his majority in 1560. Attempts at reconciliation evident at the Colloquy of Poissy in 1561 were serious but doomed to fail and arguably prevented the inevitable. The catalyst for civil war came with a Catholic massacre of Calvinists at Vassy and the civil war that it unleashed would plague French government and society for decades to come. For those reasons, Spanish pre-eminence owed much to the French monarchy's weaknesses.

Even after Câteau-Cambrésis and the onset of the civil wars, there were numerous reasons for Philip to remain attentive to French affairs. The Habsburg–Valois rivalry had lasted for decades and was fresh in the memory of both kingdoms. Domestic unrest in France may have seemed convenient for Spain, it also posed dangers. France bordered Spanish territories in the north and south and Philip was keen to ensure the security of his frontiers. The rise of Calvinism, especially in the south of France, was perceived to be a threat to Spanish security. When the rise of Dutch Calvinism caused a civil war in the Netherlands from 1566 onwards, the increasing interconnection of the French and Dutch revolts posed a serious threat (see section 'Beyond the Mediterranean' for more on the Dutch Revolt). In the late 1560s and early 1570s, the growing importance of the Calvinist Admiral Coligny at the French court raised the possibility of a joint French Catholic and Calvinist attack on the Spanish Netherlands. Coligny's assassination in 1572 put an end to this plan, but the message was clear. Philip's regime needed to monitor French events carefully. Although Admiral Coligny's 1572 plan to rally Calvinist and Catholic forces to fight against the Spanish in the Netherlands never materialised, the Dutch supported French Calvinists and vice versa. Philip was eager to ensure that the threat of Calvinism was properly contained.

Philip and his councillors feared, in particular, that if the French kingdom should come to be united under a Protestant king, then it would become a significant menace to the Spanish Netherlands. After the death of his father, Anthony of Navarre, the Calvinist **Henry of Navarre** became fourth in line to the French throne. During the St Bartholomew's Day massacres of 1572 many Calvinists lost their lives and Henry was subsequently forced to live at the French court. However, he escaped four years later, and Calvinism continued to be a potent force in France and a concern for Spain.

War and interference in France

While Spain provided occasional support for France's Catholic nobles, the death of the Duke of Alençon, the youngest brother of King Henry III (1574–89), instigated a more immediate and substantial response from Spain. Alençon's death meant that Henry of Navarre, a practising Calvinist, was now heir to the French throne. This led to the formation in 1584 of the Catholic League, whose members dedicated themselves to the expulsion of heresy from the French kingdom. The league's aristocratic members, dominated by the staunchly Catholic Guise family, signed the Treaty of Joinville with Spain in the same year. While French Catholics promised to be neutral in the event of a Spanish war with England, in return, Philip undertook to give a monthly subsidy of 50 000 écus. Calvinist rebels presented a religious and political threat to both the French and Spanish governments. The Spanish regime feared that French Calvinism might even spread into its own dominions. The Huguenots (as French Calvinists were known) also attacked Spanish communications further afield in the New World. As the religious divisions were accompanied by an escalating political crisis, Philip was left with no choice but to intervene. The Spanish were not willing to contemplate, let alone tolerate, the accession of Henry of Navarre to the French throne. When the French Catholic monk Jacques Clément assassinated Henry III in 1589, Henry nominally succeeded to the throne as Henry IV, and the Spanish felt impelled to increase their military and financial support to the Catholics. Henry's Huguenot army was a very effective force, and he defeated the Catholic League at the battles of Arques in September 1589 and Ivry in March 1590. The Spanish were determined to ensure that

> **Key term**
>
> **Princes of the blood:** The princes of the blood were Bourbons, representatives of the leading noble family in France after the ruling Valois dynasty. The senior representative, or first prince of the blood, was Anthony of Navarre. His brother, Louis, Prince de Condé, became the official protector of the French Calvinists.

the French monarchy maintained its fidelity to the Catholic faith. In due course this was achieved, as Henry would convert to Catholicism.

Yet Spanish intervention in France during the early 1590s came at a cost, for it weakened the Spanish position in the Netherlands. As early as November 1589, Philip had instructed Alexander Farnese, the Duke of Parma and governor of the Netherlands, to make the survival of the Catholic League his main priority. Between 1590 and 1592, Parma, to his credit, masterminded a couple of successful expeditions against Henry. This meant that Farnese neglected Dutch affairs and missed a tremendous opportunity to take control of Holland and Zeeland. In October 1592, Parma died, and the following March, the Spanish sent a third Spanish expedition to France from the Low Countries. The financial implications of this foreign policy were crippling for the Spanish economy. The Armada of 1588 had already cost approximately 10 million ducats and the Crown was struggling to sustain these different campaigns. Philip's army in the Netherlands remained unpaid and was becoming increasingly mutinous. During the period 1590–94, the military treasury in the Low Countries received 60.7 million guilders, but as much as 75 per cent of that sum was spent on the French expeditions and on granting subsidies to the Catholic League. Having restored Spanish control over the 10 southern provinces in the Netherlands and much of the north-east, Farnese made no additional territorial gains after 1588.

Philip's greatest mistake was to continue his military intervention in France after 1593. It ought to have become increasingly evident that Henry had no choice but to convert to Catholicism. He did so in July 1593, and the papacy validated his conversion shortly afterwards. Henry was not only a very competent soldier and commander, but he had already secured the support of Huguenots, moderate Catholics (known as *politiques*) and Henry III's supporters. With his conversion, a larger body of Catholics was likely to submit to his authority. At this very late stage, Philip attempted to promote the claims of his daughter, the Infanta Isabella Clara Eugenia, who was the niece of Henry's Valois predecessors. It was surely a mistake for Philip to challenge Henry's claim to the throne, particularly after leading Catholic nobles and the papacy had acknowledged the legitimacy of his cause. In that regard, Philip's actions suggest that he had become too ambitious, seeking to go beyond the mere defence of his own territorial possessions, and clearly overreaching himself in the process. Bizarrely, Philip did have the unanimous support of the Council of State, but as a result his key objective, the security of the Netherlands, was sacrificed to a futile policy of imperialism in France. Worse was to come.

In the spring of 1594, Henry regained control of Paris and entered the city in March. Having re-established his authority, he declared war on Spain the following January. Although Spanish forces made temporary gains, such as Calais in 1595 and Amiens in 1597, the war was economically debilitating. With their armies overstretched, the Spanish lost their earlier gains in the south (Toulouse and Marseilles) in 1596. Maurice of Nassau exploited Spanish weaknesses in 1596 by launching an offensive against Parma's dwindling army in the Netherlands. To make matters worse, Elizabeth I signed a treaty with the French king in May 1596, granting him a loan and small force of 2000 men. In 1596, both powers combined with the United Provinces to form a Triple Alliance, thereby isolating Spain diplomatically. By November 1596, Philip's regime was forced to declare its fourth and final bankruptcy of the reign. Philip had simply taken on too much and his French intervention had prevented him from making substantial progress in the Netherlands. By 1598, it was clear to both Henry and Philip that a peace treaty was mutually beneficial. The treaty of Vervins represented a restatement of the terms of Câteau-Cambrésis. All territorial gains were returned and the frontiers were reverted to 1559 lines, with the exception of the marquisate of Saluzzo. Spain was forced to abandon Calais and gains made in Picardy and Brittany, and received little in return.

Figure 4.2: England, France and the Netherlands.

Key term

Politiques: The *politiques* tended to be conciliatory in their approach to the religious troubles, and favoured a compromising stance and the avoidance of religiously motivated war rather than insisting on religious uniformity.

ACTIVITY 4.1

Reread this section on Spanish intervention in French affairs.

- Could Philip have resisted intervening in French affairs?
- Was his intervention counter-productive?
- Or did his devotion to Catholicism force his hand?

Italy

The Italian city-states (see Figure 2.8) played a significant role in Philip II's foreign policy for differing reasons. Philip directly controlled Naples, Sicily and the duchy of Milan, which explains Spain's pre-eminence on the peninsula. Of his Italian territories, Philip had only visited the duchy of Milan, and that was before he acceded to the throne, in the years 1548–51. Philip was thus dependent on his deputies, especially to ensure that each territory was both secure and able to contribute in some fashion to the empire's military campaigns. To this end, Philip created a Council of Italy in the early years of his reign – one of the few councils established by Philip during his reign. The nomination of influential secretaries on the Council, such as Diego de Vargas and Gabriel de Zayas, suggests that Philip perceived it to be important. It is scarcely insignificant that Antonio Pérez targeted the office of chief secretary on that Council. That Granvelle was a viceroy of Naples during 1571–75 and that Luis de Requesens was governor of Milan before he moved to the Netherlands to replace Alba would again suggest that Philip was eager to appoint competent representatives in the Italian territories. Leading Italian representatives, such as the Duke of Savoy, Ferrante Gonzaga of Mantua, and Andrea Doria, were considered to be councillors of the Spanish Empire.

The duchy of Milan was important on account of its substantial production of armaments for northern and southern theatres of war and for recruiting troops, particularly within Lombardy. The *tercios* of Naples, Lombardy and Sicily eventually formed the core of Alba's army in the Netherlands in the 1560s and 1570s (see Table 4.1). Given the nature of the Spanish Empire, Milan was also strategically significant because it provided a link between the Mediterranean and northern Europe. The 'Spanish road' provided a route from the Mont Cénis or Little St Bernard Pass into Savoy, then north through Franche-Comté and Lorraine to the Netherlands. Towards the east, the Valtelline and Engadine routes led, via the Swiss lands, to the Holy Roman Empire and the Austrian hereditary lands. While the former provided a connection with the Spanish Netherlands, the latter strengthened the links with the Austrian branch of the Habsburg family. Given its importance, the Spanish regime made every effort to contain and reduce the number of political problems in Milan. Governors were advised by Philip to respect the Senate, the supreme court of law, and this was overwhelmingly successful.

The kingdom of Naples was more relevant than Milan to the Spanish struggle against the Ottomans. Naples was one of the wealthiest and most densely populated of Philip's Italian territories. The viceroy, who resided in the city of Naples, seldom faced any opposition and resistance even to taxation was rare. The 1585 riots over bread prices were unusual and carefully managed by the Duke of Osuna, who used his military superiority to quell the revolt. While some sympathy was shown to the majority of the rebels, of the 820 who were brought to trial, 20 were executed, 71 were sent to work on galleys and 300 were sent into exile. The Spanish feared that rebellion might spread from the Netherlands to other parts of the Empire, so the viceroy was firm in his response. In Naples, stability reigned because the Neapolitans were ever conscious of the immediacy of the Ottoman threat, and provincial nobles accordingly maintained their own militias in coastal regions in anticipation of corsair raids. In the event of an Ottoman attack, the militias supported the royal garrisons.

The control of Sicily was also essential, given its proximity to the frontline struggle with the Ottomans. While the viceroys of Sicily had a much more difficult task, since the Sicilian parliament was more resistant, Sicily's ties with Spain were cemented by their common defence against the Ottoman Empire. In order to strengthen their position, the Spanish sought to reform the Great Court of Sicily, as well as employing Spanish jurists. In the process, largely through stealth and cunning diplomacy, the Spanish regime greatly strengthened its position in Sicily, which proved invaluable for the launching of their Mediterranean campaigns.

This firm basis of territorial control in Italy facilitated Spain's ability to mobilise forces in defence of her interests. For example, by 1568, Naples and Sicily alone were able to provide 9 and 12 squadrons of galleys respectively. The early years of Philip's rule also coincided with the signing of the Treaty of Câteau-Cambrésis with France on 3 April 1559, in which the French king Henry II renounced all territorial claims in Italy. The Spanish were strengthened by the restoration of Savoy and Piedmont to their duke, an ally of the Habsburgs, which created an obstacle to future French incursions in Italy. The French also restored the strategic island of Corsica, which they had captured in 1553, to Genoa, another Habsburg ally. The treaty marked not only the end of the Habsburg–Valois wars, but also Spain's emergence as the undisputed master of Italian peninsula. Italians, for their part, were relieved to have peace on the peninsula.

Given its ascendancy in Italy, Spain was able to gather support from the other territories. With the exception of a brief war with the Neapolitan Pope Paul IV in the years 1556–57, the papacy and Spain were largely united by their efforts to resist Ottoman expansion. While the key Tuscan cities such as Pisa, Florence and Siena were traditionally pro-French in their approach, they did not pose a direct threat to Spanish ambitions. In any case, Philip retained control of various fortresses on the Tuscan coast. The Genoese were close allies – something which Spanish merchants exploited to the full. Spain's navy also benefited from the expertise of the Genoese, most notably the military leadership provided by Andrea Doria.

The key to Philip's south Italian territories was that they represented a frontline in the struggle against the Ottomans. Spanish naval expeditions were often launched from Messina, with the key squadrons coming from Spain, Naples and Sicily. The military support from Genoa, Savoy and the papacy was often subsidised by Spain. In spite of their opposition to the Ottomans, there were underlying rifts between the different powers. Tensions between Italian and Spanish commanders, including Andrea Doria (who died in 1560), Don García de Toledo (1564–68), Don John of Austria (1571–78) and Gian Andrea Doria (1583–1606), might focus on differing priorities and strategies.

At times, it was difficult to keep the independent Italian states in coalition. Venice, the greatest Italian naval power, was particularly reluctant to engage in war, owing to its trade interests in the Far East. It had, for example, arranged commercial treaties with the Sultan, securing both the distribution of silks, cottons and spices from Alexandria and the ports of Syria and Asian Minor, and the provision of grain supplies. Venice therefore vacillated between seeking protection from its European allies and making the most of its commercial relations with the Ottomans. After the fall of Cyprus to the Ottomans in 1570, Venice was more inclined to join a Holy League, especially when the Spanish offered to supply the republic with grain.

Mediterranean relationships

Control of the Mediterranean

Spain's strategic and commercial priorities in the Mediterranean inevitably conflicted with Ottoman interests. Strategically, Spain needed to keep open communications with her key Italian dominions, Naples and Sicily, which were on the front line of the conflict. Spain also sought to maintain her scattered possessions in North Africa. Most importantly, Philip II was determined to contain the Sultan's westward expansion and defend his own Spanish coastline. Any significant naval achievements would undoubtedly benefit Spanish commerce and shipping in the Mediterranean. Having inherited the conflict from his father, Philip saw intervention as a necessity, and the circumstances in the early years of his reign seemed opportune. As Philip himself noted in 1559, 'In view of the peace concluded between me and the King of France' and the advanced 'age of the sultan and the anxiety that the discord between his sons causes him, I believe that neither negotiating nor concluding a truce with him is in my interest.'² Underlying this conflict were obvious ideological differences, namely the struggle between Catholicism and Islam.

Although the Spanish coast remained relatively secure during Philip's reign, the Ottomans remained a persistent threat. The Ottomans were feared on account of their powerful navy and the elite corps of janissaries. Their association with the **Barbary States** allowed them to threaten the western Mediterranean. Spanish survival was partly due to the winters, during which the major powers avoided lengthy military campaigns. This kept the Muslim allies apart and prevented more regular and coordinated attacks on Spanish targets. Without engaging the Spanish military in combat, the Ottomans could wreak havoc by raiding Spanish and Italian coasts, and enslaving any captives. Mediterranean commerce was severely disrupted by Muslim piracy. From the 1560s, Barbary corsairs were increasingly dominant in the western Mediterranean, operating in powerful squadrons. In contrast with Ottoman strengths, Philip had inherited a foreign policy that had become subordinated to more distant imperial objectives. Charles V's resources had been diverted to central Europe and his Mediterranean policy was neglected as a result. Initially, Philip embarked on an offensive before introducing the necessary naval reforms. In 1559, Philip launched an expedition to Tripoli that would help him to control the Mediterranean at its narrowest part. Parker takes a dim view of this decision. It 'mired Philip's dominions in a war that lasted more than eighteen years and tied down resources needed to respond effectively to threats elsewhere: how could he have made such a catastrophic miscalculation?'³ The expedition was arguably doomed to fail because it took almost six months to assemble a fleet, by which time the element of surprise had gone.

The Ottomans had noticed the concentration of ships in Sicily and this had stirred the Ottoman garrison in Tripoli to repair the city's fortifications. The Tripoli expedition retreated to Djerba, where the Turkish admiral, Piali Pasha, heavily defeated the Spanish fleet. Spain lost 42 out of its 80 vessels and a total of 18 000 men. This disaster had broader repercussions, including the withdrawal of Spanish veterans from the Netherlands in order to strengthen the defences in the Mediterranean. The following year, Barbarossa's equally competent successor, Turgut Reis (better known as Dragut), pressurised the Spanish by blockading Naples with 35 vessels. Several years later, the Ottomans sought to exploit Spanish weaknesses by besieging Malta in 1565. Despite repeated warnings, the Spanish regime and the Grand Master of the Knights Templar were taken by surprise by the scale and speed of the Ottoman offensive. Although ultimately unsuccessful, the Ottomans came close to taking the island. Noticeably outnumbered, the Christian defenders were confined to only a few forts and Malta was only saved thanks to a timely intervention from the viceroy of Naples. Malta's survival did not reduce the intensity of the Ottoman threat in the Mediterranean. In 1566, 28 Biscayan ships were lost to the Ottomans near Malaga. An Ottoman campaign against the Venetian island of Cyprus in 1570 was successful, with Nicosia falling to the Turks in September of that year. The Spanish fleet had joined a naval force, consisting of Venetian, Genoese and papal forces, but it never reached Cyprus in time.

For all its deficiencies and flaws, Philip's strategy in the Mediterranean was hardly unsuccessful. As Charles had reacted quickly to Spanish domestic problems in the early 1520s, so Philip learned from his initial mistakes in the Mediterranean. He instilled a greater sense of urgency into his Mediterranean policy by embarking on a more ambitious programme of military and naval reforms. This necessitated a more defensive strategy and the abandonment of aggressive expeditions, which allowed the Spanish navy to build up its resources. This conservation of Spanish naval strength proved to be effective when an Algerian onslaught against Oran was repelled. Between April and June 1563, the city – one of Spain's most important North African possessions – was besieged. The garrison was relieved and **Hasan Pasha**'s naval forces were decisively overwhelmed. Just two years later, Malta faced an invasion on a different scale altogether. Philip undoubtedly benefited from the foresight and brilliance of the Grand Master, Jean Parisot de la Valette. A former governor of

ACTIVITY 4.2

Class debate on Philip's actions in the Mediterranean

Using this section and your own research, draw up a timeline of the key battles between Spain and the Ottomans between 1556 and 1598. Identify the benefits and limitations of Spanish foreign policy and actions in this theatre of war. For each side, outline five key strengths and weaknesses. The motion for the debate is: 'Philip's intervention in the Mediterranean was a catastrophic miscalculation.'

Tripoli, la Valette had converted the Grand Harbour into one of most heavily defended fortresses in the Mediterranean. He had the good sense to realise that Malta's survival (and that of the Order) depended not only on his skills as a military engineer but also on the provision of adequate stores to deal with a lengthy siege. With 9000 Knights under la Valette, Malta was faced with a force of 180 Ottoman ships and 30 000 soldiers.

Despite the numbers, the Ottoman attack was neither as strong nor as well directed as it might have been. Strategically, they made the error of anchoring to the south of the island, making it more difficult for the Ottomans to break Christian lines of communication with Sicily. Yet their survival was by no means a foregone conclusion, as the defenders resisted fierce Ottoman attacks for almost four months. In the final reckoning, the Viceroy of Naples, Don García de Toledo, led a relief force of Spanish infantry from Naples and Sicily and the Ottomans were successfully repelled. The survival of Malta was of considerably strategic significance. The fall of Rhodes to the Ottomans in the early 1520s had been essential in consolidating their stranglehold over the eastern Mediterranean. The capture of Malta would have been a vital step in fulfilling their objective of securing the western Mediterranean. Although Philip had not yet undertaken a major offensive, the survival of Malta gave the Spanish renewed confidence. From 1565, a programme of naval reconstruction in Barcelona, Naples and Sicily was intensified. Having resisted Ottoman expansion to the western Mediterranean, the Spanish were better able to deal with the corsair threat. In the 1560s, Philip's policies were exclusively defensive, which was necessitated by his preoccupations at home with the *Morisco* revolt and further afield with the Dutch revolt.

Challenging the Turks

Philip's decision to move onto the offensive was encouraged by the formation of a major Christian alliance in 1571, the **Holy League**, consisting of the papacy, Venice, Genoa and Spain. The agreement was signed on 20 May. It made possible a heavy concentration of Christian forces, which was indispensable in order to challenge Ottoman naval dominance. A mixture of ideological and other motives brought the alliance together. Venice joined because of the Ottoman capture of Cyprus – her last fortress, Famagusta, fell just before the Holy League set off.

Philip had other priorities, which included the ever-present fear of potential alliances between the *Moriscos* and Muslims in the Mediterranean, so there were also significant domestic implications. Parker has implied that Philip's religious motives were subordinate to strategic objectives; Philip 'eventually agreed to join the Holy League only because he expected that, as the most powerful partner, he would be able to use the combined fleet to recover Tunis [retaken by the Ottomans in 1569], not Cyprus, and when it became clear that he might not get his way, he sought ways to back out'.[4] By the terms of the agreement, Spain, Venice and the papacy undertook to assemble a fleet of 208 galleys, 100 sailing ships, 50 000 troops and 4500 light cavalry. Spain provided the largest contingent of ships and men, resulting in the largest Christian fleet ever seen in the Mediterranean. The Spanish were helped by the fact that the Duke of Alba appeared to be in relative control of the Low Countries, and Protestant England was preoccupied with her domestic problems, dealing with the aftermath of the Northern Rebellion and a plot to murder Elizabeth I and replace her with Mary Queen of Scots. The Holy League benefited from having excellent leaders, who collaborated willingly and effectively: Don John of Austria commanded the Spanish fleet; the papal galleys were led by Marc Antonio Colonna; and Sebastiano Venier was in charge of the Venetian navy.

The Ottoman and Christian fleets were relatively balanced in numbers, though the Holy League benefited from the surprise advantage of six heavily armed Venetian **galleasses**. In the end, the battle of Lepanto was a rout. The Holy League sank 110

> **Key term**
>
> **Holy League:** The Holy League was a Christian alliance including the kingdoms of Spain, the republics of Venice and Genoa and the papacy. It was united by the common objective of containing the spread of the Ottoman Empire in the Mediterranean. While all the allies professed the Christian faith, other more secular motives were also at work, ensuring that the alliance was somewhat fragile, especially in the aftermath of the Lepanto campaign.

Ottoman galleys, captured 130 Ottoman warships and 400 pieces of artillery, almost 3500 were taken prisoner, and approximately 15 000 galley slaves were liberated. The Ottoman High Admiral, Ali Pasha, was killed in a battle with Don John's galley. Much of the success can be attributed to the excellent arquebus fire of the Spanish soldiers. The League lost only 12 galleys, though 9000 soldiers died, and 21 000 men were wounded.

The victory at Lepanto, commemorated in style by Titian, was more than symbolic. In military terms, it was decisive because the Ottoman fleet had fought at a location of its own choosing and lost. It discouraged major Ottoman expansion in the western Mediterranean and arguably marked the end of Ottoman naval supremacy. The writer Cervantes, who fought at Lepanto, reflected on 'that day, which was so happy for Christendom, because all the world then learned how mistaken it had been in believing that the Turks were invincible at sea'.[5] The Ottoman defeat triggered uprisings in Greece and Albania, which served to deflect and redirect Ottoman attention away from the Mediterranean.

Figure 4.3: Titian's Allegory on the Battle of Lepanto: Titian portrays Philip II offering the Infante Don Fernando to heaven following his victory at Lepanto.

> **ACTIVITY 4.3**
>
> Using this section and your wider reading, answer the following questions:
>
> - Was the battle of Lepanto a decisive turning point?
> - In what ways and for what reasons was the Mediterranean less important from the 1580s onwards?

Yet the Christian victory at Lepanto did not fundamentally alter the balance of power in the Mediterranean. Owing to the Holy League's losses and on account of the lateness in the campaigning season, the allied fleet had to return to their respective ports. The inability to transform a major naval victory into substantial territorial gains showed that the frontiers between Islam and Christianity had reached their natural limits. The Ottoman Empire, with its powerful military forces, remained largely untouched and Ottoman control of Cyprus was unchallenged.

While the Ottomans reassembled their forces, marked divisions increased within the Holy League. It soon became clear that its members were determined to pursue their own interests. While the Spanish sought to secure firmer territorial bases in North Africa, Venice was more eager to improve its position in the Adriatic and in the Aegean. For example, after Pope Pius V's death in May 1572, Philip ordered Don John to cancel a Spanish expedition because he refused to use Spanish resources to support Venetian interests in the eastern Mediterranean. Venice concluded a peace with the Sultan in March 1573, while Spain and the papacy continued fighting. The delicate balance of power is indicated by the various skirmishes over Tunis. In 1573, the Spanish took the city, which was placed under a native ruler. The fortifications were strengthened and a force of 8000 Spaniards and Italians defended the city. Yet it was expensive and difficult to hold, all the more so because the Spanish had not sought to annex any outlying territories. The new High Admiral, Uludj Ali, quickly brought the Ottoman navy back to strength and the Ottomans regained Tunis in 1574. The Ottoman Grand Vizier spoke confidently to a Venetian envoy, intimating that Lepanto had made no substantial difference: 'in snatching a kingdom [Cyprus] from you we have cut off your right arm. In defeating our fleet you have merely shaved our beard, and a shaven beard grows stronger than ever.'[6]

While Philip remained fearful of Ottoman attacks, particularly given the vulnerability of Spain's Italian dominions, a military stalemate was reached by the mid-1570s and the Ottomans, reluctant to engage their forces in the Mediterranean, agreed to a succession of truces in 1578, 1580, 1581, 1584 and 1587. Both Spain and the Ottomans had other priorities.

The Ottomans were preoccupied with Persia from 1578 onwards. Despite initial military successes, the Ottoman army was forced to commit to a protracted campaign against the highly competent Shah Abbas the Great. It also seemed that the North African corsairs were more reluctant collaborators than in the past, thereby weakening the Sultan's position. Similarly, the succession of truces suited the Spaniards well. From the mid-1570s, Philip's political and religious priorities were directed towards northern Europe. Don John was sent to the Netherlands in 1576. To his credit, Philip remained pragmatic and realistic after Lepanto. Rather than being driven by crusading zeal, which might have led him to follow up his victory, Philip was able to see the bigger strategic picture. There were also economic reasons why the Ottomans and Spanish did not fight in the Mediterranean. A growing economic crisis and resultant over-taxation put both empires under considerable pressure. While the Spanish economy suffered from growing inflation, the Ottomans were hampered by a weak currency and the outbreak of several peasant (*celali*) rebellions in the Anatolian heartlands. Both empires were also threatened by the growing economic challenges from the English and Dutch. In the end, economic and political weaknesses triggered a naval decline. A period of peace meant that the Ottoman navy was not properly maintained and their sailors were deprived of invaluable experience. The superiority of the Christian fleets was never again challenged.

Portugal: conquest and relationship

At a time when the Ottomans were less of a threat, Philip was provided with a tremendous opportunity in Portugal. King Sebastian of Portugal had been tempted by a disputed succession to the Moroccan throne in 1577. He set sail in June the following year, and the expedition was a disaster. King Sebastian and numerous leading Portuguese nobles were killed, their opponents having been reinforced by *Morisco* émigrés from Andalusia. While Sebastian had no direct heir, Cardinal Henry was considered to be the strongest claimant. The regency council left by Sebastian proclaimed Henry king, allowing Philip some time to win support both in Portugal and abroad for his claim to be heir presumptive and to prepare to fight in case he failed. Despite his claim, the 66-year-old Henry was unfit to rule and just before his death in 1580 supported the candidature of Philip, who was his nephew. With Portugal drained of money, and with the majority of the ruling class dead or in captivity, the country was hardly in a position to withstand a succession crisis.

Although there were pre-existing tensions between Portugal and Castile, Philip took full advantage of having a mother from the Portuguese royal family. Relations between the two countries had not always been cordial, but well-established matrimonial alliances between the Portuguese and the Habsburgs had built strong links between their respective kingdoms. Philip was obviously keen to achieve the annexation of Portugal by diplomatic means and threatened the use of force only if circumstances dictated it. His Portuguese-born adviser, Cristóbal de Moura, who played an invaluable role in the process, advised Philip in this way: 'the ideal is on the one hand to press on with negotiations and on the other to maintain the fear that we may use force'.[7]

With a lessening of the Ottoman threat, Philip's financial situation had also improved considerably. The third state bankruptcy of 1575 was followed by yet another influx of American silver, which grew to unprecedented proportions in the 1580s. There was a financial incentive to unite the Crowns, as the Portuguese and Spanish imperial economies could combine their respective resources. Portugal's empire was essentially commercial, and therefore required Spanish American gold and silver for exchange purposes. The Spanish Empire lacked the pepper, spices and silks controlled by the Portuguese East Indies. Politically, the majority of Philip's councillors supported his Portuguese enterprise.

The annexation of Portugal owed much to Philip's own decisive leadership. He appointed the highly skilful de Moura to lay the groundwork for the succession. A brilliantly orchestrated propaganda campaign promoted Philip's Portuguese credentials, to which Spanish jurists and theologians contributed. The commercial advantages of joining the empires were clearly outlined. In certain cases, bribery or the promises of money and offices were employed to convince any wavering Portuguese. Philip also exploited the procrastination of the Portuguese *Cortes*. In the end, the Portuguese were pressurised by a show of force. The Duke of Alba led an army of 37 000 Spanish troops, which crossed the frontier in June 1580. A fleet commanded by Alvaro de Bazan, the Marquis of Santa Cruz, and an army led by the Duke of Medina Sidonia supported Alba. The mobilisation of Spanish soldiers was necessary because one of the contenders for the throne, the Prior of Crato, seized the royal palace in Lisbon. Opposition was easily removed and most towns submitted to Philip's authority without fighting. Philip no doubt benefited from the inability of the two other contenders, Crato and the Duchess of Bragança, to unite. Spanish forces also conducted themselves with discretion. Alba was both cautious and diplomatic, and threatened his army with the most severe penalties if they pillaged the countryside. The Portuguese *Cortes* acknowledged Philip as King of Portugal in April 1581.

Philip was equally effective and decisive in consolidating his position in Portugal. He went on a peace offensive, helped by the Portuguese Jesuits. The Jesuits had advised Cardinal Henry and had considerable influence in Portugal, and succeeded in neutralising any significant opposition to Philip's accession from the lower clergy. Philip also won over the powerful Bragança family and his relationship with them was secured by the appointment of the **Duke of Bragança** as Constable of Portugal. Philip had also helped to ransom the Portuguese nobles held captive in Morocco, including Bragança's heir, the **Duke of Barçelos**. Philip initially prevented the latter's return to

> **ACTIVITY 4.4**
>
> Read this section on Portugal and consider the merits and possible counter-arguments to the following statement: 'Philip's annexation of Portugal was largely of his own making.'

Portugal as a threat to his candidature to the throne, but after Bragança's death made him in turn Constable of Portugal.

Crucially, Philip promised to protect Portuguese rights and customs, and to appoint only natives to important political offices. He undertook never to hold a Portuguese *Cortes* outside the kingdom and never to legislate on Portuguese affairs in a foreign assembly. He promised that the country was to be garrisoned only by Portuguese forces, and Philip's army quickly withdrew once order had been restored. The Portuguese retained control of any commerce associated with their imperial possessions. Their colonial trade was to remain unchanged, administered by Portuguese officials, conducted by Portuguese merchants, and carried in Portuguese ships. It was declared that taxes would be spent on Portuguese needs and not used to fulfil Castilian objectives.

Although the majority of Portugal's urban population and the lower ranks of clergy opposed Spanish domination, they lacked direction. Granvelle, Philip's principal adviser, insisted on a key policy change. While Philip had neglected to visit the Netherlands from the 1560s onwards, Granvelle made the necessary preparations for Philip to visit Portugal. The king waited in Extremadura until it was safe for him to enter Portugal. Philip subsequently stayed in Lisbon between 1580 and 1583 and appointed **Archduke Albert of Austria** as his representative there until 1593. Archduke Albert was later replaced by a group of four leading Portuguese notables, followed by Cristobal de Moura who was appointed the viceroy. Philip had sensibly and deliberately left most of his courtiers and ministers behind in Castile, though he did establish a Council of Portugal to facilitate the preservation of royal authority.

The advantages of the Portuguese annexation were numerous. It gave Castile even greater security and prosperity, especially with the abolition of customs barriers in 1582. Philip gained the second largest colonial empire in the world, including Brazil, parts of West Africa, the East Indies and the Azores. The Portuguese Empire rallied to Philip without presenting any opposition. Although its empire was vast, the contribution to Philip's revenues was relatively minor. This was partly due to the costs of defending these new possessions. The Spanish inherited a number of Atlantic ports, including Lisbon, which could accommodate enormous fleets, and they gained control of the Portuguese navy, which consisted of 12 fighting galleons and a large Atlantic fleet manned by experienced sailors. Above all, the Iberian Peninsula was now under one ruler for the first time in nine centuries.

Beyond the Mediterranean

Revolt in the Netherlands

There is no doubt that the Dutch Revolt was a serious dilemma for the Spanish regime. Even in normal circumstances, the Netherlands posed an obvious challenge for Philip's regime. It was a considerable distance from Spain, so making decisions, communicating and transferring resources and troops presented real obstacles for the Castilian government. Philip struggled to wield his authority from Castile and it was testing for any governor to be an effective substitute. This was especially the case where the levying of taxes was concerned, as John Lynch has noted: 'to tap the wealth of the Netherlands effectively he had to use methods of government more absolute than those of his predecessors in order to break through the constitutional restraints on his authority'.[8]

Philip's authority came to be challenged by the States General, which presented various political, religious and financial grievances in the early years of his reign. Any political concessions tended to lead to further demands. Charles's persecution of Protestantism in the Netherlands had been just as harsh, but Philip was in Castile and this made it more difficult for the government to enforce its policy and get the

Dutch to accept it. Having enjoyed earlier times of prosperity, the Dutch increasingly resented heavy taxation. Grievances also took on a proto-nationalist dimension, as some reflected on the apparent incompatibility between the Netherlanders and Spaniards. Changing attitudes also resulted from shifts in Habsburg dynastic politics. The Netherlands was now ruled not by a Holy Roman Emperor, but by a foreign king. The Dutch were subjects of Spain rather than part of a broader European empire. The Spanish, for their part, were increasingly, if not equally, apprehensive about the Dutch. From the 1560s, many of these problems started to combine. In Philip's absence, William **Prince of Orange**, the Count of Egmont and Philip of Hornes withdrew from the Council of State in 1563 and called for a relaxation of the heresy laws.

Distractions elsewhere

At the same time, Philip was faced with numerous and varied obstacles elsewhere, which prevented him from travelling to the Netherlands. One such problem was the Don Carlos crisis (see section 'Philip's character'), during which Philip had made genuine preparations for a journey to the Netherlands. The Ottoman threat persisted during the period 1559–66 and Philip struggled to focus on other affairs, with some pressure finally relieved by Suleiman's death in 1566. Philip's preoccupation with the Mediterranean obviously continued as Spain started to prepare for the Lepanto campaign. Throughout the Dutch revolt, Philip's government had to deal with the other territories (New World, Portugal and Italian dominions), foreign foes (such as England and France) and domestic unrest. Foreign intervention in the Dutch revolt accentuated the gravity of the crisis. French Calvinists became involved, in addition to English intervention. Elizabeth I sent in the Earl of Leicester with English troops at a critical time when the revolt was on the verge of collapse.

Religious tensions

Integral to the revolt was the rise and consolidation of Dutch Calvinism. Calvinism was a dynamic, radical faith and part of an international movement. As elsewhere, the icons and other religious decorations of Catholic churches were a target and in 1566 hundreds of churches and monasteries were attacked by discontented Calvinist mobs across the Netherlands: the Dutch revolt had begun. Noble support for the Dutch revolt meant that it was to be fought on a different scale from the Aragonese revolt. William of Orange's quest for a Netherlands equivalent of the 1555 Peace of Augsburg (see section 'Confessional divisions in the Holy Roman Empire') was not well received by Philip. Dutch nobles had been suspicious of any clerical reform and resistant to repressive religious policies. The tolerance or indifference of leading nobles had allowed the revolt to spread throughout the northern provinces. Although Calvinism was successful in towns and among the lower ranks of the nobility, the majority of the population remained nominally Catholic. Yet there was also a surprising amount of religious apathy. Many were willing to tolerate any religious group that opposed the Spanish.

Ultimately, Philip could not remain passive. He was a devout Catholic, so religious policies were not negotiable and compromise along the lines of the Peace of Augsburg was unimaginable. Nor could Philip abandon the Netherlands altogether because it was vital to the Spanish economy. Antwerp was the greatest commercial centre in Europe and 60 per cent of Spanish wool went to the Low Countries. Once the revolt started, governors struggled to sustain armies to put down the rebels, with the result that there were numerous mutinies – as many as 46 between the years 1572 and 1607. Mutinies greatly weakened the Spanish military campaigns, undermined Spanish political authority, forced the diversion of substantial sums into pay settlements and made a reality of Spanish tyranny.

The Dutch revolt was Philip's greatest challenge, but his regime seriously mishandled the crisis. Philip's policies partly provoked the crisis in the first instance by introducing an overly ambitious programme for ecclesiastical reorganisation. The nobility had

ACTIVITY 4.5

Read the section on the Netherlands and research in depth the following factors, with a view to explaining why the Dutch revolt posed such a profound crisis for Philip's regime: geography; religious disunity; Dutch noble opposition; Philip's decision-making and inability or refusal to visit; role, policies and actions of successive governors; financial restrictions; other preoccupations and priorities; the significance of Dutch liberties and privileges.

been unnerved by the appointment of Granvelle as Archbishop of Mechelen in 1560. The Pope had also promoted him to cardinal, so he took precedence over Orange and Egmont on the Council of State. The religious changes alienated the Dutch political elites. Many abbots were forced to resign their positions to new bishops, while magistrates in key cities objected to the introduction of inquisitors. The secrecy that surrounded these reforms greatly exacerbated the situation. As Parker noted, 'Everyone felt insulted that such a complex scheme had obviously been in preparation for many years, yet Philip had made no attempt at consultation.'[9]

Of far greater significance, and tarnishing Philip's reputation, was his failure to visit the Netherlands himself. He sought, rather unsuccessfully, to monopolise decision-making from afar, surrounded by Spanish advisers who did not understand the nature or extent of the crisis. His absence from the Netherlands allowed the situation to get out of control and gradually persuaded the Dutch that Philip was, first and foremost, King of Spain rather than their anointed sovereign. Parker is surely right in his assessment that 'only his return to Brussels could have stabilised the situation'. A number of the nobles, including Orange, fled the Netherlands in 1567; Parker points out that if they had 'refused a direct summons to explain their conduct to Philip in person, they would have lost credit both at home and abroad'.[10] There was no shortage of advisers urging him to make the journey, most notably Ruy Gomez. Philip's distance from the Netherlands may explain his pursuit of rather naive and unrealistic goals. Politically, he was determined to keep Dutch nobles away from the corridors of power and to reduce the political influence of the States General. At the same time, he wished the Dutch to accept their subordinate status. Financially, he expected the Netherlands to raise sufficient funds to maintain their government. In terms of religion, he was eager to preserve Catholicism and reluctant to negotiate with the Calvinists.

Repression

The policy of repression was counter-productive and discredited the Spanish regime. This was particularly true of the Duke of Alba's time as governor of the Netherlands (1567–73). Alba never doubted that brutal oppression was the only way of dealing with the rebellion. The Council of Troubles that he established led to the arrest of 12 300 and execution of 1100 during the years 1567–73, including Egmont and Hornes in 1568. The Council consisted of a tribunal of seven, three of whom were Spaniards, operating with almost absolute powers under Alba's presidency. It came to be deeply resented and its reputation for brutality gave it the label 'The Council of Blood'. There were numerous episodes in which Spanish troops gained a bad name. In the aftermath of the siege of Haarlem, in 1572, Alba ordered the execution of 2000 troops and city magistrates, and imposed a fine of 200 000 florins. In 1576, the violent sacking of Antwerp by mutinous Spanish troops (known as the 'Spanish Fury', with 8000 civilians dying as a result) had the effect of uniting much of the Netherlands (north and south) against Spain. Spanish brutality in the Netherlands was sufficiently extreme to be criticised even by the Austrian Habsburgs.

In 1568, William of Orange led four armies into the Netherlands to remove Alba, but the rebellion was put down by 1570. However, Alba was forced to raise funds from within the Netherlands in the early 1570s because Philip was preoccupied with his campaigns against the Ottomans in the Mediterranean. Typically, Alba decided to impose a Tenth Penny tax without the consent of the Provincial States, leading to a new uprising. As Parker argues, 'it was unconstitutional, oppressive, foreign and its proceeds were destined for the hated Spanish garrisons'.[12] The only solution was for Spanish forces to be funded by Castile. By 1575, this was costing the Castilian treasury up to 700 000 ducats per month. The sack of Antwerp followed the third Castilian state bankruptcy. Between the years 1590 and 1597, the army of Flanders cost more than 20 million ducats. Financially, it was utterly disastrous for Castile and Philip's regime was only able to support troops because of the influx of New World silver.

Worse than the financial exactions was the alienation of the Dutch nobility. Philip's earliest Council of State in the Netherlands had lacked any grandees, the traditional advisers to the king, even though they had been central to Charles V's system of governance in the Netherlands. A small group dominated the Council of State and, crucially, deprived the Dutch grandees of any significant political power. Leading nobles such as Orange and Egmont felt disenfranchised, as they had expected Philip to govern through them. Nobles were infuriated by the prospect of church reforms because church offices provided them with an invaluable source of income and patronage. When the Count of Egmont visited the Spanish court in 1564 to discuss Dutch demands, including greater religious tolerance, Philip set out to reassure him but in so doing gave a false impression of his real intentions. His rejection of Dutch demands was made manifest in his letters from the Segovia woods, written in October 1565, after which the leading nobles withdrew from the Council of State.

Philip should have empowered the well-established nobles on the Council of State and ensured that Egmont, Hornes and Orange remained loyal. The subsequent alienation of the nobility also contributed to the growth of Calvinism. The signing of the 1565 Compromise by 350 Catholic and Calvinist nobles, imploring Philip to make some religious concessions, indicates their significance. Even the more moderate Catholic nobles, despite their abhorrence of Calvinist iconoclasm, were willing to make deals with Calvinist rebels on account of their opposition to Alba's fiscal policies. In 1576, an overwhelmingly Catholic group of nobles was determined to make religious concessions at the Pacification of Ghent. Nothing united the nobility more effectively than the execution of leading nobles.

The role of the governors

The governors of the Netherlands should be partly blamed for the escalation of the crisis, especially the inconsistency in approaches. Margaret of Parma appeared to be easily manipulated by the nobility and granted full toleration under pressure. At the other extreme, the Duke of Alba and Cardinal Granvelle's brutal persecution of heretics was deeply resented and unsuccessful. It is difficult to exaggerate the damage that Alba's policies inflicted on Spain's reputation. It was common knowledge that Alba distrusted his subjects and governed through a military government of occupation, administered by Spaniards and Italians. Alba's enforcement of unpopular taxes was also counter-productive, as the States General was deprived of any role in administering taxes. Bizarrely, leading figures in the Spanish regime appeared to appreciate the significance of safeguarding the privileges and liberties of the Portuguese and Aragonese, but were reluctant to respect those of the Dutch. The Dutch were sent contrasting signals when Alba was dismissed and replaced by Luis de Requesens in 1573. This showed inconsistency in government policy and hinted

Voices from the past

Council of State

Report from the Council of State in Brussels to Philip II on the Sack of Antwerp, 1576

What ensued was a massacre of the civil guard and of the inhabitants. The Spanish soldiers set fire to several townhouses and even destroyed the city hall. The death toll in this massacre is more than eight thousand persons.[11]

Discussion points:
1. What message is the Council of State conveying to Philip II?
2. How representative were these events of Spanish actions in the Netherlands? Use evidence from this section and your own research.

> **ACTIVITY 4.6**
>
> Read this section and, using your wider reading, draw up a biographical timeline on Alessandro Farnese. How effective was he as a governor of the Netherlands?

that Alba's methods had failed. After all, Philip authorised Requesens to abolish the unpopular new taxes and the detested Council of Troubles.

Requesens also felt under pressure to negotiate with the rebels because he realised that the reconquest of Holland and Zeeland was a financial impossibility. Following Requesens's death, Don John was even more ineffective as a governor. He was far more interested in preparing an invasion of England, though at least this had the potential to cut off invaluable support for the Dutch rebels. Don John intended to marry Mary Queen of Scots and depose Elizabeth in the process. As an end goal, this would have been beneficial for the Spanish, yet the expedition would require substantial funds that the Castilian treasury lacked. The longer-term consequences of consolidating his position in England had numerous potential pitfalls and disadvantages. Above all, it diverted attention from what needed to be done in the Netherlands.

Far more competent than any of his predecessors was Alessandro Farnese, the Duke of Parma. He was a brilliant diplomat, managing to court the many southern nobles who were alarmed by Calvinist attacks on towns. He also had the good sense to choose advisers who were born in the Netherlands. In May 1579, Parma signed the Treaty of Arras with the southern Walloon Estates, in which he agreed to withdraw Spanish and foreign troops from the provinces adhering to the treaty. This was mutually beneficial, allowing Parma to employ those troops elsewhere where resistance to Spain continued. He proceeded to reduce the amount of resistance in the south-west and secured increasing support through his shrewd diplomacy. There were few death sentences for treason and loyal nobles were always rewarded. The latter were constantly reminded that their property and titles were secure and their status would be enhanced at the expense of Philip's enemies.

Parma also resorted to force and regained an impressive number of towns; Brussels and Antwerp surrendered in 1585. Unfortunately for him and for the Spanish cause in the Netherlands, Philip insisted on Spain's unnecessary intervention in France. With Farnese preoccupied with French affairs, the Dutch rebels were greatly encouraged by the defeat of the Armada and by Parma's lack of money and, more importantly, his absences in France. This helps to explain the decision of the seven northern provinces to reconstitute themselves as a free republic under Maurice of Nassau, the son of William of Orange, who had been assassinated in 1584. The Dutch rebels launched an effective campaign to regain the north-eastern provinces. This included the capture of Breda in 1590, Zutphen and Deventer in 1591, and Groningen in 1594. As a result, Calvinism was allowed to develop and assert its political identity. The Union of Utrecht between the seven northern provinces (signed in January 1579) laid strong foundations for the future, encouraging the development of a series of states increasingly Calvinist in character and anti-Spanish in policy. As Lovett commented: 'the moderate ideal of a united Netherlands, Catholic in religion but with toleration for a minority, disappeared; and in its place two unbending ideologies battled for conquest or survival'.[13] Having facilitated the growth of Calvinism, the Spanish regime was now left with only one method to deal with the movement, namely the use of military force.

Relations with England

Closely connected to the Dutch revolt was Spain's relationship with England. On the one hand, contrasting religious beliefs appeared to set the two kingdoms on a collision course. Elizabeth's Protestantism was surely irreconcilable with Philip's staunch Catholicism. Tensions mounted as Philip's regime also subsidised English Catholic seminaries on the continent. However, these religious problems were not at the forefront of their relations in the early years. Of far greater importance were their close economic ties. Historically, the commerce between England and the Netherlands was crucial to both nations, as both Philip and his father before him realised. Yet formal diplomatic relations between Spain and England did come to an end in January 1584. The Spanish ambassador, Bernardino de Mendoza, was expelled, accused of complicity in the Throckmorton plot to liberate Mary Queen of Scots and depose Elizabeth. Elizabeth's Treaty of Nonsuch with the United Provinces followed a year later. The breakdown of relations was also due to English privateering in the Atlantic; unless Spain acted, her treasure fleets were seriously endangered. As the influential secretary Idiáquez observed, 'The objective of this Armada is no less the security of the Indies than the recovery of the Netherlands.'[14]

In spite of the various problems, there were several benefits to Spain's relations with England. In particular, one should not underplay the extensive period of cordial relations between the two powers in the early decades. When Philip succeeded to the Spanish throne, he was already married to Mary Tudor. English troops had assisted the Spanish in securing the French defeat at the battle of St Quentin in 1557. Relations remained cordial between England and Spain even after Elizabeth I's accession. On several occasions, Philip intervened to oppose Elizabeth's excommunication. This was impressive given that tensions arose with some regularity. For example, in February 1569, the Spanish were outraged by the imprisonment of their ambassador in England, Don Guerau de Spes, as well as the confiscation of Genoese treasure. Subsequently, **Francis Drake**'s circumnavigation of the world during the years 1577–80 was partly funded by raiding Spanish colonies.

Conflict in Europe and the Caribbean

Philip considered launching an outright attack on England, but refrained from doing so. He was constantly tempted by the prospect of supporting English Catholics financially, promoting the claim of Mary Queen of Scots to the throne and encouraging unrest in Ireland. In spite of the mutual animosity and growing tensions, it is striking that war between Spain and England was delayed. By March 1573, Alba's negotiations bore fruit with the Convention of Nijmegen, which included a mutual agreement on property seizures, and restored trade between England and the Low Countries. Although the Spanish Armada of 1588 was a disaster and a massive psychological blow, the outcome was not decisive. England had forced Spain to rebuild her navy, but she had not won the war nor even gained mastery of the sea. Spain still controlled the crossing to the Indies. Although subsequent armadas in 1596 and 1597 came to nothing, this was mainly due to storms. The ineffectiveness of Spanish opposition to England after the Armada had more to do with Spain's preoccupation with France. After all, England greatly welcomed the peace with Spain that came shortly after Elizabeth's death. In fact, Spanish communications and defences were as strong in the last 10 years of Philip's reign as they had been in the 1560s. American silver continued to fill the royal treasury. Even the failure of the Spanish Armada was a blessing in disguise. In the longer term, Spain would have struggled to translate a naval victory into political consolidation, even more so given the execution of Mary Queen of Scots at Fotheringhay the year before.

Yet Philip's relations with England had more limitations than benefits. Philip may have been over-reliant on diplomacy and was arguably too anxious about offending Elizabeth. England's actions were a constant source of provocation well before the 1580s. In particular, the seizure of Spanish treasure on its way to Alba in the Netherlands (November 1568) led the Duke of Alba to take retaliatory measures. Alba ordered the seizure of the goods of English subjects in the Low Countries and in Spain, and English fleets were detained in Biscay and Andalucia. Similarly, the descent of the Sea Beggars on Brill and Flushing in 1572 seemed to be inspired by English collusion. In the 1580s, English privateers harassed Spanish treasure fleets, especially Francis Drake in the Caribbean. English privateering undoubtedly weakened Spain, and represented more than a minor irritation. Drake sacked Vigo and Bayona, and raided the Cape Verde Islands and attacked Santo Domingo and Cartagena in

Figure 4.4: Queen Elizabeth I.

ACTIVITY 4.7

Using this section and your broader reading, identify in tabular form the strengths and weaknesses of Spanish policies and actions. Do Philip's relations with England constitute a disastrous failure?

the Caribbean. The English expeditions led by **John Hawkins** and Francis Drake greatly disrupted Spanish commerce, particularly in the New World, and rendered the treasure fleets increasingly insecure. Closer to home, English privateers also undertook more daring raids; Cadiz was attacked the year before the Armada set sail. In the end, Spain was unable to prevent English intervention in the Netherlands. The timing of the Treaty of Nonsuch (1585) between England and Dutch Calvinists was inopportune for the Spanish, as they had started to restore royal authority. Parma had regained considerable control by that stage and perhaps England felt threatened by that, especially once Antwerp fell to the Spanish in August 1585. In the treaty with the Dutch, the English agreed to pay an annual subsidy of £126 000, as well as garrisoning Flushing, Brill and the fort of Rammekens. Parma had delayed his intended attacks against Holland and Zeeland in the north in order to devote all his resources on seizing the port of Sluys for the Spanish fleet.

The Spanish Armada

Psychologically, there was no greater loss than the Armada fiasco in 1588. There was undoubtedly some misfortune owing to poor weather and the death of the Marquis of Santa Cruz before the expedition set off. However, some of the preparations and planning were poor. The Duke of Medina Sidonia was appointed commander, even though he had limited naval experience. The dual command of Medina Sidonia and Farnese was highly problematic, for their success depended on effective communications. Philip also sought to keep in contact with both, but his remoteness made it very difficult to liaise. No clear strategy was put in place for the Armada to link up with Parma's army in the Netherlands, which would be crucial to a land invasion of England. The Spanish lacked a suitable deep water port, capable of taking the Spanish galleons, and this seriously exposed the Armada.

As early as December 1585, Philip acknowledged the seriousness of this problem to Parma, saying that without a port they could do nothing. And yet the Spanish pressed ahead with their major expedition. Unfamiliar with the Channel, the Spanish handed an early advantage to the English. Before the two sides even engaged in battle, the English managed to get windward of the Spaniards, thereby winning the weather gauge (advantageous position) and retaining it for the rest of the battle. It allowed the English fleet to dictate the terms of the battle, though the excellent seamanship, and fighting spirit of the Armada meant that the outcome was not a foregone conclusion. The Armada's troops and sailors were further weakened by their apparent disunity. Six languages were spoken and there was noticeable friction between Castilians and Portuguese. The Spanish were pressurised by the quality of English ships, built according to new designs and with greater firepower. The English fireships also played a significant role, giving the English ascendancy at the battle of Grave lines, though Medina Sidonia's leadership saved the large part of the Armada.

In the final reckoning, the English prevented the Spanish from making a rendezvous with Parma and forced them to return home via Scotland and Ireland. The Spanish failed in their objectives and England survived rather than winning a glorious victory. Spain lost over 60 ships and 9000 men. Philip also failed to learn that England could not be overwhelmed and he followed the Armada disaster with a succession of futile expeditions. In its immediate aftermath, Spanish naval dominance was under threat. In the years 1589–91, there were at least 235 English vessels between the eastern Atlantic and the New World.

Spain in the New World: the impact of empire

The New World formed a key part of Philip's foreign policy and had invaluable domestic repercussions. Religious motives were an important aspect to the expeditions, as they had been from the outset under his predecessors. With 1000 priests in the New World by 1570, and with 100 000 whites and 10 million Indians, the Spanish were eager to Christianise the natives.

Expansion, settlement and trade

The Spanish regime's policy was not overly ambitious in the New World. Having received a formidable territorial inheritance, Philip was more eager to consolidate his possessions than to increase them. There were few substantial gains during his reign, with the exception of Florida and the Philippines. As in his other territories, viceroys were appointed in Mexico and in Peru. Two were inspirational administrators: Martin Enríquez (1568–80) in Mexico and Francisco de Toledo (1569–81) in Peru, who laid excellent foundations for colonial government. Both contributed to the codification of laws, and prepared the groundwork for Indian self-government. Admittedly, the Spanish monopoly was not unchallenged, with the French in Florida, Hawkins in Mexico, and Drake attacking the silver fleet. But by 1587, there were over 100 Spanish ships in the Atlantic.

The impact of empire

The New World expeditions were primarily driven by Spanish imperialism, and especially by the financial benefits that came from improving the organisation and handling of the different territories. To that end, the administration of the New World was given high priority. The existence of the Council of the Indies was essential in this regard. Seville remained the key Spanish centre and its population increased dramatically, almost tripling during the course of the 16th century (from 50 000 to 130 000). Financially, revenues amounted to an impressive 64.5 million ducats during Philip's reign. It is difficult to disagree with Geoffrey Parker's view that Philip's territorial consolidation in the New World was one of his finest achievements.

Spain's international position by 1598: illusion or reality?

Spain's power within Europe

Before his death, Philip attempted to disengage from various foreign commitments. He was clearly conscious of how far the empire had become over-extended. He wisely and finally made peace with France in 1598. The Treaty of Vervins re-stated the terms of Câteau-Cambrésis, the 1559 peace that had concluded the Habsburg–Valois wars. Spain returned many of her conquests on the Netherlands frontier and in Brittany, and Cambrai alone was retained. Sovereignty of the Netherlands was ceded to Philip's daughter Isabella Clara Eugenia and her husband, Archduke Albert of Austria, who was also Philip's cousin. The Spanish had lost control of the northern Netherlands, for which Philip should be partly blamed. In particular, the Spanish made a grave mistake by interfering in the French civil wars in the early 1590s. An earlier peace with Henry IV would have prevented an unnecessary war that only came to an end in 1598. Under Henry's leadership, the stability of French government and society was restored after decades of civil wars. Despite its religious disunity, Spain's northern neighbour was more unified than before and Spanish ascendancy over France was lost.

Spain had obviously lost its fight with England in 1588, though this was more humiliating than strategically significant. Spain's foreign policy came at a considerable cost to the economy. However, Philip's foreign policy was far from being disastrous. He managed to annex Portugal with limited opposition, thereby unifying the entire Iberian Peninsula under his rule and also gaining the second largest colonial empire at little expense. Spain also successfully contained and brought to a definitive end the westward expansion of the Ottomans in the Mediterranean. With hindsight, the battle of Lepanto was a major turning point; the Ottomans had reached the apogee

> ### Speak like a historian
>
> ### Henry Kamen
>
> Read the following account by Henry Kamen
>
> It is plausible to maintain that Philip II's entire foreign policy was defensive. In 1586 he himself argued to the pope that 'I have no reason to allow myself to be ambitious for more kingdoms and estates'. But the requirements of defence meant that first in 1560 and then in 1580, in the Mediterranean and in the Atlantic, he was obliged to elevate Spain into a superpower, as the only way to maintain worldwide security. Once the Spanish system had been created, force and therefore aggression became an integral part of it, though there is no acceptable evidence or plausible reason to suggest that the King had expansionist dreams. Religious and dynastic considerations always remained fundamental, with the qualification that the King had his own view of what 'religion' entailed. When Philip disagreed with the Papacy and France it was precisely because he felt their policies would not best serve the universal Church.[15]
>
> #### Discussion points:
> 1. According to Kamen, what are the motives for Philip's foreign policy?
> 2. Using this chapter and your own research, do you agree with Kamen's argument?
> 3. What do you think Kamen means by the King's own view of 'religion'?

of their power of the Mediterranean, though this was partly due to Ottoman priorities elsewhere.

Spain's reach beyond Europe

The Spanish preference for consolidation rather than expansion in the New World served to strengthen and protect her interests: only Florida and the Philippines were added to her possessions. The Spanish sought to reform their colonial administration and appointed highly competent viceroys in Mexico and Peru. Their control of the high seas was certainly not unchallenged, as French and English privateers took full advantage of the vulnerability of the Spanish treasure fleets. However, the notable increase in Spanish ships operating in the Atlantic ensured that the revenues from the New World tripled during the course of Philip's reign. The regime undoubtedly benefited from their enormous colonial empire, which financed many of Philip's military exploits during his reign. The truth is that Philip's extensive empire was unrivalled at the time. He surely came close to achieving the sensible objectives described by the Venetian ambassador, Michele Suriano, in 1559: Philip's aim was 'not to wage war so that he can add to his kingdoms, but to wage peace so that he can keep the lands he has'.[16]

4 The 'Great Power', 1556–98

Practice essay questions

1. 'Spain's territorial consolidation in the New World was undoubtedly Philip's greatest foreign policy achievement.' Explain why you agree or disagree with this view.
2. 'Philip successfully promoted royal authority abroad.' Assess the validity of this view.
3. 'Spain's diplomatic and military intervention abroad was ultimately counter-productive.' Explain why you agree or disagree with this view.
4. With reference to these extracts and your understanding of the historical context, which of these two extracts provides the more convincing interpretation of Philip's achievements abroad?

Extract A

Philip's mastery of Italian affairs was if anything greater than his father's. He continued to honour the nominal independence of the north Italian states while controlling their rulers through patronage backed by the threat of force. Italy remained the strategic centre of his European empire. It was also a potential source of conflict not only with France, but with Austria, Venice, and the papacy. Some of the north Italian states were imperial fiefs, while Venice and some of the popes encouraged resistance to Spanish hegemony. In Naples and Sicily the Turks remained a threat to coastal communities as they did to those of Spain.

Source: William S. Maltby, *The Rise and Fall of the Spanish Empire*. (Palgrave, 2009), p. 102.

Extract B

But the Indies trade had its own resilience, and there was a further upswing from 1578, with years of great prosperity between 1584 and 1586. Compared to 114 ships engaged in 1576 there were 213 in 1586, and an increase in the volume of trade by 50 per cent. At the same time the most decisive progress yet made in the import of precious metals took place between the half decades 1576–1580 and 1581–1585, and was immediately reflected in the rise of Andalusian prices by 18 per cent in the six years from 1576 to 1582.

Source: Lynch, *Spain*, p. 173.

Further reading

An overview of Philip's foreign policies and actions are provided in Colin Pendrill, *Spain, 1471–1700* (Heinemann, 2002) and the Kamen and Lynch textbooks on Spain. On Spanish imperialism, see William Maltby's *The Rise and Fall of the Spanish Empire* (Palgrave Macmillan, 2009), as well as the aforementioned biographies. For the Netherlands, see the works of Geoffrey Parker, *The Dutch Revolt* (Pelican Books, 1979) and *Spain and the Netherlands*, as well as Graham Darby (ed.), *The Origins and Development of the Dutch Revolt* (Routledge, 2001). For an understanding of the varied primary sources pertinent to researching Philip's reign, see Parker's latest biography, *Imprudent King* (pages 380–385). See also J.H. Elliott's *Imperial Spain, 1469–1716* (Penguin, 1963) and *Spain and its World, 1500–1700* (Yale University Press, 1989), and Henry Kamen's *Spain's Road to Empire: The Making of a World Power, 1492–1763* (Penguin, 2009).

> ### Chapter summary
>
> By the end of this chapter you should understand:
>
> - the nature of Philip's inheritance (territorial and military) and his foreign policy objectives
> - Spanish foreign policies and relations with France, Portugal, the Netherlands, England and the Italian city-states
> - Philip's relationship to, and actions in, the Mediterranean and in the New World
> - the relative strengths and weaknesses of Spain's international position from 1556 to Philip's death in 1598.

End notes

[1] John Lynch, *Spain Under the Habsburgs, Volume 1: Empire and Absolutism, 1516–1598*. Oxford: Basil Blackwell, 1981, p. 233.
[2] Cited in Geoffrey Parker, *Imprudent King: A New Life of Philip II*. London and New York: Yale University Press, 2014, p. 137.
[3] Parker, *Imprudent King*, p. 137.
[4] Parker, *Imprudent King*, p. 203.
[5] Cited in Lynch, *Spain*, p. 245.
[6] Cited in R. Trevor Davies, *The Golden Century of Spain, 1501–1621*. Basingstoke: Macmillan, 1967, p. 175.
[7] Cited in Parker, *Imprudent King*, p. 268.
[8] Lynch, *Spain*, p. 290.
[9] Parker, *Imprudent King*, p. 142.
[10] Parker, *Imprudent King*, p. 153.
[11] Cited in Jon Cowans (ed.), *Early Modern Spain: A Documentary History*. Philadelphia: University of Pennsylvania Press, 2003, pp. 110–11.
[12] Parker, *Imprudent King*, p. 210.
[13] A. Lovett, *Early Habsburg Spain, 1517–1598*. Oxford University Press, 1986, p. 168.
[14] Cited in Lynch, *Spain*, p. 334.
[15] Henry Kamen, *Spain, 1469–1714: A Society of Conflict*. London: Longman, 2005, p. 142.
[16] Peter Pierson, *Philip II of Spain*. London: Thames & Hudson, 1975, p. 131.

Who's who

Adrian of Utrecht (1459–1523): appointed tutor to the future Charles V in 1507, Bishop of Tortosa (1516), Grand Inquisitor, appointed cardinal (1517), Charles V's Regent and Pope (1522–23).

Afonso V, King of Portugal: challenged succession of Ferdinand and Isabella, married Juana 'la Beltraneja', supported by Archbishop Carrillo, defeated in battle by Ferdinand at the battle of Toro (1476), by Treaty of Alçacovas (1479) agreed not to invade Castile again, also gained key concession of Portuguese monopoly of exploration of Africa.

Alba, third Duke of (1507–82): Fernando Álvarez de Toledo, accompanied Charles V on Tunis expedition (1535), Spanish Council of State (1545), fought at battle of Mühlberg (1547), viceroy of Naples (1556–59), governor of Netherlands (1567–73), captain-general of Portugal (1580–82).

Albert, Archduke of Austria (1559–1621): cardinal (1577–98), viceroy of Portugal (1583–93), Archbishop of Toledo (1594–98), governor of the Netherlands (1596–98), married the Infanta Isabella Clara Eugenia (1598), with whom he ruled the Netherlands as duke until his death.

Barbarossa, Hayreddin (c.1476–1546): with his brothers Ishak and Oruc took control of Algiers in 1516. Hayreddin's brother Oruc killed by Spanish in 1518. Hayreddin given the title Beylerbey by Sultan Selim I. Algiers became his headquarters, undertook numerous raids on Christian ports in the Mediterranean, later appointed admiral-in-chief of Ottoman Empire by Sultan Suleiman (1533).

Barçelos, Duke of: Teodósio (1568–1630), succeeded to his father's title as Duke of Bragança and was made Constable of Portugal in 1583.

Bragança, Duke of: Dom João (1542–83), the house of Bragança was one of the most important titles in Portugal, created in 1442 by King Afonso V of Portugal.

Carrillo, Archbishop of Toledo: contributed to Isabella of Castile's accession to the throne, though subsequently supported Juana **'la Beltraneja'** and Afonso V, even providing troops to fight against Ferdinand and Isabella, eventually made his peace following the battle of Toro in 1476.

Cassador, Guillem: Archbishop of Barcelona (1561–70), participated in the Council of Trent and quickly implemented Tridentine decrees following his return to Spain.

Castiglione, Baldassare (1478–1529): Italian diplomat, best known for his influential book on noble manners, *Book of the Courtier*, printed in 1528, worked at the courts of Mantua and Urbino.

Chinchón, Count of, Diego Fernández de Cabrera y Bobadilla (d.1608): treasurer of the councils of Aragon and Italy, councillor of state and member of the *Junta de Noche*.

Chinchón, Count of, Pedro Fernández de Cabrera y Bobadilla (d.1576): treasurer of the councils of Aragon and Italy.

Cobos, Francisco de los (d.1547): noble background, worked under King Ferdinand of Aragon (1503), appointed secretary to Charles V (1516), took charge of Castilian administration especially during Charles's frequent absences, Council of State (1529), directed affairs in Mediterranean part of the Empire.

Cortés, Hernán (1484–1547): lesser noble family, arrived in Santo Domingo in the New World (1504), worked for governor Velázquez in Cuba, put in charge of expedition to the mainland (1518), landed on Yucatán peninsula (1519), contributed to fall of Tenochtitlán (1521), further expeditions to Honduras (1525–26), further period in Mexico (1530–36), returned to Spain (1539), involved in Algiers expedition (1541).

Deza, Diego de: tutor to Prince John, son of Ferdinand and Isabella, churchman and Bishop of Zamora, Salamanca, Jaén and Palencia, Archbishop of Seville, Grand Inquisitor after Torquemada.

Don Carlos (1545–68): prince of Spain and infante, son of Philip II and Maria of Portugal. Showed signs of mental instability from childhood, considered as possible governor of Netherlands, became liability so was excluded from any important political office, eventually imprisoned owing to violent conduct and unpredictability (January 1568).

Don John of Austria (1545–78): son of Charles V by Barbara Blomberg, captain-general of the sea (1568), governor of the Netherlands (1576–78).

Doria, Andrea (1466–1560): Genoese admiral, fought against French and Spanish in Naples, fought for the French and later Charles V in the Mediterranean, put his fleet at the disposal of Charles V in 1528, appointed captain-general of the sea and councillor of state.

Dragut (1485–1565): also known as Turgut Reis, Ottoman admiral and privateer, fought numerous naval campaigns throughout the Mediterranean, fought alongside Hayreddin Barbarossa, contributed to the defeat of the Christian navy at the battle of Prevesa, governor of Djerba, appointed commander of Ottoman navy following Barbarossa's death (1546), governor of Algiers (1548), involved in the siege of Malta (1565).

Drake, Sir Francis (c.1542–95): English naval captain, captained his first ship (1565), failed expedition at San Juan de Ulúa, Mexico (1568), captured silver at Nombre de Dios, Panamá (1572), rounded Cape Horn, crossed Pacific and rounded Cape of Good Hope (1577–80). First English captain to circumnavigate the globe, knighted by Queen (April 1581), attacked Santo Domingo and Cartagena (1585–86), Cadiz raid (1587), involved in preparations for Armada campaign (1588), final voyage to West Indies (1595).

Eboli, Prince of, Ruy Gómez da Silva (1516–73): Portuguese noble brought up in Prince Philip's household, married Ana de Mendoza (1552), accompanied Philip to England, count of Melito (1555), chief minister (1559), Duke of Estremara and grandee of Spain (1568), councillor of state (1556).

Egmont, Count of (1522–68): fought for Habsburgs in victorious battles at St Quentin (1557) and Gravelines (1558), commander of the cavalry in Flanders, and councillor of state in the Netherlands (1559), led opposition to Cardinal Granvelle, arrested by Duke of Alba (September 1567), publicly executed (1568).

Erasmus, Desiderius (c.1466–1536): Dutch Christian humanist, Europe's leading scholar, ordained priest (1492), prolific author, works including *Adages, Enchiridion* (Handbook of Christian Soldier), critical edition of Lorenzo Valla's Annotations on New Testament, *Praise of Folly*, Greek edition of New Testament with Latin translation, *On Free Will* (1524) – Erasmus's response to Luther.

Farnese, Alexander, prince of Parma (1545–92): son of Margaret of Austria (illegitimate daughter of Charles V), married princess Mary of Portugal, fought at Lepanto, served in Spanish army in the Netherlands, appointed commander and governor of the Netherlands (1578–92), secured loyalty of southern provinces (Union of Arras, 1579), captured Antwerp (1585), involved in preparations for Spanish Armada, led military expeditions to France in the early 1590s.

Ferdinand I (1503–64): brother of Charles V, sent to Flanders after arrival of latter in Spain, ruler of Austrian hereditary lands from 1522, and King of Bohemia and Hungary from 1526, King of the Romans (1531–58), led campaigns against Ottomans in central Europe, largely responsible for Peace of Augsburg (1555), more pragmatic in approach to religious disunity than Charles V, involved in attempts at religious reconciliation at Colloquy of Worms (1557), Holy Roman Emperor (1556–64).

Ferrante I, King of Naples (1423–94): King of Naples (from 1458), illegitimate son of Alfonso V of Aragon, married to daughter of Prince of Taranto, most influential of Neapolitan barons, encountered frequent opposition (revolts in 1458–65, 1485–87), expelled Ottomans from Otranto (1481).

Foix, Germaine de (1488–1538): married to Ferdinand of Aragon, appointed viceroy of Valencia (1523).

Fonseca, Alfonso de (1475–1534): Archbishop of Santiago de Compostela (1507), Archbishop of Toledo (1523), member of Charles V's Royal Council, baptised Prince Philip (1527).

Francisco de Córdoba: two Spanish conquistadores by that name, one who founded Nicaragua and the other who provided the first European descriptions of the Yucatán peninsula.

Gattinara, Mercurino (1465–1530): from Piedmontese noble family, legal adviser to Duchess of Savoy (Margaret of Austria), appointed President of the Parlement of Dôle (Franche-Comté), appointed Chancellor to Charles V in Spain (1518), promoted anti-French policy, focused on Mediterranean states, appointed cardinal (1529).

Granvelle, Antoine Perrenot de (1517–86): Bishop of Arras and involved in imperial administration (1538), Archbishop of Mechelen (1560), and Cardinal Granvelle, councillor of state in the Netherlands (1559–64), Margaret of Parma's chief minister, viceroy of Naples (1571–75), President of Council of Italy (1579), and councillor of state.

Hawkins, Sir John (1532–95): English sea captain, made first slaving voyage from Sierra Leone to Hispaniola (1562), many of his ships captured by Spanish galleons at Vera Cruz (1568), entered Parliament (1571), treasurer of navy, third in command during Armada campaign (1588), last voyage to West Indies (1595).

Henry, Count of Nassau (1483–1538): travelled with Philip of Habsburg to Castile in early 1500s, became Charles V's Chamberlain (1510), member of Charles V's Privy Council.

Henry, of Navarre (1553–1610): son of Anthony of Navarre and Jeanne d'Albret, involved in military campaigns of early civil wars, married Margaret of Valois in 1572 and confined to the court after St Bartholomew's Day massacre (1572), King of Navarre (1572), escaped the royal court (1576) and reconverted to Calvinism, first King of Bourbon dynasty, Henry IV (1589–1610), succeeding to throne after Henry III's assassination, re-established royal authority after conversion to Catholicism (1593) and taking Paris (1594), and declaring war against Spain (1595), signed Edict of Nantes (1598), married Marie de Médicis (1599), assassinated (1610).

Hornes, Philip de Montmorency (1524–68): related to French Montmorency and Dutch Egmont families, served Charles

V as stadtholder of Gelderland (1555), captain of Prince Philip's bodyguard, fought at the battles of St Quentin and Gravelines, admiral-general of the Netherlands and councillor of State in the Netherlands (1559), joined opposition to Granvelle, imprisoned by duke of Alba, executed in 1568.

Idiáquez, Juan de (1540–1614): ambassador to Genoa (1573–76), ambassador to Venice (1576–78), Secretary of State for Italy (1579–85), councillor of state and war (1585), President of the Council of Military Orders (1598).

Ignatius of Loyola (1491–1556): Basque nobleman, wounded at battle of Pamplona (1521), visited Holy Land (1524), studied at Alcalá and Salamanca universities, took vows with six companions in Paris (1534), founded Society of Jesus with papal approval (1540), first General of the Order (otherwise known as the Jesuits).

Isabella, Empress (1503–39): Isabella of Portugal, Empress and Queen (1526), wife of Charles V and mother of Philip II.

Jiménez de Cisneros, Cardinal Francisco (1436–1517): Archbishop of Toledo (1495), cardinal and Inquisitor General (1507), reformed religious orders, superior of Franciscans, less tolerant to Muslim and Jewish communities than Hernando de Talavera, founded university of Alcalá (1508) and sponsored Polyglot Bible, led military expedition to Oran (1509).

St John of the Cross (1542–91): Spanish mystic and poet, friend and disciple of Teresa of Ávila, entered Carmelite Order (1563) and contributed to the reforms of Order (1565), author of numerous mystical works including *Dark Night of the Soul*.

Juana 'la Beltraneja' (1462–1530): daughter of Henry IV of Castile, married Afonso V of Portugal, claimed Castilian throne.

Machiavelli, Niccolò (1469–1527): Florentine diplomat and politician, worked for republican government (1498), head of second chancery and secretary of Ten of War in charge of foreign affairs, undertook numerous diplomatic missions to Louis XII of France, Emperor Maximilian I, Pope Julius II, and Cesare Borgia, suspected involvement in an anti-Medici plot (1513) led to his exile to small farm outside city, wrote *The Prince* that year (published posthumously), *Discourses on First Decades of Livy*, *Art of War*.

Margaret of Austria (1522–86): natural daughter of Charles V, duchess of Parma, governess (regent) of the Netherlands (1559–67).

Mary of Hungary (1505–58): daughter of Philip of Habsburg and Juana the Mad, married (1522) to Louis II, king of Hungary, Queen of Hungary (1522–26), governess of the Netherlands (1531–55).

Mary, Queen of Scots (1542–87): Mary Stuart, daughter of Mary of Guise and James V of Scotland, Queen of Scots (1542–67), dauphine (1558) and Queen of France (1559–60), involved in the Babington Plot (1586) which led to her arrest and execution at Fotheringhay Castle (1587).

Maximilian I: son of Emperor Frederick III of Habsburg, married Mary of Burgundy (1477), signed Treaty of Arras (1482) which ceded Picardy and duchy of Burgundy to Louis XI of France, retaining Franche-Comté and Netherlands for the Habsburgs, crowned King of the Romans (1486), Holy Roman Emperor (1493–1519).

Medina Sidonia, dukes of: ducal title created in 1445 for the powerful Guzmán family from Andalusia, second duke was Enrique de Guzmán (1430–92), third duke was Juan Alonso Pérez de Guzmán (1464–1507), seventh duke was Alonso Pérez de Guzmán (1550–1619), grandee of Spain, captain-general of the Coast of Andalusia and entrusted with the command of the Armada (1588), councillor of state and war (1598).

Mendoza, Luis Hurtado de (1489–1566): supported Charles V during *Comuneros* revolt, though his sister María Pacheco supported it, viceroy of Navarre (1543–46), President of Council of Indies (1546–59), President of Council of Castile (1561–63).

Mendozas: very influential family, including the duke of Infantado, the marquis of Mondejar.

Molina, Juan Vázquez de: Philip II's secretary of state, nephew of Francisco de los Cobos.

Moura, Cristóbal de (1538–1613): Portuguese by birth, visited Spain in the household of Princess Juana, sister of Philip II, ambassador to Lisbon (1578–80), acted as Philip's chief minister during his stay in Portugal (1581–83), councillor of state and war (1585), viceroy of Portugal (1598–1613).

Orange, Prince of (1533–84): William of Nassau-Dillenburg, called 'the Silent', close confidant of Charles V, councillor of state in the Netherlands (1559–67), fell out with Habsburg ministers in Brussels especially when he married Lutheran princess Anna of Saxony (1561), governor of the Franche-Comté (1561–67), took refuge abroad when Alba arrived in the Netherlands, converted to Calvinism (1573), stadtholder of Holland (1573–84), Zeeland and Utrecht, masterminded Union of Utrecht (1579), which revoked allegiance to Philip II (1581).

Pasha, Hasan: Ottoman naval commander, son of Hayreddin Barbarossa, Beylerbey of Algiers (1544–52, 1562–68).

Paul III (1468–1549): Alessandro Farnese, Pope (1534–49), from Roman noble family, bishop of Parma (1508), ordained (1519), as Pope promoted reform-minded cardinals and appointed papal commission to investigate reform, encouraged foundation of new religious orders, including Theatines, Ursulines and Jesuits, responsible for convocation of Council of Trent (1545).

Pérez, Antonio (1540–1611): Spanish royal secretary, son of royal secretary Gonzalo Pérez, secretary of state for Italy (1567–79), demise influenced by his conflict with Juan de Escobedo, secretary to Don John of Austria, Antonio accused of Escobedo's murder (1578), also implicated was Ana de Mendoza, princess of Eboli, interrogated and tortured (1585), escaped to Aragonese capital, Zaragoza (1590), later escaped to France then England.

Pérez, Gonzalo (c.1500–66): Spanish royal secretary, longest serving of Philip II's secretaries, travelled with Charles V (1527–32), assisted Charles's secretary Alfonso de Valdés, private secretary to Philip (1542), archdeacon of Segovia (1542).

Quiroga, Cardinal Gaspar de (1499–1593): bishop of Cuenca, President of Council of Italy (1563–72), Inquisitor-General (1572), Cardinal, Archbishop of Toledo (1577).

Santa Cruz, Marquis of (1526–88): Àlvaro de Bazán, captain-general of galleys of Naples (1566–78), grandee and captain-general of the Ocean Sea (1583), and of Portugal (1584), advocate of 'Enterprise of England' (Spanish Armada).

Sixtus IV (1414–84): Francesco della Rovere, Pope in the years 1471–84, commissioned the building of the Sistine Chapel, founded the Vatican Archives, helped to establish the Spanish Inquisition in 1478.

Suleiman II (c.1494–1566): the Magnificent or the 'law-giver' (*kanuni*), Ottoman sultan (1520–66), only son of Selim I, provincial governor of Kaffa (Crimea) and then Manisa (Anatolia) before he was sultan, expanded territories in Asia (overran Mesopotamia and took Baghdad), in central Europe (seizing Belgrade and much of the Hungarian lands) and in the Mediterranean (fall of Rhodes), success benefited from alliances with the French and North African corsairs.

Talavera, Hernando de (c.1430–1507): Spanish Churchman, taught philosophy at the university of Salamanca, entered Jeronimite order (1466), prior in Valladolid (c.1470), became Isabella of Castile's confessor, bishop of Ávila (1485), became first Archbishop of Granada (1493) where he pursued a more moderate policy towards the Moors, formed part of royal Council (from 1470s).

St Teresa of Ávila (1515–82): Spanish mystic and writer, entered Carmelite Order (1534), author of various mystical writings, mainly directed towards members of religious orders.

Torquemada, Tómas de (1420–98): Spanish Inquisitor General, entered Dominican Order in Valladolid, confessor to Ferdinand of Aragon and Isabella of Castile, chosen as one of the seven new inquisitors (1482), appointed Inquisitor General (1483).

Valdés, Hernando de (1483–1568): member of the Supreme Council of the Inquisition, Archbishop of Seville, Inquisitor General from 1547 to 1566, President of the Council of Castile, published *The Index of Forbidden Books*.

Vázquez, Mateo (1542–91): secretary of Cardinal Espinosa and Inquisition (1566), personal secretary of Philip II (1572–73).

Velascos: constables of Castile.

Villena, Marquis of: Juan Pacheco, supporter of Juana 'la Betraneja', daughter of Henry IV of Castile.

Wittelsbach: family of the dukes of Bavaria and rivals of the Habsburgs.

Glossary

Albaicín	one of the key districts in the city of Granada.
Alcabala	a 10 per cent sales tax levied in Castile.
Alumbrados	otherwise known as the illuminists, they were mystics who downplayed the external manifestations of religion (including Church ceremonies), thereby attracting the attention of the Inquisition.
Arquebuses	a type of firearm.
Audiencias	high courts; in the New World they became part of the government apparatus.
Auto da fé	expression meaning 'act of faith', popularly used to refer to the burning of those condemned of heresy by the Inquisition.
Barbary States	North African states, notably Algiers, which professed the Islamic faith and frequently collaborated with the Ottoman Empire. The corsairs, Muslim pirates such as the Barbarossa brothers, resided in the Barbary states.
Bureaucracy	system of administration.
Caballero	knight, belonging to the lower nobility, normally but not always propertied.
Canon Law	the Catholic Church's laws used to govern the Church and its members.
Church's Index of Forbidden Books	represents Church's list of censored books, works that were considered to contain heretical ideas.
Comunidades	refers to the communities and towns in Castile that played a prominent role in the *Comuneros* revolt. They united under a rebel government, the *Santa Junta de Comunidad*.
Conquistadores	explorers, entrepreneurs and soldiers who sought to conquer territory in the New World, such as Hernán Cortes and Francisco Pizarro.
Consulta	Reports summarising the discussions of Council meetings, which would be relayed to the King.
Conversos	New Christians, and more specifically, Jewish converts to Christianity.
Corregidor	royal official in Castilian towns.
Defenestrate	throwing an individual out of a window with a view to harming or killing them.
Despatches	documents or correspondence between representatives from different territories, especially those composed by ambassadors.
Diputación del Reyno	the permanent committee of the Aragonese Cortes, which oversaw the administration of revenues and promoted the province's liberties.
Ducats	unit of currency in Castile, though accounting was mainly processed in *maravedís* (1 ducat = 375 *maravedís*).
Elector	the Holy Roman Emperors were elected by seven Electors: the Elector of Saxony, Margrave of Brandenburg, King of Bohemia, Count of Palatine, and the Archbishops of Cologne, Mainz and Trier. The Electors were the most politically influential princes within the Empire.
Encabezamiento	system that assessed and organised collection of taxes (including the *alcabala*) in the localities.

Encomienda	as applied in the New World, a system whereby some Spanish colonists became the official protectors of large groups of natives in return for tribute, chiefly in the form of free labour.
Excusado	a tax upon properties in parishes, granted by Pope Pius V in 1567.
Galleasses	higher, larger and slower than regular galleys, galleasses played a major role in the battle of Lepanto on account of their firepower.
Germanía	the brotherhood of rebels in Valencia during the early years of Charles V's reign.
Hidalgo	Lowest rank of the nobility.
Janissaries	elite armed forces of the Ottoman Empire.
Juro	fixed sum paid by the Crown in repayment of loans.
Justiciar	the officially appointed legal protector of Aragonese rights and liberties.
Landgrave	Title of the rulers of certain territories within the Holy Roman Empire, roughly equivalent to count.
Letrado	lawyer (with university degrees in law).
Maravedí	unit of currency (see ducats).
Mayorazgo	restricting the division of inheritance so that families retained ownership of land.
Millones	a tax on meat, wine, oil and vinegar, first voted in 1589, which eventually became permanent.
Moriscos	New Christians, and more specifically, Muslim converts to Christianity.
Observant Reform	reform of Catholic religious orders, motivated by the goal of returning to, and indeed, observing the original rules of each order's founders.
Ottomans	rulers and inhabitants of the powerful Muslim Empire that stretched around the Mediterranean and into Europe in the sixteenth century, with Constantinople as its imperial capital.
Papal bull	document with papal seal declaring the commands and policies of the papacy.
Papal fief	territories handed out by the papacy in exchange for loyalty, the provision of funds and the protection of the Church.
Patronage	in this period, a hierarchical system in which kings and nobles provided income through land and office to clients who in return served them, for example, by swearing allegiance and providing military assistance when called upon to do so.
Pikes	pikes played an important role in the 16th century especially when combined with arquebuses.
Poderes	instructions which town representatives (*procuradores*) were expected to follow.
Polyglot Bible	a Bible containing side-by-side versions of the text in several different languages.
Prerogative	rights and privileges of a monarch.
Procurador	urban representatives in the Castilian Cortes.
Roman law	codified law originating in ancient Rome that contrasted with local, customary laws.
Sea Beggars	Dutch Calvinists who were privateers and opposed Spanish rule in the Netherlands.
Señorío	lordship, associated with particular area.
Subsidies	taxes voted in the *Cortes*.
Tercio	elite Spanish regiment that used a square formation combining use of arquebuses and pikes (see above).

Glossary

Trent, Council of	the eagerly awaited reforming Council of the Roman Catholic Church, which opened in 1545 and concluded in 1563. The Tridentine decrees focused on doctrines and the reform of discipline. In many countries and regions, they took decades to be implemented.
Tridentine	of or pertaining to the Council of Trent (such as its decrees or reforms).
Viceroy	governor of a particular province (such as Aragon, Naples and, later, Portugal) to whom Spanish rulers delegated their powers.

Bibliography

Chapter 1

Jon Cowans (ed.), *Early Modern Spain: A Documentary History*. Philadelphia: University of Pennsylvania Press, 2003.

John Edwards, *Ferdinand and Isabella*. London: Longman, 2005.

John Edwards, *The Spain of the Catholic Monarchs, 1474–1520*. Oxford: Blackwell, 2000.

J.H. Elliott, *Imperial Spain, 1469–1716*. London: Penguin, 2002.

Felipe Fernández-Armesto, *Ferdinand & Isabella*. London: Weidenfeld & Nicolson, 1975.

Henry Kamen, *Spain, 1469–1714: A Society of Conflict*. London: Longman, 2005.

John Lynch, *Spain under the Habsburgs: Volume I, Empire and Absolutism, 1516–1598*. Oxford: Basil Blackwell, 1981.

Colin Pendrill, *Spain, 1471–1700*. Harlow: Heinemann, 2002.

Chapter 2

Jean Bérenger, *A History of the Habsburg Empire, 1273–1700*. London and New York: Longman, 1994.

Jon Cowans (ed.), *Early Modern Spain: A Documentary History*. Philadelphia: University of Pennsylvania Press, 2003.

R. Trevor Davies, *The Golden Century of Spain, 1501–1621*. London: Macmillan, 1967.

Henry Kamen, *Spain, 1469–1714: A Society of Conflict*. London: Longman, 2005.

A. Lovett, *Early Habsburg Spain, 1517–1598*. Oxford: Oxford University Press, 1986.

John Lynch, *Spain under the Habsburgs: Volume I, Empire and Absolutism, 1516–1598*. Oxford: Basil Blackwell, 1981.

William Maltby, *The Rise and Fall of the Spanish Empire*. London: Palgrave Macmillan, 2009.

Colin Pendrill, *Spain, 1471–1700*. London: Heinemann, 2002.

James Tracy, *Emperor Charles V, Impresario of War: Campaign Strategy, International Finance and Domestic Politics*. Cambridge: Cambridge University Press, 2002.

Chapter 3

R. Trevor Davies, *The Golden Century of Spain, 1501–1621*. London: Macmillan, 1967.

Henry Kamen, *Spain, 1469–1714: A Society of Conflict*. London: Longman, 2005.

A. Lovett, *Early Habsburg Spain, 1515–1598*. Oxford: Oxford University Press, 1986.

John Lynch, *Spain under the Habsburgs, Volume 1: Empire and Absolutism, 1516–1598*. Oxford: Basil Blackwell, 1981.

William Maltby, *The Rise and Fall of the Spanish Empire*. London: Palgrave Macmillan, 2009.

Geoffrey Parker, *Imprudent King: A New Life of Philip II*. London and New Haven: Yale University Press, 2014.

Chapter 4

Thomas F. Arnold, *The Renaissance at War*. London: Cassell, 2002.

R. Trevor Davies, *The Golden Century of Spain, 1501–1621*. London: Macmillan, 1967.

A. Lovett, *Early Habsburg Spain, 1517–1598*. Oxford: Oxford University Press, 1986.

John Lynch, *Spain under the Habsburgs, Volume 1: Empire and Absolutism, 1516–1598*. Oxford: Basil Blackwell, 1981.

Geoffrey Parker, *Imprudent King: A New Life of Philip II*. London and New York: Yale University Press, 2014.

Peter Pierson, *Philip II of Spain*. London: Thames & Hudson, 1975.

Acknowledgements

The authors and publishers acknowledge the following sources of copyright material and are grateful for the permissions granted. While every effort has been made, it has not always been possible to identify the sources of all the material used, or to trace all copyright holders. If any omissions are brought to our notice, we will be happy to include the appropriate acknowledgements on reprinting.

The publisher would like to thank the following for permission to reproduce their photographs (numbers refer to figure numbers, unless otherwise stated):

Cover image Paolo Giocoso/SOPA RF/SOPA/Corbis **Chapter 1 opener** Peter Barritt / Alamy. **1.5** The Art Archive / Alamy. **1.6** Classic Image / Alamy. **1.7** GL Archive / Alamy. **1.8** PRISMA ARCHIVO / Alamy. **Chapter 2 opener:** The Art Archive / Alamy. **2.1** World History Archive / Alamy. **2.4** PRISMA ARCHIVO / Alamy. **2.5** Art Reserve / Alamy. **2.9** Lebrecht Music and Arts Photo Library / Alamy. **Chapter 3 opener:** Michelle Chaplow / Alamy. **3.1** Peter Horree / Alamy. **3.4** Albert Knapp / Alamy. **3.5** VPC Photo / Alamy. **3.7** Author's Image Ltd / Alamy. **Chapter 4 opener** Classic Image / Alamy. **4.1** DEA / G. DAGLI ORT / Getty Images. **4.3** The Art Archive / Alamy. **4.4** World History Archive / Alamy.

The publisher would like to thank the following for permission to reproduce extracts from their texts:

Extract Chapter 1 from Edwards, J. (2005) *Ferdinand and Isabella,* 1st edn, pub Longman, pp.ix-x, 168, reproduced with permission from Taylor & Francis Group; **Extract Chapter 1** from Kamen, H (1991) *Spain, 1469-1714: A Society of Conflict*, pub. Longman, pp.60, reproduced with permission from Taylor & Francis Group; **Extract Chapter 2** from William S. Maltby, *The Rise and Fall of the Spanish Empire*, 2009, Palgrave Macmillan, reproduced with permission of Palgrave Macmillan; **Extract Chapter 2** from Tracy, J. (2002) *Emperor Charles V, Impresario of War: Campaign Strategy, International Finance, and Domestic Politics*, p.289, reproduced with permission from Cambridge University Press; **Extract Chapter 2** from Lovett, A. W. (1986) *Early Habsburg Spain, 1517-1598*, p.39, by permission of Oxford University Press; **Extract Chapter 3** from Parker, G. (2014) *Imprudent King: A New Life of Philip II*, p.xvxviii, reproduced with permission from Yale University Press; **Extract Chapter 3** from Kamen, H. (1998) *Philip of Spain*, p.212, reproduced with permission from Yale University Press; Extract Chapter 3 from *Philip II of Spain* by Peter Pierson, © 1975 Thames and Hudson Limited, London. Reproduced by kind permission of Thames & Hudson, Ltd; **Extract Chapter 4** from Kamen, H (1991) *Spain, 1469-1714: A Society of Conflict*, pub. Longman, pp.60, reproduced with permission from Taylor & Francis Group; **Extract Chapter 4** from William S. Maltby, *The Rise and Fall of the Spanish Empire*, 2009, Palgrave Macmillan, reproduced with permission of Palgrave Macmillan; **Extract Chapter 4** Lynch, J. (1981) *Spain Under the Habsburgs, Volume 1: Empire and Absolutism, 1516–1598*, pub. Basil Blackwell, p 173, reproduced with permission from John Wiley & Sons.

Index

Acosta, José de 76
Adrian of Utrecht 29, 30, 32, 47, 105
Afonso V 4, 105
Alba, third Duke of 41, 55, 59, 61, 62, 73, 87, 90, 93–5, 96, 105
Albaicín 64, 109
Albert, Archduke of Austria 94, 101, 105
alcabala 20, 24, 30, 38, 51, 73
Alcáçovas, Treaty of 5, 6, 22
Alcalá University 46, 48
alumbrados 47, 109
anti-Semitism 15–17
Aragon 2–5, 7–11, 20, 22–3, 35, 38, 58–62, 64–7
Aragonese revolt 62, 64–7
Arbues, Pedro de 16, 17
Armada 74, 83, 86, 98, 99, 100
army 83–4
arquebuses 39, 109
audiencias 8, 35, 109
auto da fé 16, 17, 109
Aztecs 49

Barbarossa, Hayreddin 45, 46, 48, 105
Barbary States 89, 109
Barçelos, Duke of 93, 105
Bible, Polyglot 12, 24, 47, 76, 110
Bragança, Duke of 93, 105
bureaucracy 35–7, 109

caballeros 30, 109
Calvinism 70, 72–77, 82–5, 95–8
Canon Law 15, 107
Carranza, Archbishop of Toledo 68, 70
Carrillo, Archbishop of Toledo 3, 4, 105
Casas, Bartolomé de las 50
Cassador, Guillem 70, 105
Castiglione, Baldassare 6, 105
Castile 2–10, 19, 21–3, 32, 35, 36, 37, 47, 51, 59, 74
Câteau-Cambrésis, Treaty of 82, 84, 86
Catholic League 74, 85
Catholicism 43, 48, 57, 68–70, 72, 86, 89, 96, 98
censorship 75–7
Cervantes, Miguel de 76, 91
Charles V 27–33, 34–8, 39–47, 49–50
Charles VIII 9, 21
Chinchón, Count of 59, 105
Christian mysticism 72
Christianity 15, 16, 17, 48, 63, 92
Church 11–12, 38, 42–7, 68–72, 77

Church's Index of Forbidden Books 47, 72, 109
Cisneros, Cardinal 11, 15, 21, 29, 46, 107
Cobos, Francisco de los 32, 35, 36, 37, 38, 51, 105
Columbus, Christopher 12, 19, 22–3, 24, 48
Comuneros revolt 29–33, 37
Comunidades 29, 109
conquistadores 23, 46–9, 109
consultas 60, 109
conversos 15, 16, 17, 109
corregidores 7, 11, 15, 32, 109
Cortes 3, 7–8, 29, 30, 35, 37, 60, 61, 66
Cortés, Hernán 45, 49, 105
Council of Trent 11, 43, 70–1, 111
cruzada tax 12, 13, 58

Deza, Diego de 11, 105
Diputación del Reyno 67, 109
Don Carlos 55, 56, 57, 61, 95, 105
Don John of Austria 55, 59, 63, 65, 88, 90, 105
Don Quixote 75–6
Doria, Andrea 45, 82, 87, 88, 105
Dragut (Turgut Reis) 46, 89, 105
Drake, Sir Francis 99, 100, 106
Dutch Calvinism 85, 95
Dutch Revolt 55, 82, 94–8

Eboli, Prince of 55, 61, 106
economy 3–4, 17–23, 37–9, 72–4
Egmont, Count of 55, 95, 97, 106
Electors 42, 109
Elizabeth I 69, 82, 86, 90, 95, 98, 99
empire 48–50, 101–2
encabezamiento 38, 109
encomienda 50, 110
England 20, 62, 69, 95, 98–100
Erasmus, Desiderius 47, 48, 106
Escobedo, Juan de 57, 62
Europe 81–3, 87–9, 99–101
excusado tax 74, 110

Farnese, Alexander 59, 73, 86, 98, 100, 106
Ferdinand I 3–11, 12–15, 17, 19–24, 26, 106
Ferrante I 22, 106
fifth column 48, 63
Foix, Germaine de 9, 21, 22, 32, 33, 106
Fonseca, Alfonso de 46, 106
foreign relations 20–23, 39–45
France 2, 9, 20, 21, 38, 39, 40, 41, 81–4, 98
Francis I 40, 42
Francis II 84

Francisco de Córdoba 64, 106
Franco, General Francisco 18
Fuggers 29, 38, 51, 73

galleasses 90, 110
Gattinara, Mercurino 28, 33, 106
Germanía revolt 31–2, 33, 48, 51, 110
Gómez da Silva, Ruy (Prince of Eboli) 61, 106
Granada 8, 10, 12–14, 20
Granvelle, Antoine Perrenot de 33, 36, 87, 94, 96, 97, 106

Hawkins, Sir John 100, 101, 106
Henry, Count of Nassau 37, 106
Henry, of Navarre 85, 106
Henry II 44, 82, 84
Henry IV 85, 101
hidalgos 31, 37, 110
Holy League 88–9, 90
Hornes, Philip de Montmorency 57, 95, 96, 106
Huguenots 85, 86
humanism 46

Idiáquez, Juan de 59, 60, 99, 107
Ignatius of Loyola 47, 68, 107
Imperial Diets 43
Incas 49
Index of Forbidden Books 47, 72, 109
Inquisition 16–17, 47, 63, 71, 75–6
Isabella, Empress 3–11, 12–15, 17, 19–22, 24, 35, 107
Italy 41, 42, 87–90, 103

janissaries 44, 110
Jews 15–17, 18, 19
Jiménez de Cisneros, Francisco 11, 12, 107
St John of the Cross 72, 107
Juana 'la Beltraneja' 4, 24, 29, 107
Junta de Noche 59
juros 38, 110
Justiciar 8, 66, 67, 110

landgrave 43, 110
Lepanto, battle of 83, 90, 91, 92, 101
letrados 35, 110
Luther, Martin 12, 42, 43, 76
Lutheranism 12, 43, 44, 47, 82

Machiavelli, Niccolò 5, 107
Malta 89–90
maravedís 14, 19, 110
Margaret of Austria 21, 107

Index

Mary of Hungary 33, 107
Mary, Queen of Scots 69, 84, 90, 98, 99, 107
Mary Tudor 61, 81, 99
Maximilian I 21, 22, 107
mayorazgo 10, 110
Medina Sidonia, dukes of 6, 9, 14, 60, 100, 107
Mediterranean relations 88–94
Mendoza, Diego Hurtado de 32, 72
Mendoza, Luis Hurtado de 58, 107
Mendozas 6, 9, 61, 107
Mexico 48, 101, 102
Milan 42, 87
military orders 6
millones tax 74, 110
Molina, Juan Vázquez de 36, 107
Moors 12–13, 14, 17, 48–9
Moriscos 12, 15, 33, 45–6, 48, 63–5, 90, 110
Moura, Cristóbal de 59, 93, 94, 107

Naples 22, 38, 87, 88
navy 83
Netherlands 81, 83–6, 92–5, 99
New World 22–3, 48–51, 74–5, 81, 100–103
nobility 9–10, 35–7, 95

Observant Reform 12, 110
Orange, Prince of 57, 65, 95–8, 107
Ottomans 13, 20, 21, 44–6, 63, 64, 82, 87–90, 92, 96, 101, 110
Ovando, Nicolas 12, 23

papal bulls 12, 16, 71, 110
papal fief 22, 110
patronage 10, 13, 110
Paul III, Pope 43, 107
Paul IV, Pope 69, 70, 88
Peace of Augsburg 82, 95
peasantry 10
Pérez, Antonio 57, 60, 61, 66, 87, 108
Pérez, Gonzalo 36, 60, 108
Peru 45, 49, 101, 102
Philip of Habsburg 9, 10, 24
Philip II
 Aragonese revolt 64–7
 character 55–7
 Dutch Revolt 93–6
 factions 61–2
 impact of empire 98–9
 inheritance 57–8, 72–3, 80–2
 relations with Europe 82–7, 91–3, 97–100
 religion and society 67–71
 as ruler 55–61
 and Turks 88, 90, 91
pikes 39, 110
Pius V, Pope 55, 69, 72

Pizarro, Francisco 45–9
poderes 60, 110
Polyglot Bible 12, 24, 47, 76, 110
Portugal 4, 92–4, 101
princes of the blood 84
procurador 29, 110

Quiroga, Cardinal Gaspar de 60, 70, 108

Reconquista 10, 12, 15, 17, 18
religion 4, 12–14, 46–8, 68–72, 77, 95–6
religious minorities 12–17
Roman Curia 70
Roman law 16, 110
royal authority 4–9

Santa Cruz, Marquis of 59, 108
Santa Hermandad 6, 8, 10, 14
Schmalkaldic League 43, 44
Sea Beggars 73, 99, 110
señorios 15, 110
Sepúlveda, Juan Ginés de 60
Sicily 87, 89
Sixtus IV, Pope 14, 16, 17, 108
social developments 9–12, 23–4, 75–6
Spanish Armada 72, 81, 84, 86, 97, 99
Spanish Inquisition 16–17, 46, 63, 71, 74–5
subsidies 30, 110
subsidio tax 38, 73
Suleiman II, the Magnificent 44, 45, 81, 94, 108

Talavera, Hernando de 11, 15, 46, 108
taxation 18–19, 38, 73–4
tercios 39, 110
St Teresa of Ávila 68, 72, 73, 108
Titian 28, 91
Toledo, Don García de 70, 82, 88, 90
Torquemada, Tómas de 16, 108
trade 37–9, 101
Treaty of Alcáçovas 5, 6, 22
Treaty of Câteau-Cambrésis 84, 88
Treaty of Nonsuch 99, 100
Treaty of Vervins 86, 101
Trent, Council of 11, 43, 70–1, 111
Turks 44–6, 90–3

Valdés, Hernando de 71, 108
Vázquez, Mateo 59–62, 108
Velascos 6, 108
Venice 81, 88, 90, 92
Vervins, Treaty of 86, 101
Villena, Marquis of 4, 108

William of Orange 57, 65, 95–8, 107
Wittelsbachs 44, 108

115